MASTER YOUR MONEY BUILD WEALTH WITH PROVEN STRATEGIES

UNLEASE YOUR POTENTIAL FOR
FINANCIAL FREEDOM, LEARN TO TRADE
OPTIONS WITH CONFIDENCE AND
INCREASE PROFITS WITH RISK MITIGATION
FOR YOUNG ADULTS AND BEGINNERS

MAXX LIONESZ

Table of Contents

OPTIONS TRADING FOR BEGINNERS

FINANCIAL FREEDOM

MASTER MONEY MANAGEMENT AND BUILD WEALTH WITH PROVEN STRATEGIES

FOR YOUNG ADULTS

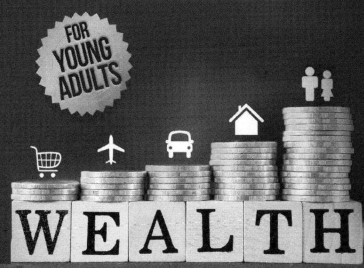

WEALTH

MAXX LIONESZ

Introduction

Let's get real: Achieving financial independence isn't just a distant dream; it's a tangible reality that you can start working toward right now. In a world where financial advice is often overwhelming and impersonal, I bring you a fresh, practical approach to mastering your money.

I am the founder of **LIONESZ PUBLISHING**, a brand born from a deep-seated passion for financial literacy and a commitment to empowering others to achieve financial independence and stability. Our wide array of publications covers everything, from basic budgeting to sophisticated investing strategies, and aims to make financial wisdom accessible and actionable.

This book is designed specifically for you, the young adults of today who are ready to lay the groundwork for lifelong wealth. Money management is not just about managing your money but about transforming your relationship with your finances. We'll start with the basics and progressively work toward more complex concepts, ensuring you have a solid foundation before moving on to advanced tactics. Real-world examples, strategic tips, and visual aids like line art images, graphics, and tables are peppered throughout this book to boost your understanding and engagement.

What sets this book apart is its ability to not only inform but also inspire. It's crafted to shift your mindset about money, from viewing it as a source of stress to viewing it as a tool for creating the life you want. I would recommend checking out "BE R.E.A.L: The Mindset to Achieve The Winning Lifestyle You Desire," my book on fostering the ideal mindset for success to understand how a shift in your mindset can work wonders in your life. It includes practical tips and exercises that will come in handy when you're working on cultivating the ideal mindset for financial freedom.

Moreover, this guide recognizes that generic advice is rarely sufficient and offers personalized strategies to address your unique financial situations and aspirations.

I understand if you're skeptical. Maybe you've tried other financial guides only to find yourself back at square one. That's why I've included features like interactive content and QR codes for accessing supplementary online resources to make this journey as engaging and enriching as possible.

Achieving financial freedom is not a solo mission. I'll show you how to tap into communities and find mentors who can guide you through the maze of personal finance. You're not just reading a book; you're joining a network of support.

As you turn each page, envision yourself applying the principles within, making informed decisions, and confidently stepping toward financial empowerment. This book is more than a guide; it's a gateway to financial freedom and success.

So, are you ready to take control of your finances? Then, join me on this transformative journey. Let's break free from financial uncertainty together and unlock a world of possibilities. With each chapter, you'll not only gain the knowledge but also the power to create a prosperous and secure future. Let's make your financial independence a reality.

BUILDING A FOUNDATION

 SAVINGS/INVESTMENTS

 EMERGENCY FUNDS

MANAGE DEBT/REDUCE LIABILITY

LIFE INSURANCE PROTECTION

HEALTH CARE PROTECTION

INCREASE CASH FLOW

Chapter 1:

Building a Foundation

Welcome to the first step on your path to financial freedom. Think of your current financial knowledge as a raw block of marble. This chapter will provide the tools you'll need to sculpt a more defined and empowered understanding of finances. We'll start by laying down a solid foundation of knowledge to support your immediate financial decisions and your long-term financial health. Whether you're making your first investment or signing your first loan agreement, understanding the basic financial terms and concepts is crucial. This isn't just about learning definitions but about applying the knowledge in a way that benefits you daily, turning complexity into clarity and anxiety into smart financial actions.

1.1 Decoding Financial Jargon: Essential Terms Every Young Adult Should Know

In every area of life, the right words can open doors. In finance, they can do even more: They can unlock opportunities. Let's start by demystifying some of the most common financial jargon that often sounds more intimidating than it is.

Annual Percentage Rate (APR): Think of APR as the total cost you pay each year for borrowing money, including interest and fees. It's like the full price tag on a loan. For example, if you're considering a credit card with an APR of 18%, you'll owe 18% of your balance in interest and fees for the year. Understanding APR helps you compare different loans and credit cards, ensuring you choose the most cost-effective option.

Compound Interest: This is your money's best friend. Compound interest means earning interest on your interest. Here's how it works: Imagine you invest $1,000 (this is your principal amount) at an interest rate of 5% per year. The first year, you earn $50 in interest, which adds to your principal amount, so the next year, you earn 5% on $1,050, which comes to $52.50. Over time, compounding can significantly increase your savings or investments without any extra effort from you.

Diversification: This term simply means don't put all your eggs in one basket. Diversification involves spreading your investments across various assets to reduce risk. For instance, instead of investing all your money in tech stocks, you might split it between stocks, bonds, real estate, and other investments. If one market dips, you won't lose everything.

Liquidity: Liquidity refers to how seamlessly you can convert assets into cash without significant loss in value. Cash itself is the most liquid asset. Stocks are generally liquid, but something like real estate, which can take months to sell, is considered less liquid. Knowing the liquidity of your assets is crucial when you need quick access to cash, especially in emergencies.

Quick-Reference Glossary

- APR or annual percentage rate: The annual cost of borrowing money, including interest and fees, expressed as a percentage.

- Compound Interest: Earning interest on both the initial principal and the accumulated interest from previous periods.

- Diversification: Reducing investment risks by allocating investments among various financial instruments.

- Liquidity: The ease with which an asset can be converted into cash without affecting its market price.

Understanding these terms helps you make smarter, more informed decisions about your money. When you understand the terms of a loan agreement or the principles guiding your investment choices, you hold the power to navigate the financial landscape confidently and competently.

When you know exactly what you're getting into financially, you can manage and grow your wealth effectively. Each term you master adds another feather to your hat, enabling you to construct a robust and prosperous economic future. This basic knowledge not only prepares you to tackle more complex financial challenges but also lays the groundwork for ongoing financial success.

1.2 Crafting Your First Budget: A Step-by-Step Guide for Beginners

⊙ CALCULATE INCOME   ⊙ SET SAVINGS GOALS

⊙ CATEGORIZE EXPENSES   ⊙ REVIEW BUDGET

Creating your first budget is a pivotal moment in your life, akin to drawing a map before embarking on a journey. It's about plotting your course with precision and care, ensuring every dollar earned plays a role in the larger narrative of your financial independence. Let's walk through this process step by step, ensuring you have a firm grasp of where your money comes from and where it goes. The first step in crafting a budget is to list all sources of income, including salary, freelance payments, and any passive income streams. This gives you a clear picture of what you're working with.

Next, categorize your expenses into fixed and variable. Fixed expenses are those that don't change every month, like rent or mortgage payments, while variable expenses can fluctuate, like groceries or entertainment. This distinction is crucial, as it highlights areas where adjustments can be made if needed. From here, the critical step is setting aside a portion of your income for savings—an act that not only builds your wealth but also secures your finances against unexpected setbacks.

Several methods can be employed to manage your budget effectively. Each has its merits and limitations, tailored to different lifestyles and financial goals. The envelope system, for example, involves allocating cash for various spending categories into envelopes. It's a tangible method that physically limits spending in each category to the cash you've assigned to it, making it ideal for those who benefit from seeing and feeling their budget. However, it might not suit those who are more digitally inclined or have more complex financial portfolios.

The 50/30/20 rule offers a broader approach, advocating that 50% of your income goes to necessities, 30% to wants, and 20% to savings and debt repayment. This method provides a simple framework for balancing enjoyment and responsibility without meticulously tracking every penny. It's suitable for those who seek a more straightforward, big-picture budgeting approach.

Conversely, the zero-based budgeting method requires you to account for every dollar you earn, assigning each one a specific job, from living expenses to investment. While this method ensures comprehensive financial oversight, it demands time and effort, which might be daunting for budgeting novices.

Consider the case of a recent college graduate working their first job. They might opt for the 50/30/20 rule to ensure they can handle rent and student loan payments while still enjoying life and saving for future goals. In contrast, a couple saving for a down payment on a home might find zero-based budgeting more effective, as it can highlight unnecessary expenses that could be redirected toward their savings goal.

To streamline budgeting, numerous digital tools and apps are available, offering functionalities that range from basic expense tracking to full financial management. Apps like Mint allow you to track purchases in real time and categorize expenses. It even offers personalized insights into your spending patterns. Others, like You Need a Budget (YNAB), embrace the zero-based budgeting method, offering tools to give every dollar a purpose and adjust budgets on the fly. These tools not only simplify the budgeting process but also help in building long-term habits, ensuring you stay on track with your financial goals.

By integrating these tools into your budgeting process, you enhance the accuracy and effectiveness of your budget. With the right tool, real-time updates, and data-driven insights, you can avoid common pitfalls and make informed decisions that align with your long-term financial aspirations. Visit https://www.rocketmoney.com or Scan the QR code below for a favorite money management application for your day-to-day finances.

1.3 The Power of an Emergency Fund: Strategies to Build and Maintain It

In the unpredictable journey of life, financial surprises are more a question of "when" than "if." Whether it's a sudden job loss, unexpected medical bills, or urgent car repairs, unforeseen expenses can destabilize even the most carefully planned budgets. This is where an emergency fund becomes not just beneficial but essential to maintaining financial stability. An emergency fund acts as a financial buffer that can keep you afloat in times of need without having to rely on credit cards or high-interest loans that can plunge you deeper into debt.

The first step in establishing this fund is determining its size. Conventional wisdom suggests saving enough to cover three to six months of living expenses. This range provides a solid buffer for most financial emergencies. To tailor this to your circumstances, start by calculating your monthly expenses, including everything from rent or mortgage payments, utilities, groceries, and any other recurring payments. Once you have a clear picture of your monthly outgoings, multiply this number by three, four, five, or six based on your current job stability, health, and lifestyle. For instance, if you're a freelancer with a fluctuating income, aiming for six months' worth of expenses might be prudent. Conversely, if you have a stable job and health insurance, three months could suffice.

Building this fund might seem daunting, especially if you're starting from scratch. However, you can employ several strategies to grow your emergency savings gradually. One such strategy involves automating your savings, which is a highly effective and painless method. Set up an automatic transfer from your checking account to a savings account specifically designated for emergencies. Time these transactions with your paycheck. Even small amounts can build up over time. Additionally, scrutinize your monthly expenses to identify non-essential items that can be cut to free up more money for your emergency fund. Perhaps, there's a subscription you rarely use or you dine out too many times. Another avenue is to look for additional sources of income. This could be anything from taking up freelance gigs, selling unused items, or taking on any side hustle that fits into your schedule.

When it comes to managing your emergency fund, accessibility is key. Your fund needs to be easily accessible, but it should also be kept separate from your regular checking account to avoid the temptation to dip into it for everyday expenses. High-yield savings accounts are ideal for emergency funds. They offer higher interest rates than regular savings accounts, which means your money grows while it sits, and they provide the flexibility to withdraw funds without penalties when an emergency strikes. This strategic placement ensures your emergency fund is both growing and readily available, providing a dual benefit that enhances your financial security.

Building and maintaining an emergency fund is a fundamental aspect of sound financial management. It's about more than just having money set aside—it's also about securing your peace of mind. Knowing you have a financial cushion can relieve stress and give you the freedom to focus on other long-term financial goals. With each deposit into this fund, you fortify your financial resilience, paving the way for a more stable and secure future.

1.4 Understanding Credit and How to Use It Wisely

Navigating the world of credit can often feel like walking through a maze blindfolded. Understanding credit scores, how to manage credit cards, and the influence of credit on major life decisions guides you through this maze and sets you firmly on the route to financial empowerment. Let's break down these concepts, starting with the cornerstone of most financial evaluations: the credit score.

A credit score is a numerical representation of your creditworthiness based on your past and current financial behaviors. It factors in elements like your payment history, the amounts owed, the length of your credit history, new credit, and the types of credit in use. Essentially, it tells lenders how likely you are to repay borrowed money. Accessing your credit report, which details your credit history and the basis of your credit score, is straightforward and free through major national credit reporting agencies. This report doesn't just affect how you're viewed by lenders but also influences your job applications, rental agreements, and insurance premiums. Thus, understanding and regularly reviewing your credit report helps you catch inaccuracies that could drag your score down, ensuring you are always ready for your next big financial decision.

Let's move on to credit cards. They are not just a means of payment but of building your financial reputation. Responsible credit card use is pivotal. This means paying off your balances in full each month to avoid interest charges and not spending more than you can afford. The benefits of this approach extend beyond avoiding debt to impact your credit score by keeping your credit utilization rate low. However, pitfalls like high interest rates and the temptation to overspend can turn credit cards from a financial tool to a financial burden. It's crucial to understand the terms of your credit card, such as the APR and other fees, and use the card strategically—for instance, benefiting from cashback offers or points without falling into the trap of accruing interest.

The impact of your credit history stretches far beyond the immediate future. When you decide to make significant life purchases, such as a home or a car, your credit score comes under scrutiny. A higher credit score can secure you lower interest rates, potentially saving you thousands of dollars in loan repayment. Conversely, a lower credit score might result in higher interest rates or your loan application being declined outright. Therefore, managing your credit score is managing your future possibilities. It's about keeping doors open and ensuring you have the best possible options available when you need them.

Finally, let's discuss strategies to build or improve your credit score. For those just starting or needing to rebuild their credit, secured credit cards are a viable option. These cards are backed by a cash deposit you make upfront; the deposit amount typically becomes your credit limit. This reduces the risk to the issuer, making it easier for individuals with no credit or poor credit to get approved. Regular payments on this card, as with any form of credit, are crucial. They demonstrate to creditors your reliability and intention to handle debt responsibly. Moreover, rectifying errors on your credit report, from small inaccuracies to fraudulent accounts, is vital in maintaining your credit health. Regular monitoring allows you to identify and address these issues promptly, thereby protecting your credit score.

By integrating disciplined credit card usage with strategic credit building and maintenance practices, you can safeguard your current financial health and set the stage for future financial success. Whether it's renting your dream apartment, owning a car, or securing loans with favorable terms, a robust credit score opens up a spectrum of financial opportunities. It's about taking control of your financial narrative to reflect your true financial responsibility and potential.

1.5 Smart Debt Management: Tips to Overcome Overwhelming Student Loans

Navigating the landscape of student loans can often feel like steering through a thick fog—challenging and fraught with uncertainty. Understanding the nuances of different loans, repayment options, and strategies for management can clear this fog, revealing a path to financial relief and control.

Student loans, typically categorized into federal and private, come with their own sets of rules and flexibility that can significantly impact your repayment strategy. Federal loans, backed by the government, usually offer lower interest rates and more flexible repayment options compared to private loans, which are sourced from banks, credit unions, or other private entities and tend to have higher interest rates and less flexible terms.

For federal student loans, several repayment plans can cater to your changing financial circumstances. Plans such as the standard repayment plan offer a fixed amount over ten years, while graduated repayment plans start with lower payments that increase over time. Income-driven repayment plans adjust your monthly payments based on your income and family size, which can be particularly beneficial if you're starting with a lower salary that's expected to rise. Understanding these options allows you to tailor your repayments to fit your financial situation, reducing the strain on your budget.

Private student loans do not usually offer income-based repayment plans and are less likely to provide forbearance or deferment options, which allow you to temporarily stop making payments without accruing interest. This makes choosing the right private loan and paying close attention to the terms, interest rates, and the reputation of the lender crucial from the outset. If you're juggling both federal and private loans, prioritize payments toward private loans given their typically higher and variable interest rates and less flexible repayment options.

Exploring forgiveness programs can also offer avenues for reducing your student loan burden. Programs like Public Service Loan Forgiveness are designed to forgive the remaining balance on your direct loans after you've made 120 qualifying monthly payments under a qualifying repayment plan while working full-time for a qualifying employer, typically in public service. Understanding the qualifying criteria and ensuring you adhere to them from the start can lead to significant financial relief.

Developing a smart repayment strategy involves more than just understanding the types of loans and repayment plans. It also involves integrating your student loan repayments into your broader financial goals and obligations. Prioritizing student loan repayments in your budget is crucial, but so is balancing other financial needs such as emergency savings, retirement funds, and personal investments. This balanced approach ensures that while you are diligent in paying off student debt, you are also building a financial cushion and securing your future.

Maintaining financial awareness plays a critical role in managing student loans effectively. Regularly reviewing your loan terms, keeping tabs on interest rates, and staying informed about changes in federal regulations can help you optimize your repayment strategy. For instance, during the COVID-19 pandemic, federal student loan interest rates were temporarily set to zero and payments were suspended as part of the U.S. government's relief efforts; those who stayed informed could make educated decisions about how to manage their loans during this period.

Setting up alerts for payment deadlines, keeping records of payments made, and monitoring your loan balance over time are all part of this active management approach. Additionally, if you encounter financial difficulties, understanding options such as deferment and forbearance can prevent the kind of defaults that lead to ballooning balances and damaged credit.

The road to overcoming the burden of student loans is paved with informed decisions, balanced financial planning, and consistent oversight. By understanding the details of your student loans and integrating this knowledge into a comprehensive financial strategy, you not only work toward freeing yourself from debt but also toward realizing your broader financial goals. With each payment, you are more than just closer to being debt-free; you are building a foundation of financial discipline that will benefit you throughout your life.

1.6 Setting Achievable Financial Goals: Short-Term vs. Long-Term Goals

Understanding the distinction between short-term and long-term financial goals is like recognizing the difference between sprinting and running a marathon. Short-term goals are your sprints—achievable within a year or less. They provide immediate satisfaction and momentum and might include saving for a vacation, paying off a small credit card debt, or purchasing a new laptop. Long-term goals are your marathons, requiring sustained effort and endurance. They often include substantial objectives like buying a home, funding your retirement, or paying off your student loans. Both types of goals are crucial; short-term goals keep you motivated and financially fluid, while long-term goals ensure you are working toward your future.

To effectively set these goals, employ the SMART—Specific, Measurable, Achievable, Relevant, Time-bound—goal-setting method. This approach transforms vague ambitions into clear, actionable goals. For instance, instead of the vague desire to "Save more money," a SMART goal would be "Save $5,000 for a down payment on a new car by the end of next year." This method not only clarifies what success looks like but also provides a timeline and measurable milestones to track progress.

Strategic planning is essential in achieving your goals. It begins with a thorough assessment of your financial situation—understanding your income, expenses, debts, and savings. From there, establish

16

prioritization strategies. While it's tempting to tackle multiple goals at once, spreading yourself too thin can lead to frustration and burnout. Instead, prioritize based on urgency and importance. For example, if you have high-interest debt, it might be prudent to focus on paying this down before aggressively saving for a vacation. Use tools like budget planners and financial management apps to allocate resources effectively and stay on track. These tools can help you adjust your monthly spending and visualize different scenarios where you can reallocate funds from non-essential expenses to your goal funds.

Regularly reviewing and adjusting your financial goals are as important as setting them. Life is dynamic—financial markets fluctuate, personal situations change, and new opportunities and challenges arise. Bi-annual reviews of your financial plan allow you to adjust your sails according to the changing winds, ensuring you remain aligned with your goals. During these reviews, ask yourself the following:

- Are my goals still relevant?

- Am I on track to achieve them?

- Do I need to adjust my timelines or strategies?

This ongoing process keeps your financial plans relevant and keeps you engaged and proactive about your financial health.

An active and structured approach to setting and achieving financial goals does more than just improve your financial condition; it also enhances your overall life satisfaction. By setting achievable targets, you create a series of successes that boost your confidence and competence in managing money. These victories, small and large, compile over time, building a solid foundation of financial stability and independence. With each goal met, you're checking a box and paving a path toward a more secure and fulfilling life. A proactive and mindful approach to financial planning ensures you are not only dreaming about a better future but also actively constructing it.

CHAPTER 2

ADVANCED MONEY
MANAGEMENT TECHNIQUES

Chapter 2:

Advanced Money Management

Techniques

Mastering your money requires more than just sticking to the basics; you must also adopt advanced techniques that refine and perfect your ability to manage your finances with precision and foresight. Think of it as upgrading from a manual gearbox to an automatic; it's about optimizing processes and ensuring every dollar works effectively toward achieving your financial goals. This chapter delves into sophisticated strategies that streamline your financial operations and amplify your capacity to build wealth with less effort and more control.

2.1 Zero-Based Budgeting: Plan Every Dollar

Understanding Zero-Based Budgeting

Zero-based budgeting stands out as a meticulous and laser-focused budgeting technique where every dollar of your income has a purpose—be it expenses, savings, or debt repayment—leaving zero at the end of the month. This method forces you to justify every expense and ensures that your money is working precisely as you intend it to. Unlike traditional budgeting methods, which might start with the expenses from the previous month as a baseline, zero-based budgeting requires a fresh evaluation of every cost, every month. You start from scratch and ask, "What do my financial priorities need to be this month?"

Implementing Zero-Based Budgeting

To set up a zero-based budget, begin by listing your monthly income from all sources. Next, list your expenses, starting with the essentials like rent, utilities, and groceries, followed by debt payments and savings contributions. Finally, allocate any remaining funds to other planned expenses, such as entertainment or personal care. The goal is to ensure that your income minus your expenses equals zero by the end of the month. This practice might require you to track your expenses more diligently and frequently adjust your budget categories to reflect your actual spending and keep the budget balanced.

Advantages and Challenges

One significant advantage of zero-based budgeting is the complete control it provides over your financial flow. Each dollar has a purpose, which can dramatically cut down on wasteful spending and improve savings rates. It's particularly effective for reaching specific financial goals quickly, such as saving for a down payment or paying off a significant debt. However, the meticulous nature of zero-based budgeting can also be its drawback. Justifying every expense and allocating every dollar can be time-consuming and may require a daily commitment to tracking and adjusting expenditures, which might be daunting for some.

Practical Examples

Consider a freelancer with an irregular income who adopts zero-based budgeting to handle their fluctuating financial landscape. By assigning every dollar a job each month based on actual income received, they can ensure that essential expenses are covered, and any extra money is directed toward their fluctuating tax obligations and a business emergency fund. Conversely, a family with a stable monthly income might use zero-based budgeting to maximize their savings. By rigorously allocating funds toward specific savings goals after covering their regular expenses, they can accelerate their financial progress toward larger objectives, like funding college educations or investing in real estate.

Case Study: Freelancer With Irregular Income

To provide a concrete example, let's examine the case of Alex, a freelance graphic designer with an unpredictable income stream. Alex's earnings vary significantly from month to month, making traditional budgeting methods less effective. By implementing zero-based budgeting, Alex begins each month by projecting their minimum expected income and plans essential expenses accordingly. They prioritize rent, utilities, and minimum debt payments. In months where Alex earns more than anticipated, the additional income is allocated toward an emergency fund and retirement savings, ensuring that these extra dollars are not spent frivolously but are instead enhancing Alex's financial security and future stability. This disciplined approach not only keeps Alex's finances in check but also builds a buffer that smooths out the financial ups and downs typical of freelance income.

Zero-based budgeting, with its rigorous and disciplined approach, offers a powerful strategy for those ready to take an active role in managing their finances. Whether you're dealing with variable income or looking to supercharge your savings, this method provides the structure and clarity needed to make every dollar count. As you implement this budgeting strategy, remember that its success lies in consistent application and regular adjustment, ensuring that it remains aligned with your evolving financial goals and circumstances.

2.2 Automating Your Finances to Build Wealth Effortlessly

Imagine a world where managing your finances is as effortless as setting your favorite playlist on repeat. That's the power of financial automation—it transforms money management from a daily chore into a seamless, almost invisible background process, enhancing your financial health without constant oversight. Automating your finances means setting up systems to handle savings, bill payments, and investments automatically, which saves time and ensures important financial transactions are never overlooked or delayed.

The beauty of automation lies in its simplicity and the peace of mind it brings. You can automate most aspects of your financial life, including depositing your paycheck directly into your bank account, scheduling your monthly bill payments, and routing a portion of your income into a retirement account or investment fund. These automated transactions ensure that your bills are paid on time, which could help avoid late fees and the potential negative impacts on your credit score. Similarly, by automating transfers to savings or investment accounts, you're effectively paying yourself first, a cornerstone principle of personal finance that prioritizes saving overspending.

To get started, review your bank's online services and apps, as most financial institutions now offer features that support automation. Apps like Mint or Personal Capital not only track your spending and investments but also provide tools to automate savings based on your spending patterns and financial goals. Investment platforms such as Acorns or Robinhood allow for automatic contributions to investment accounts, which can be set up to recur regularly, aligning with your payday. This ensures that you consistently invest without having to manually transfer funds each time.

Setting up these automated systems usually involves a simple one-time setup process. Begin by logging into your online banking platform or financial app. Navigate to the payments or transfer section, where you can set up recurring payments for bills like your mortgage, utilities, and credit card charges, specifying the amount and the date for each month. Similarly, establish automatic transfers to your savings and investment accounts. Decide on a percentage of your income that you want to save or invest and set up automatic transfers to occur right after payday. Thus, you will reduce the risk of human error and the temptation to spend the money elsewhere.

The psychological benefits of automating your finances are profound. By reducing the need for daily decisions about where and when to use your money, you eliminate emotional spending, which can often derail financial goals. Automation creates a built-in discipline that can help you stick to your savings and investment plans, making it easier to reach your financial goals without succumbing to impulse purchases. Moreover, the predictability and consistency of automation can significantly reduce financial anxiety. Knowing that your bills will be paid on time and your savings goals will be met can provide a sense of security and control over your finances.

In essence, automating your finances changes your relationship with money. It shifts your role from being an active participant in every financial transaction to an overseer who sets goals and achieves them systematically. Automation ensures your financial plan is executed without fail, turning your aspirations from mere intentions to tangible outcomes. It's like having a personal financial assistant dedicated to keeping your finances on track while you focus on living your life to the fullest. Through this seamless integration of technology and personal finance, you can effortlessly build wealth and ensure long-term financial stability.

2.3 Breaking Down Investment Types: Stocks, Bonds, and Mutual Funds

Navigating the investment landscape can often feel like exploring a vast, complex world. Understanding the basic types of investments—stocks, bonds, and mutual funds—is, therefore, crucial to making informed decisions that align with your financial goals. Let's break down these essential investment vehicles, exploring their unique characteristics, risks, and potential returns.

Understanding Stocks, Bonds, and Mutual Funds

Stocks represent ownership in a company. When you buy a stock, you're purchasing a share of that company's earnings and assets. The allure of stocks lies in their potential for significant returns. Companies can grow their earnings over time, increasing the value of your shares.

However, stocks are also subject to market volatility, meaning their prices can fluctuate dramatically based on everything, from company performance to economic conditions. This makes stocks a higher-risk investment, suitable for those who have a longer time horizon and a tolerance for market swings.

Bonds are akin to loans that you give to corporations or governments in exchange for periodic interest payments plus the return of the bond's face value at maturity. They are generally considered safer than stocks because they provide predictable income and are less vulnerable to market fluctuations. However, bonds typically offer lower returns compared to stocks, which makes them more appealing to conservative investors or those nearing retirement who prioritize stability over growth.

Mutual funds are investment programs funded by shareholders that trade in diversified, professionally managed holdings. By pooling your money with other investors, you can invest in a portfolio of stocks, bonds, or other securities, depending on the fund's focus, without having to choose each investment individually. This diversification reduces risk, making mutual funds a good option for novice investors or those looking to simplify their investment strategy. However, mutual funds come with management fees, which can vary widely and impact the overall return on your investment.

Criteria for Choosing Investments

Begin by understanding your risk tolerance, time horizon, and financial goals. Risk tolerance is how much market volatility you can handle without panicking. It's crucial because it can help you avoid impulsive decisions during market downturns. Time horizon refers to the amount of time you plan to hold an investment before taking the money out. Generally, the longer your time horizon, the more risk you can afford to take, as you have more time to recover from any losses. Finally, aligning your investments with your financial goals—whether saving for a down payment, funding a child's education, or building a retirement nest egg—ensures that your investment strategy supports what you're ultimately trying to achieve.

Strategies for Diversification

Diversification is a key strategy to reduce risk in your investment portfolio. It involves spreading your investments across various asset classes (like stocks, bonds, and real estate) and within asset classes (such as different sectors, industries, and geographies). For example, instead of investing only in technology stocks, you would invest across different sectors like healthcare, finance, and consumer goods. This strategy helps mitigate the risk that a single failing investment could adversely affect your overall portfolio. Effective diversification is not just about owning different investments; it's also about owning investments that react differently to the same economic event—when one part of your portfolio is down, another might be up, balancing out the overall risk and return.

Case Studies: Real-Life Investment Scenarios

To illustrate these concepts, let's consider two hypothetical investors: Emily and John. Emily is a young professional with high-risk tolerance and a long time horizon. She invests heavily in stocks with a focus on high-growth tech companies. While her portfolio experiences significant volatility, it also sees substantial growth during bull markets. John, nearing retirement, prioritizes stability. He chooses a conservative portfolio dominated by bonds and a balanced mutual fund that includes stocks and bonds for slight growth potential but limited risk exposure. Both strategies align well with their respective risk tolerances, time horizons, and financial goals, showcasing the importance of tailoring your investment approach to your financial situation.

By understanding the characteristics of different investment types and how they can be combined to achieve diversification, you're better equipped to build a portfolio that reflects your personal risk tolerance, time horizon, and financial goals. Whether you're drawn to the potential high returns of stocks, the stability of bonds, or the diversified approach of mutual funds, the key is to choose investments that not only aim to increase your wealth but also match your overall financial strategy. This tailored approach helps ensure that your investment decisions are both strategic and effective, paving the way for financial success.

2.4 Advanced Debt Repayment Strategies: Snowball and Avalanche Methods

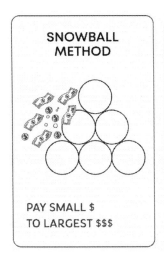

Repaying your debt isn't as simple as making payments; you must also choose a strategy that aligns with your financial situation and psychological comfort. Two popular methods, the debt snowball and avalanche, offer distinct approaches to managing and eliminating debt. Understanding the mechanics and psychological impacts of each can help you select a method that not only accelerates your debt repayment but also integrates seamlessly with your financial habits and goals.

The Debt Snowball Method

The debt snowball method focuses on paying off debts from the smallest to the largest, regardless of the interest rates. This means you make only minimum payments on all your debts except for the smallest one, which you target with any extra money you have. Once the smallest debt is paid off, you roll the amount you were paying on that debt into the next smallest debt, creating a "snowball" effect as your available funds for debt repayment grow larger with each debt you eliminate.

Advantages: Clearing the smallest debts first can give you quick wins, boosting your motivation and sense of accomplishment. This can be incredibly valuable if you find it challenging to stick with a long-term debt repayment plan. Seeing debts disappear one by one can reinforce your commitment to your financial strategy and keep you engaged in the process.

Disadvantages: It might cost you more over time, especially if your larger debts also carry higher interest rates. By focusing on the balance rather than the cost of the debt (interest rate), you may end up paying more in interest over the life of your debts.

The Debt Avalanche Method

In contrast, the debt avalanche method prioritizes debts with the highest interest rates, regardless of the balance. You focus on paying as much as you can toward the debt with the highest interest rate while making minimum payments on others. Once the highest-interest debt is paid off, you move on to the debt with the next highest interest rate, and so on. This method is mathematically optimal for minimizing interest payments and reducing the total cost of your debt.

Advantages: It is cost-effective, saving you money in the long run by reducing the amount you pay in interest, and particularly beneficial if you have high-interest debts like credit card balances or payday loans. Eliminating high-interest debts first decreases the overall accumulating interest, which can significantly speed up the debt repayment process.

Disadvantages: It can take longer to see the results if your highest-interest debt also has a large balance. This might impact your motivation to stick with the plan, especially if you don't see many debts being fully paid off for a considerable amount of time.

Simulation Scenarios

To illustrate these methods in action, consider two individuals: Sarah and Mike. Sarah has three debts: a $500 medical bill at 5% interest, a $2,000 credit card balance at 20% interest, and a $10,000 student loan at 6% interest. Using the snowball method, she would pay off the $500 medical bill first, followed by the $2,000 credit card debt, and finally the $10,000 student loan. This strategy helps Sarah quickly reduce her debts, providing motivational boosts throughout her repayment journey.

Mike decides to use the avalanche method for his similar debts. He targets the $2,000 credit card balance first due to its high interest rate, followed by the $10,000 student loan, and ends with the $500 medical bill. This approach saves Mike more money in interest over time, even though it takes longer to fully pay off each debt.

Customizing Your Approach

While both strategies have their merits, you might find that a combination of the two methods works best for your situation. For instance, you could start with the snowball method to quickly knock out a couple of small debts for psychological wins and then switch to the avalanche method to minimize interest payments on the larger, more costly debts. Alternatively, you could decide to tackle a high-interest small debt first to blend the benefits of both strategies.

Understanding and choosing the right debt repayment strategy can significantly affect how quickly and cost-effectively you become debt-free. Whether you prefer the quick wins of the snowball method or the cost-saving focus of the avalanche method, the key is to stick with a plan that aligns with your financial goals and psychological needs. As you implement these strategies, remember that the best approach should not only make mathematical sense but also keep you motivated and committed on your journey toward financial freedom.

Visit https://www.nerdwallet.com/article/finance/pay-off-debt or Scan the QR code below for strategies to pay off debts and avoid widening interest pitfalls.

2.5 The Role of Insurance in Wealth Building: What You Need to Know

Insurance is often viewed simply as a safeguard—a way to mitigate the financial fallout from unexpected events. However, when integrated into a comprehensive financial plan, certain types of insurance can also act as powerful tools for wealth building. Understanding the basics of different types of insurance and how they can protect and enhance your financial resources is crucial.

Life, health, and property insurance are the fundamental types of insurance that serve distinct purposes. Life insurance provides for your dependents in the event of your death, offering peace of mind and financial security. Health insurance protects against the often-exorbitant costs of medical care, safeguarding your savings and preventing bankruptcy due to medical debts. Property insurance, covering assets like your home and car, shields you from financial loss due to damage or theft, ensuring that a disaster doesn't derail your financial stability.

Moving beyond basic protection, certain types of life insurance, such as whole life and universal life, can be utilized as part of a broader wealth-building strategy. These policies not only provide a death benefit but also include a tax-deferred, cash-value component that grows over time. You can borrow against the cash value or even withdraw it during your lifetime, providing financial flexibility. This feature makes it a dual-purpose tool—it protects your family while also serving as a potential source of funds for future needs.

Carefully evaluate your personal and family circumstances to choose the right insurance. Factors to consider include your current financial situation, expected future income, and specific financial goals. It's also important to consider the stability and reputation of the insurance provider. Look for companies with strong financial health as indicated by ratings from agencies like AM Best or S&P Global Ratings, which reflect an insurer's ability to pay claims.

You must also consider the flexibility of the policy. For instance, some life insurance policies offer riders or additional benefits that can be tailored to your needs, such as accelerated death benefits or coverage for chronic illness. Evaluating these options can help ensure that you not only choose a policy that meets your current needs but one that can also adapt to your changing circumstances.

Real-life case studies highlight the critical role of adequate insurance coverage and the potential repercussions of inadequate planning. Consider the story of a young entrepreneur, Linda, who, in the rush of starting her own business, overlooked the importance of health insurance. When faced with unexpected health issues, the lack of coverage led to substantial medical bills that not only wiped out her savings but also forced her into debt, severely impacting her business operations and personal finances. This situation underscores the importance of health insurance in protecting against unforeseen medical costs that can have far-reaching effects on your financial well-being.

Another example involves a family that neglected to update their home insurance policy after extensive renovations that significantly increased the value of their home. When a natural disaster struck, their outdated policy didn't cover the full cost of the damages, leading to substantial out-of-pocket expenses for repairs. This case highlights the necessity of regularly reviewing and updating insurance policies to reflect current values and conditions, ensuring adequate coverage when it's most needed.

These examples illustrate key lessons about the importance of not only having insurance but ensuring that it is adequate and up to date. To effectively use insurance as a financial tool, you must understand the specific benefits and limitations of the different types of policies, regularly assess your coverage needs, and choose reputable providers that offer the flexibility to adapt to your evolving financial landscape. Integrating insurance into your overall financial strategy protects against potential losses and allows you to leverage certain policies to contribute to your wealth-building efforts. This proactive approach to insurance can shield your assets, secure your future, and provide peace of mind.

2.6 Tax Planning and Optimization for Maximum Savings

Tax planning is a critical component of financial management that involves strategizing how to minimize tax liability and maximize after-tax income. Understanding and utilizing various tax laws and regulations can significantly increase the amount of money you retain each year, which can then be reinvested toward your financial goals. Effective tax planning requires a proactive approach, ensuring that all deductions, credits, and savings strategies are fully leveraged throughout the year, not just as an afterthought during tax season.

Strategies for Reducing Taxable Income

One of the most effective strategies for reducing taxable income is through contributions to retirement accounts. Traditional individual retirement accounts (IRAs) and 401(k)s are particularly beneficial because the money you contribute is deducted from your yearly taxable income. For instance, if you earn $50,000 annually and contribute $5,000 to your 401(k), only $45,000 of your income will be subject to income tax. Additionally, investing in a health savings account (HSA) not only allows you to deduct contributions from your taxable income but also offers the benefit of tax-free withdrawals for qualified medical expenses, which can be a significant financial advantage.

Another sophisticated strategy is tax-loss harvesting, used primarily in investment portfolios. This involves selling investments that have incurred losses to offset gains you've received from other investments. For example, if you sold an investment with a $5,000 gain this year and another with a $5,000 loss, the loss would cancel out the gain for tax purposes, meaning you owe no capital gains tax. This method can be particularly useful in years where you have high gains from investments, as it can substantially lower your tax obligation.

Leveraging Tax Credits and Deductions

Understanding the various tax credits and deductions available can also lead to substantial tax savings. Tax credits, such as the American opportunity tax credit for higher education expenses, directly reduce the amount of tax you owe, dollar for dollar. Tax deductions decrease your taxable income. For instance, if you're eligible for a $1,000 tax deduction and you're in the 22% tax bracket, that deduction saves you $220 in taxes. Common deductions include those for student loan interest, certain business expenses for self-employed individuals, and charitable contributions. By carefully planning your expenses around these credits and deductions, you can maximize your tax savings each year.

Tools and Resources for Tax Planning

Several tools and resources can help optimize your tax strategies. Tax software programs like TurboTax or H&R Block can guide you through the complexities of your tax return, ensuring you take advantage of all possible deductions and credits. For more personalized assistance, consulting with a tax professional or a certified public accountant (CPA) can be invaluable, especially if you have multiple income streams, complex investments, or significant assets. These professionals stay abreast of the latest tax laws and can provide tailored advice on reducing your tax liability based on your specific financial situation.

In addition to software and professional advice, staying informed through reliable financial news sources and the Internal Revenue Service (IRS) website can help you keep up with new tax laws and provisions that might affect your finances. Regularly updating your knowledge allows you to adjust your tax strategies and avoid missing out on opportunities to reduce your tax burden.

Through diligent tax planning and the strategic use of deductions, credits, and other tax-saving mechanisms, you can retain a larger portion of your earnings and accelerate your progress toward financial independence. This proactive approach not only ensures compliance with tax laws but also aligns your tax practices with your broader financial objectives, fostering long-term stability and growth in your personal finances.

As we conclude this chapter, remember that understanding and applying the principles of advanced money management can transform your approach to personal finance. From implementing advanced budgeting and debt repayment techniques to optimizing your tax strategy, each step is designed to enhance your financial acumen and independence. As we progress to the next chapter, we'll explore even more sophisticated strategies that can accelerate your journey to financial independence, empowering you to make informed decisions that pave the way for a prosperous future.

INVESTMENT STRATEGIES
BEYOND THE BASICS

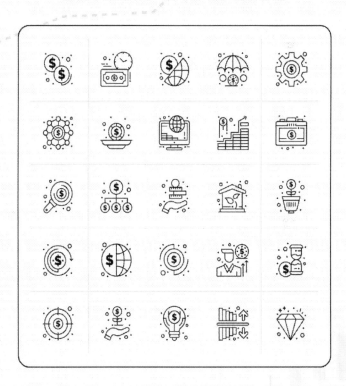

Chapter 3:

Investment Strategies Beyond the

Basics

Imagine waking up to a world where your investments work for you, generating income even as you sleep. This isn't just a dream for the wealthy elite; it's a tangible reality that you can achieve with strategic investment choices, particularly in real estate. Real estate investment is often touted as one of the most effective ways to generate passive income and build substantial wealth over time. It's not without its complexities and challenges, but with the right approach, even beginners can navigate this lucrative field successfully.

3.1 Real Estate Investment for Beginners: Getting Started With Rental Properties

Overview of Real Estate Investment

Investing in real estate involves purchasing properties to generate income, either by renting them out or selling them at a higher price. It's a powerful wealth-building tool for several reasons. Firstly, real estate tends to appreciate over time, meaning the property you buy today could be worth significantly more in the future. Secondly, rental properties provide a steady stream of passive income, which can help cover mortgage costs and generate profit. Finally, real estate offers unique tax advantages, such as deductions for mortgage interest, property taxes, and depreciation, which can significantly reduce your tax burden.

Steps to Purchasing Your First Rental Property

Start with thorough research and planning. First, define your investment goals. Are you looking for quick profits through house flipping, or do you prefer a steady income from rentals? Once your goals are clear, focus on location. The adage "location, location, location" holds particularly true in real estate. Look for areas with growing job markets, good schools, low crime rates, and amenities such as parks, restaurants, and public transport. These features attract tenants and contribute to property appreciation.

Second, dive into market research. Analyze the local real estate market trends, including average rent prices, property values, and occupancy rates. Tools like Zillow, Trulia, and local real estate websites can provide valuable data. Additionally, attending local real estate investment meetings or joining online forums can offer insights and networking opportunities.

Third, consider your finances. Most investors don't pay in cash but take out a mortgage. Explore different financing options and compare mortgage rates from various lenders to find the best deal. Consider your budget and ensure the rental income will cover your mortgage payments and property expenses, including maintenance, taxes, and insurance.

Risk Management in Real Estate

Investing in real estate is not without risks. Market fluctuations can affect property values and rental rates, while unexpected repairs can disrupt your cash flow. To mitigate these risks, conduct a thorough inspection of the property before purchasing to identify any potential issues. Additionally, build a financial cushion to cover unexpected expenses, such as emergency repairs or vacancies between tenants.

Insurance is also a vital part of risk management. Ensure you have adequate property insurance, including specific coverage for landlords, which can protect you from financial losses due to damage or liability claims.

Tips for Successful Property Management

Effective property management is key to turning your investment into a profitable venture. Start with rigorous tenant screening. Check potential tenants' credit scores, employment history, and references to ensure they are reliable and can afford the rent. Drawing up a comprehensive lease agreement is also crucial. The lease should clearly outline the terms of the tenancy, including rent amount, payment deadlines, rules regarding pets, and maintenance responsibilities.

Regular maintenance of the property keeps it in good condition and helps retain its value. Establish a schedule for regular inspections and maintenance tasks, such as landscaping, checking smoke detectors, and servicing heating systems. Building a good relationship with your tenants can also make property management smoother. Responsive and respectful communication can encourage tenants to take better care of your property and notify you promptly of any issues.

In conclusion, real estate investment offers a fantastic avenue for building wealth, especially for young investors willing to do their homework and take a proactive approach. By understanding the market, managing risks wisely, and maintaining properties effectively, you can turn real estate investments into a significant source of income and a cornerstone of your financial independence strategy. As you explore this exciting opportunity, remember that every property you purchase is not just an investment in real estate but an investment in your future financial freedom.

Visit https://www.realtor.com/marketing/resources/successful-property-management or Scan the QR code below for some useful tips on successful property management.

3.2 Exploring Crowdfunding and Peer-to-Peer Lending as Investment Options

Crowdfunding and peer-to-peer (P2P) lending represent a shift in how individuals can engage with the financial markets, democratizing the process of funding and investing. Crowdfunding platforms allow entrepreneurs and creatives to raise capital directly from the public, bypassing traditional financial institutions. This process not only helps bring diverse projects to life but also opens up new investment avenues for you. Similarly, P2P lending platforms connect borrowers directly with investors, offering an alternative to conventional bank loans. Here, you can contribute to funding personal loans, business ventures, or even green initiatives, often receiving higher returns than typical savings or fixed deposit accounts would offer.

The allure of these platforms lies in their ability to offer both investors and borrowers benefits that traditional banking channels might not. For investors, the appeal includes potentially higher returns on investment and the ability to directly impact the success of innovative projects or individuals. For borrowers, it provides access to funds that might not be available through standard channels, often with more flexible repayment terms. Additionally, these platforms generally use advanced algorithms to assess risk, providing an extra layer of security and reassurance for your investments.

Evaluating opportunities within crowdfunding and P2P lending requires a keen eye. When considering an investment, assess the project or borrower's background comprehensively. Look into the history and credibility of the person or team behind the request. Many platforms provide ratings or reviews of borrowers based on their repayment history, which can be a valuable resource. Furthermore, understand the risk associated with each investment. Unlike traditional investments, those in crowdfunding and P2P lending are typically not insured or guaranteed, meaning you could lose your capital if the project fails or the borrower defaults. Diversification is crucial here; spreading your investments across various projects and loans can mitigate potential losses.

Legal and regulatory considerations are paramount when investing through these platforms. Crowdfunding and P2P lending are subject to a range of laws that vary significantly from one jurisdiction to another. These regulations are designed to protect both borrowers and lenders from fraud and ensure transparency in all transactions. Before investing, familiarize yourself with the regulations that apply to the platform and the jurisdiction it operates in. This might include rules about who can invest, how much they can invest, and how returns are taxed. Many platforms provide detailed information about these aspects, but consulting with a financial advisor can also provide clarity and ensure compliance.

To effectively incorporate crowdfunding and P2P lending into your investment portfolio, consider how these options fit with your broader investment strategy. The key to successful investment diversification is understanding how different investments correlate with each other. Investments in crowdfunding and P2P lending should be balanced with more traditional investments like stocks, bonds, and real estate. This strategy helps spread risk and create a more resilient investment portfolio. For instance, while stocks may provide good returns over time, they can be volatile. Conversely, P2P loans can offer steady, predictable returns, which can buffer the volatility of the stock market.

By understanding how crowdfunding and P2P lending work, assessing the risks and returns, complying with legal requirements, and strategically diversifying your investment portfolio, you can tap into these modern financial avenues effectively. They not only offer the potential for financial returns but also the opportunity to partake in innovative projects and personal stories, adding a fulfilling dimension to your investment activities. As you explore these options, take a calculated approach, do thorough research, and always keep your financial goals in sight, ensuring that every investment moves you closer to your aspirations of financial growth and stability.

3.3 The Basics of Cryptocurrency: What It Is and How to Invest Safely

Cryptocurrency has surged from a niche interest to a major player in global finance, revolutionizing how we think about money and investment. At its core, cryptocurrency is a digital or virtual currency that uses cryptography for security, making it nearly impossible to counterfeit. The backbone of most cryptocurrencies is a technology called blockchain, a decentralized technology spread across many computers that manages and records transactions. Think of it as a highly secure, transparent digital ledger. This innovation not only supports cryptocurrencies like Bitcoin and Ethereum but is also capable of executing smart contracts and running decentralized applications, or DApps.

The role of cryptocurrencies in modern finance is expanding rapidly. Initially viewed as speculative investments, they are increasingly seen as valuable tools for diverse financial activities, including remittances and online transactions. Moreover, their potential to provide financial services to the unbanked populations of the world showcases their broader socio-economic impact.

If you're considering diving into the world of cryptocurrencies, the first step is selecting a reputable trading platform. Platforms like Coinbase, Binance, and Kraken offer user-friendly interfaces that cater to beginners and advanced traders alike. When choosing a platform, consider factors such as security measures, transaction fees, the range of available cryptocurrencies, and the quality of customer support. Once you've chosen a platform, the next steps involve setting up an account, securing it preferably with two-factor authentication, and linking a payment method such as a bank account or credit card.

Purchasing cryptocurrencies can be as simple as buying stocks. You decide how much you want to invest and buy the crypto at its current market price (or set a price at which you want to buy it). After the purchase, your cryptocurrencies will be stored in a digital wallet. Security here cannot be overstressed; ensure that your investments are protected by using wallets that allow you to keep control of your private keys—a critical piece of information used to authorize outgoing transactions on the blockchain network. Options include hardware wallets like Ledger and Trezor, which store your keys offline and away from potential online threats.

Cryptocurrencies are not without risks. Their prices can be highly volatile. Sharp price movements can result in significant gains but equally substantial losses. Effective risk management is crucial. One approach is to invest only what you can afford to lose. Diversification, by spreading your investment across different cryptocurrencies, can also help manage risk. Additionally, keeping a pulse on market trends, technological advancements, and regulatory changes can provide you with the insights needed to make informed decisions.

Cryptocurrencies are also paving the way for innovative financial applications. Bitcoin, for example, has emerged as an alternative store of value, with proponents likening it to digital gold due to its finite supply and resistance to inflation. Ethereum has introduced smart contracts that execute automatically when conditions are met, opening possibilities from decentralized finance (DeFi) to non-fungible tokens, or NFTs, which are revolutionizing art and collectibles markets.

Investing in cryptocurrencies offers a unique blend of risks and opportunities not found in traditional financial assets. By understanding the underlying technology, choosing the right trading platform, and employing sound investment strategies, you can confidently navigate this exciting new landscape.

Cryptocurrencies may represent a transformative technology that could redefine global finance for years to come.

3.4 Art and Collectibles as Alternative Investments

The allure of art and collectibles as investment avenues is not just in their aesthetic value but also in their potential to appreciate over time, offering a unique blend of personal and economic gratification. Unlike conventional stocks or bonds, investing in art and collectibles introduces you to a dynamic market where passion meets profit. The value of these items isn't tied solely to economic conditions but also to factors like rarity, historical significance, and cultural trends, making them a fascinating investment option.

Understanding the dynamics of this market requires a keen eye and a deep appreciation of the items' intrinsic qualities. The art market, for instance, fluctuates based on trends, artist reputation, and critical acclaim, much like fashion. Collectibles, which can range from vintage cars to rare stamps, derive their value from their historical significance, their condition, and the nostalgia they evoke. The rarity of a piece can significantly enhance its value, as collectors prize unique items for their exclusivity. However, the market for art and collectibles is less liquid than traditional investment markets. Selling these items can take time, and prices can be highly subjective—dependent on finding the right buyer who appreciates the item's worth as much as you do.

If you want to invest in this avenue, start with research. Familiarize yourself with the market by going to art shows, auctions, and galleries, and subscribing to databases that track sales and valuation trends. Understanding past price movements of similar items can give you insights into potential future appreciation. Also, engaging with communities of collectors and experts can be invaluable in helping you gauge the sentiment around certain pieces or artists.

Purchasing art and collectibles usually involves different channels. Auctions, both traditional and online, are popular venues where items are sold to the highest bidder. Auction houses like Sotheby's and Christie's provide opportunities to acquire rare pieces, but understanding the auction process is crucial. This includes knowing the buyer's premium (a percentage of the final bid price that you pay on top of the bid), and other potential fees. Galleries offer a more personal buying experience, with staff who can provide detailed backgrounds on the pieces and artists. Online platforms have also become prevalent, democratizing access to art and collectibles, allowing more people to participate in this market from anywhere in the world.

Authenticity and provenance are the cornerstones of value in art and collectibles. Authenticity refers to the verification that a piece is indeed what it is claimed to be, while provenance is the history of the item's ownership. Both factors can significantly affect an item's market value. Ensuring authenticity might involve scientific tests or expert evaluations, especially for ancient artifacts or signature pieces from renowned artists. Provenance, documented through a chain of ownership, helps establish an item's history and authenticity. For high-value items, provenance can also include historical records, receipts, and even letters or photos that connect the piece to its previous owners.

Investing in art and collectibles carries a set of risks alongside its potential for high rewards. The market's volatility can be driven by changes in cultural trends or consumer sentiment, which are less predictable than economic indicators that drive traditional investment markets. The subjective nature of valuation, influenced by factors like an artist's current popularity or the historical significance of a collectible, adds another layer of risk. Additionally, the lack of a quick liquidation option means that you may not be able to sell the item quickly or for a fair price in a pinch.

Despite these risks, the potential rewards are compelling. Apart from financial gain, investing in art and collectibles can bring emotional and aesthetic satisfaction, allowing you to enjoy your investment visually and emotionally. Moreover, for those passionate about history, art, or culture, this form of investing allows a deeper connection to their interests, making it a uniquely gratifying way to diversify an investment portfolio. As you consider adding art or collectibles to your investment array, weigh the emotional and financial aspects carefully, ensuring that each piece not only adds beauty to your collection but also holds the promise of increased value over time.

3.5 Understanding Real Estate Investment Trusts and Their Role in a Diversified Portfolio

Real Estate Investment Trusts (REITs) serve as a gateway for you to engage with large-scale real estate assets without the complexities and capital requirements of direct property ownership. Essentially, REITs are companies that own, operate, or finance income-producing real estate across a range of property sectors. These can include shopping malls, office buildings, apartments, hospitals, and hotels. By investing in a REIT, you are purchasing a share of a professionally managed portfolio of real estate, allowing you to earn a share of the income produced through real estate investment without having to buy, manage, or finance any properties yourself.

One of the most compelling reasons to include REITs in your investment portfolio is their ability to generate regular income streams. Most REITs pay out at least 90% of their taxable income to shareholders in the form of dividends, and many pay out 100%. This can provide investors with a regular income stream, which is particularly appealing if you're looking for passive income or need steady cash flow.

The accessibility of REITs is another significant advantage. They are traded on major stock exchanges just like any other stock, which means you can buy and sell REIT shares easily, providing liquidity that direct real estate investments generally lack. This feature makes REITs an excellent option for diversifying your investment portfolio while maintaining the flexibility to adjust your investment exposure as needed.

REITs are generally classified into three types, each with distinctive characteristics and investment profiles.

- Equity REITs, the most common type, own and operate income-generating real estate. The revenue primarily comes from leasing space and collecting rents on the properties they own, which is then passed on to shareholders in the form of dividends.

- Mortgage REITs provide funding for income-producing real estate by purchasing or originating mortgages and mortgage-backed securities. They earn income from the interest on these financial assets.

- Hybrid REITs combine the investment strategies of equity and mortgage REITs by investing in both properties and mortgages.

Incorporating REITs into your investment portfolio can significantly enhance its diversification. Real estate often reacts differently to economic cycles compared to other assets like stocks or bonds. REITs can provide a buffer against volatility in your portfolio, as the real estate market doesn't always move in tandem with stock or bond markets. Moreover, REITs offer exposure to a broad array of property sectors, which can help spread and manage investment risk. For instance, if the retail sector is suffering due to an economic downturn, other sectors like health care or residential might still perform well, balancing the impact on your REIT investments.

While the benefits are substantial, managing risks is crucial. Interest rate fluctuations can impact REITs, particularly mortgage REITs. When interest rates rise, financing costs can increase, and property values may decline, which could affect the performance of equity REITs. To manage these risks, consider diversifying not only across different types of REITs but also across different geographies and property sectors. This strategy can help mitigate the impact of downturns in any single market or sector on your overall investment.

REITs stand out as a practical choice for investors looking to diversify their portfolios and improve potential returns through regular dividend payments. They offer a unique combination of income generation, liquidity, and exposure to the real estate market, all while providing a convenient and less capital-intensive way to benefit from real estate investments. As you consider integrating REITs into your portfolio, evaluate how their characteristics align with your overall investment goals and risk tolerance. This careful consideration will ensure that your investments not only grow but also align seamlessly with your broader financial strategies, helping you build a robust and resilient investment portfolio.

3.6 Strategies for Investing in Startups and Small Businesses

Venture capital and angel investing represent pivotal avenues through which you can engage directly with the innovation economy, providing capital to startups and small businesses that promise high growth potential. Venture capital firms typically pool money from various investors to fund startups in exchange for equity, or partial ownership, while angel investors, often affluent individuals, invest their personal funds. Both forms of investment are crucial during different stages of a startup's lifecycle, from conception to early business operations. Angel investments usually come in early, helping startups get off the ground, while venture capital tends to play a vital role in scaling the business.

If you'd like to invest in this avenue, you must learn to evaluate potential startups. This starts with understanding the business model: How does the startup intend to make money? Is their model sustainable in the long term? Next comes assessing the market potential: Is there a demand for this product or service? How large is the target market? Finally, and most critically, evaluate the experience and capability of the founding team. A committed, knowledgeable team with complementary skills is often the linchpin in a startup's success.

You'll have to consider the risks too. The stark reality is that many startups fail, and investments can be lost. Liquidity is another concern; money invested in a startup may be tied up for years without any guarantee of return. Mitigating these risks begins with due diligence regarding the startup's business plan, market research, and financial projections. Diversify your investments across various sectors and stages of business to spread risk. Additionally, stay actively involved where possible. Many angel investors provide not just capital but also mentoring and advice, leveraging their experience and networks to guide the startup toward success.

Exit strategies are essential to investing in startups—defining how you can eventually realize the financial return on your investment. The most common exit strategies include initial public offerings, or IPOs, where a startup goes public and its shares are sold on a stock exchange, and acquisitions, where a larger company purchases the startup. Less commonly, a buyout might occur, where the startup's founders or management buy back the shares held by investors. Understanding these strategies and discussing potential exit routes with the startup early in your investment relationship can help align expectations and potentially secure your investment returns.

Venture capital and angel investments also offer the exhilarating experience of being part of a startup's journey from an idea to a fully operational business. This form of investment allows you to contribute to innovation and entrepreneurship, potentially changing industries and impacting the economy. As you explore these exciting opportunities, approach each potential investment while carefully balancing enthusiasm and analytical rigor so you are well-positioned to contribute and benefit from the next wave of business innovations.

As we wrap up this exploration into the dynamic world of investing in startups and small businesses, remember the blend of risk and opportunity that characterizes these investments. Venture capital and angel investments require not just financial capital but also a commitment toward due diligence and active involvement. By understanding the fundamentals of how these investments work, assessing opportunities carefully, and managing risks intelligently, you can engage with this exciting aspect of the financial world effectively. This chapter sets the stage for the innovative financial vehicles discussed next, each offering distinct opportunities and challenges in your quest for financial growth and independence.

ENTREPRENEURSHIP AND SIDE HUSTLES

Chapter 4:

Entrepreneurship and Side Hustles

In a world where traditional career paths often seem pre-paved and somewhat predictable, carving out your own niche through entrepreneurship and side hustles presents an exciting challenge and opens doors to financial independence and personal fulfillment. This chapter isn't just about making extra cash; it's also about transforming your passions and skills into profitable ventures. Whether you're looking to turn a hobby into a revenue stream or launch a startup that could change the market landscape, the initial steps you take can set the tone for your success.

4.1 Identifying Lucrative Side Hustles Tailored to Your Skills

Before diving into the vast ocean of side hustles, it's crucial to anchor yourself by assessing your own unique set of skills and interests. Start by conducting a thorough self-assessment. What are you good at? More importantly, what do you enjoy doing? Perhaps, you have a knack for graphic design, a passion for vintage clothing restoration, or a talent for tutoring math. List these skills and passions clearly. Remember, the most successful side hustles often stem from genuine interests and innate talents because that's where your intrinsic motivation resides.

Once you've pinpointed your skills, the next step is to analyze the market demand. Which of your skills has the potential to meet a need or solve a problem? Conducting market research might sound daunting, but in the age of the internet, it is more accessible than ever. Use online tools like Google Trends or social media platforms to gauge what people are talking about, what problems they are facing, and what kinds of services or products are trending. Subreddits relevant to your interests can also be goldmines of information, offering insights into what potential customers might be looking for.

Idea Validation

Validating your idea before fully committing your resources is crucial. Start small. For instance, if you think there's a market for your handmade jewelry, try selling a few pieces on platforms like Etsy or at local craft fairs to see how they are received. Feedback from these initial sales can be invaluable in learning whether there's interest in your product and scope for improvement. This phase is about learning and adapting, not about making instant profits.

Leverage Existing Networks

While breaking into new markets is always an option, leveraging your existing networks can provide a quicker and often more reliable path to early sales. Reach out to family, friends, and professional contacts who might be interested in your side hustle or know someone who would be. Utilize platforms like LinkedIn to announce your new venture or join Facebook groups where your target audience is likely to be active. Networking is not about making sales pitches to every acquaintance but about creating genuine connections that can naturally lead to business opportunities.

Embarking on a side hustle is a dynamic way to enhance your financial independence and personal satisfaction. It allows you to take control of your time and earnings while doing something that adds value to your life beyond just monetary gain. As you navigate through these initial steps, remember that patience and persistence are your allies. Every major success story started with a single step, and every global brand began as an idea. Yours is no different. Embrace the learning curve, adapt to feedback, and persist through challenges. The world of entrepreneurship and side hustles is as rewarding as it is demanding, and your journey through it is bound to be one of the most exhilarating parts of your financial narrative.

4.2 Steps to Launching a Successful Online Business

In today's digital age, launching an online business offers unparalleled opportunities for reaching a global audience and scaling with relatively low startup costs. However, the key to harnessing these opportunities lies in making well-informed decisions about where and how to establish your online presence. Choosing the right platform is the first crucial step. Each platform, whether it's a dedicated e-commerce site, a social media channel, or an online marketplace, comes with its unique set of advantages and challenges. Dedicated e-commerce platforms like Shopify or BigCommerce provide robust tools tailored for online selling, including customizable templates, integrated payment processing, and inventory management systems. These platforms are designed to handle a high volume of transactions and provide a high level of control over the user experience. However, they also require more time and technical know-how to set up and manage. Conversely, marketplaces like Etsy or eBay offer ease of entry, with simpler setup processes and built-in audiences. The trade-off, however, is less control over branding and higher competition from other sellers. Social media platforms like Instagram and Facebook have evolved into powerful selling tools with features like shoppable posts and marketplace functions. These platforms benefit from vast, engaged audiences and integrated advertising tools but often serve better as supplementary channels for driving traffic to a primary e-commerce site.

Once you've selected the ideal platform, building an impactful online presence is your next step. The cornerstone of a strong online presence is engaging content. This means high-quality photos, compelling product descriptions, and interactive elements like videos or blogs that provide value to your visitors. Effective branding is equally important; your brand's visual and narrative identity should resonate with your target audience, creating a memorable impression that encourages loyalty and word-of-mouth promotion.

Digital marketing techniques such as search engine optimization (SEO), pay-per-click (PPC) advertising, and email marketing are critical tools for attracting and retaining customers. SEO involves optimizing your website's content and structure to rank higher in search engine results, which is essential for driving organic traffic. PPC offers an opportunity to appear in front of potential customers through targeted ads, while email marketing helps in building relationships and keeping your audience engaged with updates, promotions, and personalized content.

Handling the logistics of an e-commerce operation is no small feat and includes managing inventory, processing payments, and shipping products. Effective inventory management ensures that you have enough products to meet customer demand but not so much that you tie up valuable resources in unsold goods. Software solutions can help track your inventory levels in real time and predict demand based on historical data. Payment processing must be secure and efficient with clear terms and conditions to ensure trust and compliance with financial regulations. Shipping presents its own set of challenges, from choosing the right carriers and packaging to managing shipping costs and tracking deliveries. Offering clear, concise shipping policies and options can significantly enhance customer satisfaction and encourage repeat business.

Lastly, utilizing online tools and resources can significantly streamline the process of running an online business. Tools like Zapier can automate workflows between apps, saving time and reducing errors. Project management tools such as Asana or Trello help keep your tasks and projects organized and on track. Customer relationship management (CRM) systems like Salesforce or HubSpot integrate sales, customer service, and marketing in one platform, providing a holistic view of your customer interactions and improving service delivery. Additionally, analytics tools such as Google Analytics provide crucial insights into your website's performance and customer behavior, enabling data-driven decisions that can enhance your marketing strategies and boost your business growth.

Launching a successful online business requires careful planning, from selecting the right platform and building a strong online presence to managing logistics and utilizing efficient tools. Each step involves a series of strategic decisions and actions that, when executed well, can build a robust online business capable of thriving in the competitive digital marketplace. As you embark on this venture, focus on creating a seamless user experience and maintaining a strong commitment to meeting your customers' needs and expectations, which are central to achieving long-term success in the online business arena.

4.3 Balancing a Side Hustle With Full-Time Employment

Managing both a full-time job and a side hustle demands more than just hard work; it also demands strategic planning and a commitment to maintaining balance. The key to success lies in integrating effective time management strategies that allow you to excel in your career while growing your side hustle.

Prioritization and scheduling become your best tools. Start by clearly defining the boundaries between your job and your side hustle. Establish specific times dedicated to each, ensuring that one does not bleed into the other. Utilize tools such as digital calendars to block out time for each activity, setting reminders and alerts to keep you on track. This methodical approach helps in maintaining focus and efficiency, ensuring that time spent on your side hustle is productive and does not detract from your primary employment responsibilities.

Moreover, setting realistic goals for your side hustle is crucial to prevent overcommitment, which can lead to burnout. These goals should be SMART.

For instance, instead of vaguely aiming to *increase sales*, set a precise target to *grow sales by 30% within six months by increasing online marketing efforts and expanding product lines*. Such clear objectives guide your actions and help you measure progress, making adjustments as needed. It's important to remember that side hustles, while offering financial and personal growth opportunities, should not compromise your health or primary job performance. They should rather complement your career, providing a creative outlet and a potential additional income stream.

Navigating the legal and ethical considerations is another pivotal aspect of juggling employment with entrepreneurship. Be aware of any potential conflicts of interest and ensure that your side hustle does not violate the terms of your employment contract. Many companies have policies regarding external engagements and intellectual property that employees must adhere to. Review your employment contract or consult with HR to understand these stipulations. Transparency with your employer about your side hustle, especially if it could intersect with your professional life, can prevent complications. It's also wise to keep your side business activities separate from your job, using your own resources and time rather than those of your employer to maintain clear ethical boundaries.

Balancing your work, side hustle, and personal life is perhaps the most challenging part. You must manage time effectively but also reserve time for rest. Maintaining a healthy lifestyle—regular exercise, adequate sleep, and proper nutrition—is vital. Remember, the value of a side hustle extends beyond additional income to include the personal satisfaction and empowerment that comes from entrepreneurship. Allocate time for family, hobbies, and relaxation to keep life balanced and enjoyable. This holistic approach not only enhances your well-being but also energizes you, increasing productivity in all areas of life.

Balancing a full-time job with a side hustle is an art that requires you to be proactive, organized, and disciplined. It allows you to explore your passions and increase your earnings while maintaining career security. By mastering time management, setting realistic goals, understanding legal boundaries, and nurturing your well-being, you can make both your job and your side hustle successful and fulfilling. As you continue to develop your entrepreneurial skills alongside your career, you'll not only achieve greater financial independence but also enrich your professional and personal life.

4.4 Legal and Financial Considerations for New Entrepreneurs

The entrepreneurial path has myriad legal and financial responsibilities that, if managed wisely, can pave the way for a business's success and sustainability. Understanding how to structure your business is the first critical decision you'll make, as it affects everything from your liability and taxes to your ability to raise funds.

For instance, operating as a sole proprietorship is the simplest form of business structure, making it an attractive option for many new entrepreneurs. It requires less paperwork, and in many jurisdictions, you can operate under your own name or a registered business name. However, the major downside is that there is no legal distinction between you and your business. This means your personal assets could be at risk if your business is sued or incurs debt.

Forming a Limited Liability Company (LLC) can protect from personal liability while maintaining operational flexibility. An LLC is a hybrid structure that allows the profits and losses of the business to pass through to your personal income without facing corporate taxes. However, the cost to establish and maintain an LLC is higher than running a sole proprietorship, and the regulatory requirements can be more complex, involving annual reports and other compliance obligations.

Corporations, while more complex and costly to set up, offer the greatest protection from personal liability and are favored by businesses that plan to seek investment or go public. They can sell shares of stock to raise capital, and shareholders are typically not liable for corporate debts or liabilities. However, they are subject to more stringent regulatory requirements, including corporate governance and detailed record-keeping.

Once your business structure is decided, the next crucial step is understanding your tax obligations. Running a business means you'll need to manage a range of taxes, from income tax to sales tax, depending on what your business does and where it operates. If your business is home-based or operates online, you might have different tax liabilities than a business with a physical storefront. For example, if you sell goods online, you may need to collect sales tax from customers in certain states. Understanding these nuances is crucial. Utilizing accounting software or consulting with a tax professional can help you navigate these complexities, ensuring you meet your tax obligations without overpaying.

Navigating licenses and permits is another fundamental step. Almost every business will need some form of license or permit to operate legally, but the requirements vary significantly based on industry, state, and locality. For instance, a home-based consulting business may only need a local business license, while a restaurant might need health permits, liquor licenses, and more. Failing to obtain the necessary licenses can result in fines and even cause your business to be shut down. Therefore, it's crucial to research the specific requirements for your business type and location by consulting local government websites or legal advisors.

Risk management should also be a priority for any new entrepreneur. Along with securing the premises or safeguarding digital data, risk management includes the strategic use of insurance to protect your business from financial losses. General liability insurance, for example, can protect against financial loss as a result of bodily injury, property damage, or lawsuits. Professional liability insurance, also known as errors and omissions insurance, is crucial for businesses that provide services or advice, as it covers damages that arise from professional mistakes or failure to perform. Depending on your business, you might also consider product liability insurance or commercial property insurance.

Effective risk management also involves planning for the unexpected. This means having a financial buffer to handle emergencies or slow periods, which can be crucial for maintaining your business operations under any circumstances. Additionally, consider the long-term risks and opportunities in your industry. Is your sector growing, or is it threatened by new developments and technologies? How will you adapt your business to these changes? Regularly assessing the external environment and adjusting your business plan accordingly can help mitigate risks and leverage opportunities, securing your business's future in a rapidly changing world.

Navigating the legal and financial aspects of a business venture can seem daunting, but with the right information and resources, you can lay a solid foundation for your venture. By carefully considering your business structure, staying compliant with tax laws and licenses, and employing robust risk management strategies, you set the stage for your business to thrive. Remember, the decisions you make now will impact not just your current operations but also your business's ability to grow and adapt in the future.

4.5 Scaling Your Side Hustle Into a Full-Time Business

Deciding when to transform your side hustle into a full-time business isn't just a pivotal moment—it's a calculated shift that hinges on understanding both your venture's financial health and your personal readiness to commit. Recognizing the optimal time for this transition involves closely monitoring specific financial metrics that indicate your business's capacity to sustain you.

Key indicators include consistent revenue growth, profitability, and cash flow stability. For instance, a good rule of thumb could be achieving a revenue that not only covers your business costs but also matches or exceeds your current salary, maintained consistently over several months. This financial buffer assures that you can handle the uncertainties of business without compromising your personal financial security.

Beyond financial metrics, personal readiness is equally crucial. It includes your ability to bear risks and your emotional and mental preparedness to invest more time and energy into the business. It's about feeling confident in your venture's direction and your capability to steer it toward continued growth. Transitioning to full-time also means being prepared to leave the security of a regular paycheck, which can be a significant emotional and financial step. Ensuring you have a clear understanding of your business's operations, the market conditions, and the growth potential is essential before making this leap.

Once you've decided to scale, identifying effective growth strategies becomes your next focus. Expanding your product line or service offerings is a common approach. This might involve introducing new products that complement the existing ones, thus attracting a broader customer base while maximizing the revenue from current customers.

For instance, if your side hustle involves selling bespoke candles, consider introducing related products such as handmade incense or essential oils. Another powerful strategy is franchising, which allows you to expand your business's footprint more quickly without the need to manage new locations directly. This can be particularly effective if your business model is unique, replicable, and appealing to potential franchisees.

Expanding into new markets is another growth strategy—whether it's targeting new geographies or tapping into different customer segments— and requires careful research to understand the new market's dynamics and consumer behaviors. Digital marketing can play a crucial role here in reaching new audiences efficiently through SEO, social media marketing, and online advertising. However, you must ensure your business infrastructure, from supply chains to customer service, can handle this expansion without compromising the quality of your products or services.

Hiring the right employees is critical as you scale. You're not merely filling positions; you're seeking individuals who possess the necessary skills and share your vision and enthusiasm for the business. Start by clearly defining the roles and responsibilities for each position. This clarity helps in attracting the right candidates and sets clear expectations from the start. During the recruitment process, focus on both skills and cultural fit, considering how potential employees align with your business's values and goals.

Onboarding new employees effectively is just as important as hiring them. A structured onboarding process helps new hires understand their roles, the business operations, and the company culture, which can significantly boost their productivity and job satisfaction. Regular training and professional development opportunities can also motivate employees and enhance their contributions to the business.

Compliance with labor laws is a non-negotiable aspect of hiring. This includes understanding and implementing regulations related to wages, benefits, workplace safety, and anti-discrimination policies. Failure to comply can result in legal issues and can damage your business's reputation. Therefore, staying informed about the legal obligations in your jurisdiction and possibly consulting with an HR professional or lawyer is advisable to ensure compliance.

As your business grows, sustaining this growth through continuous improvement and innovation is crucial. This involves regularly reviewing and refining your business processes to increase efficiency, reduce costs, and improve customer satisfaction. Encourage feedback from customers and employees alike, as this feedback can be invaluable in identifying areas for improvement. Additionally, staying adaptable and responsive to market changes can help you maintain a competitive edge. This might mean updating your technology, adopting new business practices, or changing your business strategy in response to consumer trends or economic shifts.

Fostering customer loyalty is another vital aspect of sustained growth. This can be achieved through excellent customer service, regular engagement via social media or email newsletters, and loyalty programs that reward repeat customers. By building strong relationships with your customers, you not only boost your current sales but also enhance your business's reputation through positive word-of-mouth.

Transitioning your side hustle into a full-time business is a journey fraught with challenges but also rich with rewards. By carefully planning this transition, employing effective growth strategies, and fostering an environment of continuous improvement, you can build a thriving business that not only meets your financial goals but also brings personal fulfillment. As you move forward, keep your eyes on both the details and the big picture, ensuring that every step you take is a step toward greater success.

4.6 Case Studies of Successful Millennial Entrepreneurial Ventures

Millennial entrepreneurship speaks of innovation, resilience, and strategic acumen. Through a collection of inspiring case studies, we uncover the pathways several young entrepreneurs have navigated to carve out niches in diverse industries. These stories highlight the triumphs and challenges and extract the essence of what propels a modern business to success.

Take the story of Maya, who launched a sustainable fashion brand right out of college. Recognizing the growing consumer interest in cco-friendly products, Maya used her passion for environmental activism to create a line of clothing made entirely from recycled materials. Her success wasn't just due to her innovative product line but also her savvy use of social media to market her brand. By engaging directly with her audience through platforms like Instagram and Pinterest, she built a loyal customer base. Maya's journey underscores the power of aligning a business with broader social values and the effectiveness of digital platforms in building brand identity.

Then there's Liam, a software developer whose side project turned into a leading tech startup. Liam developed a mobile app that uses artificial intelligence (AI) to help people manage their mental health. What started as a personal project to deal with his own challenges soon caught the attention of investors. Key to his success was his commitment to continuous improvement and user feedback, which he integrated into each update of the app. Liam's approach demonstrates the importance of adaptability and customer-focused innovation in the tech industry.

Elena and Raj, a duo who started a food delivery service that connects people with home-cooked meals from their neighbors, set their business apart with originality and a strategic approach to operations. They implemented a robust business model that included a revenue-sharing system with home cooks and a dynamic pricing model that adjusted for peak times. Their clear, well-planned business model and attention to operational details were crucial in scaling their service across multiple cities.

These entrepreneurs from different sectors share common success factors—innovation, a keen understanding of market needs, and robust business planning. Each story is a testament to the idea that successful entrepreneurship often involves more than just a great product or service; it requires a holistic approach that encompasses market understanding, customer engagement, and continuous evolution and adaptation.

From these narratives emerge lessons about the importance of resilience and flexibility. Many of these entrepreneurs faced significant challenges, from financial constraints to market competition and operational hurdles. However, their ability to pivot and adapt to changing circumstances played a critical role in their success. Their stories showcase how embracing innovation, leveraging new technologies, and responding to societal shifts can pave the way to successful and sustainable business ventures. For any young individual looking to embark on an entrepreneurial venture, these examples illuminate the path to potential success and personal and professional growth. Visit https://www.thepennyhoarder.com/make-money/side-gigs/best-side-hustles/ or Scan the code below for a list of unique and creative ideas for a side hustle. Who knows, you may just find your calling among these ideas!

As we round off this exploration into the vibrant world of millennial entrepreneurship, we connect these narratives back to the broader theme of this book—empowering you to take active steps toward financial independence and business success. Each story adds a layer of understanding about what it takes to transform a vision into reality in today's fast-paced and ever-evolving market landscape.

We're nearly halfway through the book, and I just wanted to check how you're feeling about everything so far. We've already discussed so much, from budgeting to entrepreneurship, and there's still so much to discuss!

Make a Difference With Your Review

Unlock the Power of Generosity

"Money can't buy happiness, but giving it away can." - Freddie Mercury

People who give without expecting anything in return live longer, happier lives and often find success along the way. Are you willing to assist someone unfamiliar if it meant receiving no recognition? Who is the person, you ask? They are like you. Or, at least, like you used to be. Curious, exploring new technologies, wanting to make a difference, and needing help but not sure where to look.

Our mission is to make **FINANCIAL FREEDOM** accessible to everyone. All our efforts are grounded in this endeavor, intending to reach a broad audience, and this is where you play a vital part. Most people do, in fact, judge a book by its cover (and its reviews). On behalf of those young adults, you've not met:

Your review for this book would be greatly appreciated. This small act could significantly affect others, potentially aiding local businesses, supporting entrepreneurs, or helping individuals achieve their dreams. Your willingness to leave feedback makes a world of difference and can be accomplished easily by scanning the QR code below or using this link: https://www.amazon.com/review/review-your-purchases/?asin=B0DCJXC3QP.

Join us if making a difference anonymously resonates with you. Thank you for your consideration. Remember, adding value to others' lives enhances your own value to them. If you believe this book might help someone, please pass it along.

THE DIGITAL AGE OF
PERSONAL FINANCE

Chapter 5:

The Digital Age of Personal Finance

In this era where technology seamlessly integrates into every aspect of our lives, mastering the digital tools that manage our money is not just an advantage—it's a necessity. As young adults stepping boldly into the complexities of financial independence, the power to manage, multiply, and monitor your finances is literally at your fingertips. Through innovative financial apps, you can keep up with the digital age and harness its potential to craft a future where financial clarity and growth are constant companions on your path to wealth.

5.1 Financial Apps That Revolutionize Money Management

The landscape of personal finance apps is as varied as it is dynamic, offering tools that cater not only to diverse financial needs but also to differing financial acumen. Among the plethora of options, apps like Mint, You Need a Budget (YNAB), and Acorns stand out due to their robust functionalities that simplify budgeting, investing, and expense tracking. Mint has carved a niche for itself by offering a comprehensive overview of your financial picture. It allows you to connect all your accounts in one place, track your spending, and set budgets that alert you when they're nearing their limits.

YNAB takes a proactive approach, focusing on giving every dollar a job to ensure that you're always planning for your next dollar rather than just tracking what you've already spent. Acorns introduces you to the world of investing by rounding up your daily purchases to the nearest dollar and investing the difference in a diversified portfolio.

The benefits of these apps extend beyond mere convenience. Real-time budget tracking helps you see where your money goes as it happens, enabling you to make immediate adjustments to avoid overspending. Automated savings take the guesswork out of financial planning so you're consistently setting aside a portion of your income toward your financial goals. Investment features in apps like Acorns make the stock market accessible and less intimidating for new investors by allowing you to start small and learn as you grow.

Comparing these apps, you'll find that each offers a unique user experience designed to meet specific financial needs. Mint is ideal for someone who wants a broad overview and regular updates on all their financial activities, while YNAB appeals to those who need a more hands-on approach in active budget management. Acorns provides a user-friendly platform for those new to investing by simplifying the investment process and making it an almost invisible part of daily life. The cost of these apps varies with some offering basic services for free and more advanced services with a subscription. Choosing the right app depends on your financial situation and goals. Do you need comprehensive financial oversight or just help with specific aspects like budgeting or investing?

User Testimonials and Case Studies

The practical benefits of these apps become most evident through the stories of those who use them. Take, for example, Samantha, a recent college graduate who struggled to keep her spending in check and save money. With Mint, she could visualize her spending patterns through colorful charts and receive alerts for unusual transactions, which significantly improved her financial habits. Then there's Jake, who was skeptical about investing but decided to give Acorns a try. The app's approach of using spare change to invest made the process less daunting, and over time, Jake grew more comfortable with his growing portfolio. These stories highlight just how transformative these tools can be in turning passive money management into proactive financial growth.

Embracing these financial apps helps in taking control of your finances. As you navigate through the options, consider what aspects of your finances need the most attention and choose tools accordingly. The right app can not only streamline your financial tasks but also open up new avenues for saving and investing that you might not have considered before.

In the next sections, we'll continue to explore other digital tools and platforms that can help you enhance your financial management skills so you're well-equipped to thrive in the digital age of personal finance.

5.2 Leveraging Social Media for Business and Branding

In today's digital ecosystem, social media stands out as a dynamic tool for building personal and business brands. Platforms like Instagram, Twitter, and LinkedIn have transcended their roles as networking sites to become powerful channels for marketing and brand engagement. For you, the aspiring entrepreneur or established business owner, these platforms offer fertile ground to sow the seeds of your brand's identity and watch them flourish through strategic engagement and monetization techniques.

Building a compelling brand on social media can seem daunting, but all you need is consistency and authenticity. Start by clearly defining your brand's voice and aesthetic—it could be professional and authoritative on LinkedIn and casual and witty on Twitter. The key is to ensure that your brand's messaging resonates with your target audience while reflecting your core values and mission.

Instagram, with its visual-centric format, is ideal for brands that can showcase their appeal through images and videos, such as fashion labels or travel agencies. Twitter's fast-paced, text-driven environment is perfect for brands that thrive on immediate engagement—think quick customer service responses or timely commentary on current events.

The next step is cultivating engagement. This is where the magic happens. Engagement on social media isn't just about garnering likes or shares—it's also about fostering a community and sparking conversations that keep your audience coming back. Start by creating content that adds value. This could be a blog post series shared on LinkedIn that addresses common industry challenges or Instagram tutorials that showcase your product in action. Use features like polls or Q&A sessions to encourage interaction, and don't forget to jump into discussions—engaging with your followers builds community and loyalty.

Hashtags and collaborations can exponentially increase your visibility and engagement. Use targeted hashtags to reach beyond your existing followers to a broader audience interested in similar topics. Collaborating with influencers or other brands can also be a game-changer. Choose collaborators who share your brand values and have an audience that might benefit from your products or services. These partnerships can lead to shared content that introduces your brand to an entirely new group of potential customers, effectively doubling your visibility.

Monetizing your social media presence is the next challenge. As your brand gains traction, opportunities to monetize will emerge. Sponsored posts are a direct way to earn revenue; brands will pay you to promote their content if your audience demographics align with their target market. Affiliate marketing is another lucrative model—promoting other brands' products and earning a commission for each sale made through your referral. Finally, consider leveraging your social media platforms to sell your products directly. Instagram and Facebook, for example, offer integrated shopping features that allow users to purchase products without leaving the app, streamlining the buying process and keeping everything within your branded ecosystem.

Case Studies of Successful Social Media Campaigns

Consider the success of Ella, a freelance graphic designer who used Instagram to transform her one-person operation into a thriving design studio. By posting her projects regularly and using hashtags like #GraphicDesign and #BrandIdentity, she attracted a diverse client base. Collaborations with content creators in the tech industry further boosted her visibility, leading to a 50% increase in project inquiries within six months.

There's also the small coffee shop that leveraged Twitter to drive engagement and sales. By tweeting daily specials and hosting weekly Q&A sessions about coffee sourcing and brewing techniques, they established themselves as a go-to source for coffee lovers in the area. They also used Twitter to promote live events and seasonal offers, which increased foot traffic and strengthened their customer base.

These examples underscore the transformative potential of social media in building and scaling your brand. By strategically leveraging these platforms, you can create a robust online presence that enhances your brand's visibility and drives business. As you continue to explore and integrate these social media strategies, remember that authenticity is your greatest asset. Let your brand's genuine personality shine through every post, tweet, or pin, and watch as your digital footprint expands, bringing with it increased recognition and revenue.

5.3 E-commerce: Turning a Hobby Into an Online Store

Transforming your hobby into a thriving online store is an exhilarating way to channel your passion into profit. With the rise of e-commerce platforms, setting up an online store has become accessible for many, allowing you to reach a global audience from the comfort of your home. The first step in this venture is to select the right platform. Choices range from comprehensive solutions like Shopify, which offers extensive customization and support for a variety of payment gateways, to more niche platforms like Etsy, which caters specifically to handmade goods and vintage items. Consider what suits your product type and what kind of customer experience you want to offer. For instance, Shopify might be the best fit if you're looking at a large-scale operation with a diverse inventory, while Etsy could be ideal for personalized crafts.

Understanding the basics of e-commerce is crucial. This includes knowledge of online payment systems, website design, and customer service. A user-friendly design with clear navigation and high-quality product images can significantly enhance the shopping experience and influence buying decisions. Integrating reliable payment systems that ensure secure transactions will build trust with your customers. Additionally, setting up an efficient customer service system, including clear policies on returns and exchanges, will help manage customer expectations and enhance overall brand satisfaction.

Marketing your online store effectively is key to attracting and retaining customers. Start with SEO to ensure your store appears in search results when potential customers are looking for products you sell. This involves using the right keywords in your product descriptions and titles, optimizing website images, and ensuring your site is mobile-friendly.

Email marketing is another powerful tool. By collecting email addresses either through sign-ups or at checkout, you can keep your customers informed about new products, promotions, and content. Well-crafted emails that offer genuine value can help in building customer loyalty and encouraging repeat purchases.

Social media advertising also plays a crucial role. Platforms like Facebook and Instagram offer powerful targeting options to reach potential customers based on their interests, behaviors, and more. Running targeted ads can drive traffic to your store and increase sales.

Logistics and fulfillment are the backbone of any e-commerce business. Efficient inventory management, order processing, shipping, and returns are vital for customer satisfaction and operational scalability. Implementing an inventory management system can help track stock levels, manage orders efficiently, and reduce the risk of overselling. When it comes to shipping, offering multiple options can cater to different customer needs and budgets. Partnering with reliable couriers that provide tracking information ensures transparency and builds trust with customers. Lastly, a clear and straightforward returns policy can alleviate potential concerns for new customers about ordering from your store.

Success Stories

Consider the story of Julia, who turned her passion for jewelry making into a lucrative online business. By starting small on Etsy, she gradually expanded her business by setting up her own website powered by Shopify. Her success was not just due to her unique designs but also her strategic use of Instagram for marketing. By posting engaging content and utilizing Instagram Shopping, she was able to significantly increase her visibility and sales.

Mark created an online store for his woodworking projects. He focused on producing high-quality custom furniture and used YouTube to share the crafting process. This not only showcased his expertise and craftsmanship but also helped him build a community of followers who were keen to buy his products. His detailed tutorials and the transparent display of his work process helped create a trusted brand.

These stories prove that with the right strategies, turning a hobby into a profitable e-commerce business is very achievable. They underscore the importance of choosing the right platform, understanding e-commerce fundamentals, effectively marketing your store, and managing logistics efficiently.

As we wrap up this exploration of turning hobbies into online stores, remember that the success of your e-commerce venture lies in your ability to seamlessly integrate passion with business acumen. By understanding your market, leveraging the right digital tools, and consistently delivering value to your customers, you can transform your hobby into a flourishing online business. This journey into e-commerce not only opens up a pathway to financial independence but also allows you to make a living doing what you love.

5.4 Online Platforms for Freelancers: Maximizing Your Earnings

Freelancing has become not just a viable career option but a preferred choice for many, especially millennials and Gen Zers who cherish flexibility and autonomy over their work. Platforms like Upwork, Freelancer, and Fiverr have emerged as bustling marketplaces where freelancers can connect with clients from all over the world needing everything, from graphic design and writing to software development and marketing. These platforms are not just about matching skills with needs; they're about creating opportunities for freelancers to manage their careers as independent entrepreneurs.

Creating a standout profile on these platforms is your first step toward attracting potential clients. Think of your profile as your storefront. It needs to be compelling, professional, and clear. Start with a friendly, professional photo and a headline that succinctly showcases your expertise. Your profile summary should clearly articulate what you do, how you can help clients, and what makes you different from other freelancers in your field. Highlight your skills with specific keywords that potential clients might use to search for services like yours.

For instance, instead of just listing 'writer', specify 'SEO content writer' or 'technical writer' to attract more targeted job offers. Including a portfolio of your work is crucial. This visual proof of your abilities can be the deciding factor in a client's decision to hire you. If you're a graphic designer, show a range of your projects from logos to websites. If you're a writer, include links to your published articles or blog posts. Each item in your portfolio should reflect the quality and range of your work, ensuring potential clients know exactly what you can deliver.

Bidding on projects is the next crucial step, and it requires a balance of strategy and an understanding of your worth and the market. When you find projects that interest you, tailor your proposals specifically to each job. Avoid generic bids; a personalized approach shows potential clients that you understand their project and are genuinely interested in helping them achieve their goals.

Your proposal should clearly outline how you plan to tackle the project, the timeline, and why you are the best fit for the job. Be realistic and clear about your rates. It's often tempting to undervalue your work in an attempt to win more jobs. However, setting fair rates not only ensures you are adequately compensated for your time and skills but also helps set client expectations about the quality of work you provide. As you build relationships, consider negotiating longer-term contracts or retainer agreements with clients who have ongoing needs. This can provide more stability and predictability in your income—a common challenge in freelance work.

Managing your income as a freelancer is fundamentally different from receiving a paycheck as an employee. Your income can fluctuate, which makes financial planning all the more critical. Start by setting up a separate bank account for your freelancing business. This makes tracking your income and expenses easier, simplifying tax filing and financial management. Develop a budget based on your average monthly earnings and be sure to include a line item for taxes.

In many locations, freelancers need to pay estimated taxes quarterly. Failing to plan for these can lead to a large tax bill at the end of the year. Additionally, consider using accounting software designed for freelancers which can help you track your invoices, expenses, and taxes. This software often includes features that allow you to send professional invoices and set up payment reminders for clients, streamlining your financial operations.

Financial stability as a freelancer also involves preparing for the unexpected. Establish an emergency fund that can cover at least three to six months of living expenses. This fund can be a lifeline during slow periods or if you need to take time off for any reason. Investing in health insurance and retirement plans is also crucial. As a freelancer, you're responsible for your own benefits, and neglecting them can have long-term consequences on your financial health. Various retirement accounts that cater specifically to self-employed individuals are available, offering tax advantages that can significantly boost your savings over time.

Navigating the freelance economy requires not just talent and hard work but a strategic approach to profile creation, client engagement, and financial management. By building a presence on freelance platforms, you can attract more clients and better projects. Coupled with savvy financial planning and client relationship management, these strategies will help you build a successful and sustainable freelancing career, turning your professional aspirations into reality while enjoying the autonomy and flexibility that freelancing offers. Visit https://www.upwork.com/resources/best-freelance-websites or Scan the QR code below for a list of great freelancer platforms that connect clients with talent.

5.5 The Impact of Blockchain Technology on Personal Finance

Blockchain technology has emerged as a novel innovation and transformative force reshaping how transactions are conducted and recorded. At its core, blockchain is a decentralized digital ledger that records transactions across multiple computers so the registered transactions cannot be altered retroactively. This foundational aspect of blockchain is what underpins cryptocurrencies, a class of digital assets poised to potentially redefine the concept of money.

Blockchain's primary appeal lies in its ability to foster a level of transparency and security that traditional financial systems struggle to match. Every transaction on a blockchain is recorded with an immutable cryptographic signature called a hash. This not only makes transactions virtually tamper-proof but also publicly verifiable, fostering a new degree of trust in financial activities. For anyone navigating the complexities of personal finance, the implications are profound. Blockchain introduces a scenario where you can trace the authenticity of your transactions without relying solely on external validations from banks or other financial institutions.

The applications of blockchain in finance extend beyond cryptocurrencies. Smart contracts, self-executing contractual states stored on the blockchain, automate agreements without intermediaries. This can revolutionize everything from mortgage approvals to insurance claims, reducing the potential for disputes and the delay in execution. DeFi further exemplifies blockchain's impact. It uses smart contracts to create protocols that replicate existing financial services more transparently. You could participate in lending, borrowing, trading, and earning interest on your assets, all governed by transparent smart contracts and accessible to anyone with an internet connection.

However, engaging with blockchain technologies has its own challenges and risks. The very features that make blockchain revolutionary also give rise to significant considerations. One of the most glaring is market volatility. Cryptocurrencies, for instance, can experience extreme fluctuations in value within short periods. While this can yield high returns, the risk of significant losses is equally high. Moreover, the regulatory landscape for blockchain and cryptocurrencies is still in flux. Different countries have varying degrees of openness to these technologies, ranging from outright bans to enthusiastic support. This regulatory uncertainty can affect your ability to use and benefit from blockchain technologies, depending on your location and the nature of your transactions.

Furthermore, while blockchain offers enhanced security features, it is not completely immune to risks. The technology is relatively new and complex, which can make it a target for sophisticated cyber-attacks. For instance, while the blockchain itself may be secure, digital wallets and exchanges where cryptocurrencies are stored can be vulnerable. Hackers have exploited vulnerabilities in these platforms to steal vast amounts of cryptocurrency, leading to significant financial losses for users.

You must navigate the blockchain landscape carefully. Educating yourself about how blockchain works and the specific risks and benefits associated with its various applications is crucial. Stay updated with the latest developments in blockchain technology and regulatory changes and consult with financial advisors who are knowledgeable about this new terrain. As you consider incorporating blockchain technologies into your personal finance strategy, weigh the potential benefits against the risks. Consider how features like transparency, security, and the potential for smart contracts could impact your financial dealings. Always be vigilant about the volatility, regulatory uncertainties, and security challenges that come with this technology.

Blockchain holds the promise to redefine elements of personal finance significantly. Whether it's enhancing how we perform transactions, ensuring the security of our financial dealings, or providing new ways to invest and manage assets, its potential is undeniable. As you explore this innovative technology, keep in mind that like any financial decision, a balanced approach and thorough understanding are your best strategies for harnessing the benefits while mitigating the risks.

5.6 Cybersecurity: Protecting Your Financial Data Online

The importance of cybersecurity cannot be overstated, especially when it comes to protecting your financial information. Think of cybersecurity as the digital equivalent of locking your doors and windows; it's essential for keeping your personal and financial data safe from intruders. As we navigate various platforms, from mobile banking apps to online shopping sites, our financial data becomes susceptible to cyber threats. Understanding these threats and how to guard against them is crucial to safeguard your money, protect your identity, and maintain your financial health.

One of the most common and dangerous threats is phishing. This tactic involves fraudsters impersonating legitimate institutions, such as your bank or a well-known retailer, to trick you into providing sensitive information. These phishing attempts often come in the form of emails or texts that appear urgent, prompting you to click on a link that leads to a fake website designed to steal your data.

Another prevalent threat is malware, or malicious software, which can be installed on your device without your knowledge simply by visiting a compromised website or downloading an infected attachment. Once installed, malware can wreak havoc, from monitoring your keystrokes to access passwords to directly stealing funds from your accounts. Identity theft is another significant risk, where cybercriminals use the data they've stolen to impersonate you, opening accounts in your name and potentially ruining your credit score and financial standing.

To protect yourself from these threats, use strong, unique passwords for each of your online accounts. Avoid common words or easily guessable combinations; instead, opt for a mix of letters, numbers, and symbols, and consider using a password manager to keep track of them all. Two-factor authentication adds another layer of security. This method requires your password *and* a second piece of information— often a code sent to your phone or generated by an app—for access. This means that even if someone does get hold of your password, they won't be able to access your account without also having your phone or other second-factor device.

Securing your Wi-Fi connection is also critical. Use a strong, unique password for your home network and consider setting up a guest network for visitors to protect the main network that connects your personal devices and stores your sensitive information. Be cautious when connecting to public Wi-Fi networks; avoid accessing financial accounts or making transactions over these networks since they can be easily intercepted by cybercriminals. For added security, use a virtual private network, or VPN, which encrypts your internet connection and hides your online activity from prying eyes, whether you're at home or on the go.

Staying informed about cybersecurity trends and best practices is the final piece of the puzzle. Cyber threats are constantly evolving as are the technologies and strategies to combat them. Regularly updating your software and apps ensures you have the latest security patches. Educate yourself about the newest scams and learn how to recognize the signs of a phishing attempt or other malicious activities. Many financial institutions and cybersecurity organizations offer resources and alerts to help keep you informed and one step ahead of fraudsters.

Incorporating these cybersecurity practices into your daily digital routine can significantly reduce your risk of falling victim to cybercrime. As you continue to navigate the complexities of the digital world, remember that protecting your financial information is an ongoing process that requires vigilance, awareness, and proactive measures. By taking these steps, you empower yourself to move confidently through online spaces, secure in the knowledge that your financial data is well-protected.

The next chapter will delve into more specialized areas of personal finance, ensuring you have a holistic understanding of the financial tools and strategies at your disposal to secure and grow your wealth.

MINDSET AND PERSONAL DEVELOPMENT

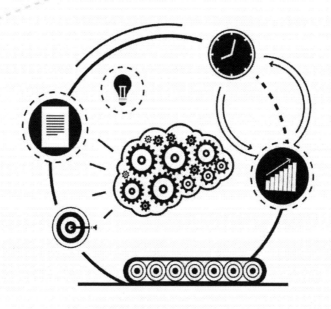

Chapter 6:

Mindset and Personal Development

Imagine your financial success as a skyscraper. The structural integrity of this towering achievement not only includes steel beams and glass panes but also a deeply embedded architectural blueprint—your mindset.

I have spoken extensively about the power and benefits of having the ideal mindset in my book, "BE R.E.A.L: The Mindset to Achieve The Winning Lifestyle You Desire," which offers a comprehensive, guided approach to building a growth mindset. This chapter, however, will focus more on cultivating the ideal mindset for financial freedom. We'll talk about financial strategies, reshaping their foundation, and transforming invisible barriers into launchpads for growth and success. Visit https://www.amazon.com/BE-R-L-Mindset-Lifestyle/dp/B0D8WNX1FH or Scan the QR code below to find "BE R.E.A.L: The Mindset to Achieve The Winning Lifestyle You Desire."

6.1 Developing a Wealth Mindset: Overcoming Mental Barriers

Identify Common Mental Barriers

Our journey toward financial mastery often encounters hidden snags. Among the most insidious are the mental barriers that can derail even the best-laid financial plans. Common culprits include the fear of failure, a scarcity mindset, and social stigmas around discussing money.

Fear of failure might manifest as hesitation to invest or explore new financial opportunities. This fear often stems from past mistakes or societal narratives that equate financial risk with irresponsibility.

A scarcity mindset, which can be ingrained from experiences of financial hardship, persuades you to view life as a finite pie. From this perspective, every gain by another is a loss for you, stifling generosity and bold financial moves.

Social stigmas about discussing finances openly can prevent the sharing of knowledge and support that could catalyze financial growth. Each of these barriers not only shackles your financial potential but also clouds your ability to see and seize opportunities.

A Shift From Scarcity to Abundance

Transitioning from a scarcity mindset to one of abundance marks a profound pivot in your financial narrative. An abundance mindset opens up the world, transforming how you engage with money and wealth. It encourages the view that there are enough resources and successes to share around. From this vantage point, financial decisions shift from protective hoarding to strategic, growth-oriented investments. Opportunities for collaboration and innovation emerge, revealing new paths to wealth that were previously obscured by fear and competition. Embracing abundance also fosters a deeper sense of gratitude and contentment, which studies suggest can lead to smarter financial decisions and greater wealth in the long term.

Role of Positive Affirmations

One tool to cultivate and reinforce an abundance mindset is the use of positive affirmations. These short, powerful statements, when spoken with conviction and regularity, can reprogram your subconscious mind, shifting your concept of self and what's possible financially. Statements like "I am capable of mastering my financial future" or "There is always more than enough for everyone" can recalibrate your internal dialogue. They act as mental armor, shielding you against the barrage of negativity and doubt that can arise in daily life and during financial setbacks. Integrating these affirmations into your daily routine can fortify your mental resilience and pave the way for a healthier relationship with money.

Impact of Mindset on Financial Decisions

The transformation in mindset directly influences your financial decision-making. With an empowered, abundant approach, risks are more likely to be viewed as calculated investments rather than reckless gambles. A wealth mindset doesn't just alter your reactions to financial opportunities; it also actively shapes the opportunities you believe are available to you. Psychological studies affirm that those who adopt a positive financial outlook are more likely to recognize and act upon opportunities for wealth creation. Moreover, they are generally more resilient in the face of financial adversity, viewing setbacks as temporary and instructive rather than definitive failures. This resilient outlook ensures that each financial decision, whether successful or not, enriches your understanding and enhances your strategic approach to wealth building.

In this dynamic landscape of personal finance, your mindset is the lens through which you view every challenge and opportunity. By recognizing and reshaping mental barriers, embracing an abundance mindset, using positive affirmations, and understanding the profound impact of your outlook on your financial decisions, you equip yourself with more than just financial tools and strategies. You shape a mindset that can envision and achieve remarkable wealth. As you continue to engage with and refine this mindset, remember that each step forward, each thought recalibrated, and each fear confronted is building you a wealthier future and a profound legacy of financial empowerment and success.

6.2 The Importance of Financial Literacy in Personal Growth

Understanding financial literacy means grasping more than just the ability to balance a checkbook or understanding annual percentage rates. It encapsulates a comprehensive knowledge of how to make informed choices about saving, investing, and managing money efficiently. This skill empowers you to navigate the financial landscape with confidence, making decisions that align with both your immediate needs and long-term goals. The importance of being financially literate cannot be overstated—it is a fundamental stepping stone toward achieving personal and financial freedom. By mastering this skill, you position yourself to take control of your finances rather than letting them control you.

The correlation between financial literacy and personal development stretches far beyond just dollars and cents. Enhancing your financial knowledge can lead to a profound increase in self-confidence. When you understand financial concepts and how they apply to your life, you're likely to feel more competent and secure in your financial decisions. This boost in confidence can spill over into other areas of your life, enhancing your overall sense of self-efficacy.

Furthermore, financial literacy significantly contributes to better stress management. Money-related issues are a common source of stress for many, but when you comprehend financial principles and apply them effectively, you mitigate the anxieties associated with unexpected expenses or economic downturns. Additionally, financial knowledge encourages a proactive approach to life. Instead of reacting to financial situations as they arise, you'll find yourself planning and preparing for future financial needs, which can lead to a more organized and goal-oriented lifestyle.

The world of finance is constantly evolving, with new products, technologies, and regulations emerging regularly. Staying informed through books, podcasts, and seminars not only keeps you updated but also deepens your understanding and application of financial concepts. For instance, reading books such as "Rich Dad Poor Dad" by Robert Kiyosaki or "The Total Money Makeover" by Dave Ramsey can transform your thinking about money and investing. Podcasts like "So Money" with Farnoosh Torabi offer insights into modern financial trends and tips from leading experts. Attending seminars and workshops provides a platform to engage with financial professionals and expand your network, which can be invaluable in your personal and professional development.

To illustrate the transformative power of financial literacy, consider the experiences of individuals like Laura and Michael.

Laura, a recent college graduate, found herself overwhelmed by her student loan debt and from living paycheck to paycheck. By dedicating time to learning about personal finance, she developed a budget that allowed her to manage her expenses more effectively and even start saving for retirement. This knowledge not only improved her financial situation but also reduced her stress levels and increased her optimism about the future.

Michael, a young professional, earned a decent salary but had no idea how to invest his money. After attending a financial planning workshop, he began to invest in stocks and mutual funds, which helped him build a substantial nest egg. His newfound financial literacy not only increased his wealth but also empowered him to make informed financial decisions confidently.

These cases underscore the profound impact that financial literacy can have on an individual's life. It not only equips you with the skills to improve your financial well-being but also enhances your overall personal development, leading to a more fulfilled and purposeful life.

As you continue to explore and expand your financial knowledge, remember that each piece of information acquired is a stepping stone toward financial independence and a richer, more empowered existence.

6.3 Stress Management Techniques for Financial Worries

The ebbs and flows of your bank account can often lead to emotional highs and lows. Recognizing the sources of financial stress is the first step in managing them effectively. Common triggers include the stress of overwhelming debt, the fear of not having enough savings, and the instability of an uncertain economic climate. Such stressors are not just numbers on a page; they evoke deep emotional responses that can affect your overall well-being. Debt, for instance, is often seen as a financial burden and a personal failure, insufficient savings can trigger anxiety about future security, and economic instability can cause a constant state of worry about the unknown.

Addressing these stressors begins with adopting tailored stress management techniques. Mindfulness, a practice rooted in being present and engaged in the current moment without judgment, has been shown to significantly lessen the anxiety associated with financial uncertainty. By focusing on the here and now, mindfulness exercises can help you detach from worries about past financial mistakes and future repercussions, allowing for a clearer perspective on how to manage your finances today. Structured problem-solving is another effective technique where financial challenges are broken down into manageable steps. This approach transforms overwhelming problems into a series of actionable steps, reducing the mental burden and promoting a sense of accomplishment as you tackle each one.

Developing a financial buffer can significantly alleviate financial stress. An emergency fund, for instance, provides a safety net that can cover unexpected expenses, reducing the need to accrue high-interest debt. The psychological peace of mind that comes from having a financial cushion cannot be overstated. It transforms the fear of potential financial disasters into a confident assurance that you can handle challenges without derailing your financial stability. This buffer does more than just provide monetary security; it also enables a mental space where you can make decisions from a place of strength and calm, rather than from panic and desperation.

At times, however, the weight of financial stress might feel too heavy to manage alone, and that's when seeking professional help becomes invaluable. Financial advisors can offer strategies and insights that you might not have considered, helping to restructure debt or optimize savings in ways that align with your financial goals. Moreover, if financial stress is causing significant anxiety or depression, consulting with a therapist can be crucial. Mental health professionals specialize in helping you develop coping strategies to manage stress effectively, ensuring that your financial worries do not overwhelm your daily life. This step, often overlooked, is vital in maintaining not just financial health but overall well-being.

As you continue to navigate through these financial pressures, remember that managing stress is not about eliminating it completely but about developing the resilience and tools needed to deal with challenges effectively. By understanding the sources of your financial stress, employing targeted techniques to mitigate it, ensuring you have a financial safety net, and seeking professional guidance when needed, you equip yourself with a robust toolkit to handle the financial ups and downs. These strategies not only foster a healthier relationship with money but also enhance your capacity to enjoy life's journey, irrespective of the financial landscape.

6.4 Goal Setting and Visualization for Financial Success

Principles of Effective Goal Setting

Goal setting is not just about defining what you want to achieve; it's about clarifying your intentions, focusing your efforts, and setting a benchmark for success. Setting SMART goals is crucial to financial planning.

A specific goal pinpoints exactly what you want to achieve, such as saving $10,000 for a down payment on a house. Making it measurable means you can track your progress; for example, by saving $500 each month. It's achievable because it's realistic; it stretches your capabilities without being out of reach. The goal is relevant if it aligns with your broader financial objectives, like owning a home, and it's time-bound by having a clear deadline—say, in 20 months. This structured approach not only organizes your financial ambitions but also boosts your motivation and focus, providing clear milestones and an actionable roadmap to follow.

Visualization Techniques

Beyond setting goals, visualization is a potent tool that can enhance your ability to achieve them. This technique involves creating a vivid mental image of achieving your financial goals, engaging all your senses to deepen the experience. Imagine the feeling of making the final payment on your student debt or the pride of reaching your investment target for retirement. Visualization isn't just daydreaming; it's a practice supported by neuroscience. By regularly visualizing your financial success, you reinforce your brain's ability to recognize and act upon opportunities that align with your goals. This mental rehearsal primes you to navigate the path to these outcomes with more confidence and clarity, effectively programming your subconscious to recognize and seize opportunities that might otherwise go unnoticed.

Creating a Vision Board

A financial vision board can serve as a constant visual reminder of your goals. Start by gathering images, quotes, and symbols that represent your financial aspirations. These could range from pictures of your dream home or destinations for future travels to motivational quotes about financial freedom. Arrange these elements on a board in a way that feels inspiring. Place this vision board somewhere you'll see it daily—like by your desk or on your bedroom wall. This visual representation serves as a daily reminder of your goals, keeping them at the forefront of your mind and subtly steering your decisions and actions toward those outcomes. The process of selecting and arranging these images can also help clarify and prioritize your goals, making them more tangible and attainable. Visit https://www.masterclass.com/articles/how-to-make-a-vision-board or Scan the QR code below to get some tips on how to create a compelling vision board for yourself.

Monitoring Progress

Regularly reviewing and adjusting your financial goals is essential to ensure they remain aligned with your evolving financial situation and aspirations. Tools and methods such as financial tracking apps or regular check-ins with a financial planner can help monitor progress. These tools not only help you stay on track with your savings and investment plans but also provide valuable insights into your spending habits and financial health. They can alert you to potential issues before they become serious, allowing you to adjust your spending or saving strategies accordingly. This proactive approach to financial management not only helps you stay aligned with your immediate financial goals but also builds a strong foundation for long-term financial success. By continuously engaging with your financial plan, you maintain momentum toward your goals and adapt more swiftly to any changes in your financial landscape, ensuring that your financial growth remains on course.

In essence, setting goals with precision, visualizing success, creating tangible reminders, and keeping track of your progress are more than just steps—they are the scaffoldings that support the construction of your financially healthy future. By embedding these practices into your strategy, you enhance your ability to envision and achieve a prosperous financial life.

6.5 Learning From Financial Mistakes: Resilience in Personal Finance

Mistakes are not merely missteps but pivotal learning opportunities that forge a path to greater wisdom and stability. Embracing the inevitability of financial errors, not as defeats but as integral components of your financial education, is crucial. In every error, there is a lesson that, once learned, can illuminate your financial decisions moving forward. Whether it's an investment that didn't pan out or a budget that fell short of needs, each mistake carries invaluable insights that sharpen your financial acumen.

The process of normalizing financial mistakes begins with understanding that everyone—no matter their level of expertise—makes them. This realization is liberating, dispelling the paralyzing fear of failure that often stops you from taking necessary risks or trying new strategies. By reframing mistakes as natural and universal, you remove the stigma that often surrounds financial errors, fostering a more open, inquisitive approach to money management. Recognize that the most successful financial figures have navigated through numerous setbacks to arrive at their achievements. This perspective encourages a healthier, more proactive relationship with financial learning, where the focus shifts from avoiding errors to extracting value from them.

Analyzing your financial missteps requires a balanced approach; it's about being critical enough to learn but not so harsh as to be discouraged. Begin by pinpointing exactly where things went awry. Was it a lack of research before investing? Perhaps an overestimation of how much you could afford to spend? Or maybe it was a failure to save for unforeseen expenses? Identifying the specific decision or assumption that led to the error is the first step.

Next, consider what could have been done differently. This might involve seeking more thorough financial advice, adjusting your spending habits, or setting up a more realistic budget. The key is to convert these insights into actionable lessons that refine your strategies and enhance your decision-making processes. This methodical review not only prevents repetitions of the same mistakes but also strengthens your overall financial strategy.

Building resilience in personal finance is akin to strengthening a muscle—it develops through consistent effort and adaptability. One practical strategy is diversifying your income sources. Just as a portfolio of mixed investments spreads out the financial risk, multiple income streams protect you from being overly reliant on one financial avenue. This might mean balancing a full-time job with a side hustle, investing in stocks, or earning rental income. Such diversification not only safeguards against financial uncertainty but also provides additional avenues for wealth accumulation.

Resilience is also fostered by maintaining a growth mindset—a belief that your abilities and understanding can expand over time. This mindset encourages continuous learning and adaptation, which are key components in navigating the financial landscape successfully. A growth mindset transforms challenges into opportunities for growth and reinforces the understanding that capability is not fixed but changeable through effort and learning.

The stories of those who have faced and overcome significant financial setbacks further underscore the power of resilience. Consider the tale of a young entrepreneur—let's call them Anna—whose startup floundered due to unforeseen market changes. Despite the initial financial loss, Anna thoroughly analyzed the failure, gaining insights into market volatility and the importance of adaptable business models. Using this knowledge, she launched a new venture that was robust, flexible, and ultimately successful.

Another inspiring story is of an individual—let's call them Dean—who accumulated considerable credit card debt due to unchecked spending habits. By recognizing his mistakes, Dean not only worked his way out of debt but also became a financial advisor to help others avoid similar pitfalls. These narratives highlight that recovery from financial setbacks is not only possible but can also be a profound turning point toward better financial management.

As you forge ahead, remember that each mistake holds the potential to refine your strategies, broaden your understanding, and strengthen your resilience. Embrace these experiences, analyze them critically, and let them teach you invaluable lessons that will enhance your financial prowess. In doing so, you transform your financial narrative from one of fear and avoidance to one of empowerment and growth.

6.6 The Role of Mentorship in Achieving Financial Independence

The path to financial independence is often rugged and uncharted, making the guidance of a seasoned mentor not just a luxury but a game-changer. Financial mentorship goes beyond mere advice on money management to encompass coaching on strategic decision-making, providing moral support during setbacks, and offering insights into leveraging networks effectively.

The benefits are manifold: mentors can help demystify the complex finance world, keep you motivated during your fiscal journey, and connect you with individuals and opportunities that can propel your financial growth. Their experience in navigating financial pitfalls and successes provides a real-world education that textbooks or articles cannot replicate.

Finding the right mentor is pivotal and can be a thoughtful reflection of where you see your financial journey heading. Start by identifying what you need guidance on—be it investing, debt management, or wealth building—and seek out professionals who excel in these areas. Networking events, professional associations, and even social media platforms like LinkedIn are fertile grounds for connecting with potential mentors. When choosing a mentor, consider their financial acumen, mentoring style, and personal integrity. A good mentor should have a successful track record and exhibit qualities such as patience, empathy, and effective communication. They should be someone interested in your personal and professional growth as opposed to just another business connection.

Being an effective mentee is equally important in this relationship. It involves being proactive in your learning, open to feedback, and respectful of your mentor's time and insights. Prepare for your interactions with thoughtful questions and preliminary research. Show initiative by setting goals for what you hope to learn and achieve through the mentorship and be receptive to tasks or advice your mentor may provide. Remember, a mentor–mentee relationship is a two-way street; your engagement and responsiveness can significantly impact the dynamics and outcomes of this partnership.

Mentorship can also take unconventional forms, adapting to the digital age and varying personal needs and schedules. Online communities, for example, offer platforms where you can receive guidance from multiple experienced individuals at your convenience. Platforms like Reddit and specific finance-related forums host a wealth of knowledge and are often willing to offer guidance and share personal experiences. Peer groups, often formed on social media or through professional networks, offer mutual support systems where individuals can learn from each other's experiences. Virtual mentorship, connecting with mentors through video calls or messaging, breaks geographical barriers and opens up a global network of advisors. These alternative forms of mentorship retain the core benefits of traditional mentorship while adding flexibility and a broader scope of perspectives and experiences.

In embracing the power of mentorship, you unlock a pivotal resource in your quest for financial independence. Mentors do not just guide; they inspire, challenge, and broaden your financial horizons. Whether through traditional one-on-one sessions or innovative online forums, mentor–mentee relationships enrich your financial journey, making the climb toward your financial goals a more informed and supported process.

SOCIALLY RESPONSIBLE AND ETHICAL INVESTING

Chapter 7:

Socially Responsible and Ethical

Investing

Imagine investing not just for personal gain but as a profound expression of your values and vision for the world. This is the heart of socially responsible investing (SRI)—a strategy that merges the pursuit of financial returns with the desire to positively impact society, the environment, and corporate governance. It's about placing your money where your morals are, ensuring that your investments reflect your ethical standards and contribute to a sustainable future. For many of you, especially those aged 18–35, the resonance of SRI comes from a deep-seated desire to see change in the world, a change you are ready to support in words and through action.

7.1 Introduction to SRI

Define SRI: What It Means to Invest Responsibly

SRI encompasses a range of investment practices that consider environmental, social, and corporate governance (ESG) criteria to generate long-term competitive financial returns and positive societal impact. At its core, SRI is about making conscious choices to invest in companies that align with your ethical beliefs, whether that involves advancing environmental sustainability, promoting human rights, or ensuring effective corporate governance. Unlike traditional investing, where decisions are primarily based on financial factors, SRI involves evaluating investments based on both their financial potential and contribution to societal goods.

Historical Context and Growth: The Evolution of SRI

The roots of SRI can be traced back several decades when it began as a niche practice among investors looking to exclude stocks or entire industries that conflicted with their values, such as tobacco or firearms. Over the years, SRI has evolved from simple exclusionary tactics to a more integrated approach that thoroughly assesses ESG criteria as a core part of investment analysis. Significant milestones in its development include establishing the principles for responsible investment by the United Nations in 2006, which provided a framework for incorporating ESG issues into investment practice.

Today, SRI is experiencing unprecedented growth, driven by an increasing awareness of environmental issues like climate change, and a growing recognition that ESG factors can significantly impact the financial performance of investments. This shift is particularly pronounced among younger investors, like yourselves, who not only demand transparency and sustainability in investment choices but also view these factors as critical to achieving long-term financial returns.

SRI Strategies: How to Invest Responsibly

Implementing SRI involves several strategies that can be tailored to individual ethical preferences and financial goals. One common approach is the use of exclusionary screens, where you might choose to avoid investments in companies or industries that do not meet certain ethical thresholds. Another strategy is ESG integration, where ESG factors are incorporated into the traditional financial evaluation process to identify companies that are leaders in responsible business practices. Finally, shareholder advocacy provides a proactive pathway to influence corporate behaviors from within. By using your rights as a shareholder, you can propose and vote on initiatives aimed at improving company policies and practices on environmental and social issues.

Benefits and Challenges: Navigating the Complexities of SRI

The benefits of SRI extend beyond personal satisfaction and into the realm of financial gains and societal impacts. Studies have increasingly shown that companies with robust ESG practices display better risk management and long-term resilience, translating to stronger financial performance over time. Additionally, by investing in these companies, you contribute to the promotion of sustainable practices that can lead to widespread social and environmental benefits, aligning your portfolio with a vision for a better world.

However, navigating SRI comes with its challenges. One of the primary concerns is the potential limitation on diversification since excluding certain companies or sectors can narrow the investment pool. Moreover, the varying definitions of what constitutes *socially responsible* can lead to inconsistencies in ESG reporting and assessment, making it crucial to rely on credible sources and rigorous analysis when evaluating potential investments. Despite these challenges, the strategic integration of SRI principles offers a compelling pathway to align your investment practices with your deepest values while aiming for solid financial returns.

In your hands, investing becomes a powerful tool for change, sculpting a portfolio that mirrors your principles and aspirations for the future. By choosing SRI, you are not just choosing where to put your money; you are making a statement about the kind of world you want to live in. It's a method that empowers you to infuse your financial activities with your values, ensuring that your investments work not only for your benefit but also for the betterment of society.

7.2 Combining Philanthropy With Investment Strategies

Philanthropic Investing Explained

Think of philanthropic investing as a bridge where the world of finance meets altruistic goals, providing a unique opportunity for you to support charitable causes while also aiming for financial returns. This investment strategy diverges from traditional philanthropy where the primary focus is on donating money without expecting any financial benefits. Philanthropic investing, instead, allows you to invest capital in ways that generate social or environmental benefits yet also offer potential financial gains. It's an approach that reflects a shift in how modern investors, particularly among the younger generations, perceive the role of money in society. You're not just choosing where to invest but also aiming to make a difference through your investments. This dual-purpose strategy is increasingly appealing in a world where financial resources are seen not just as a means to personal wealth but as essential tools for global betterment.

Examples of Philanthropic Investments

A practical example of philanthropic investments is community bonds, which is an innovative financial tool that allows you to invest directly in local projects for social or environmental benefits. These bonds might fund the development of community centers, green infrastructure, or affordable housing projects. They typically offer a fixed return, and by investing, you contribute directly to tangible assets that improve community welfare. Similarly, social impact bonds are designed to fund programs that address societal issues, such as reducing homelessness or improving education. Investors fund projects delivered by service providers with proven impact, and returns are based on the achievement of agreed-upon outcomes, thus aligning financial returns with social impact. These investment opportunities allow you to see the direct correlation between your financial input and societal benefit, making your investment choices profoundly impactful.

Creating a Philanthropic Investment Plan

To begin aligning your philanthropic goals with your investment strategies, start by defining what success looks like for you both financially and socially. What causes are you passionate about? Is it environmental sustainability, education, health, or community development? Once you've identified your key interest areas, the next step is setting clear objectives. For instance, if you choose to focus on environmental sustainability, your goal could be to invest in green technologies or conservation projects that aim for specific environmental outcomes along with financial returns. After setting these objectives, selecting the right assets is crucial. This might involve choosing stocks, bonds, or funds that align with your goals. Finally, measuring the impact of your investments is essential. This can involve tracking financial performance and also assessing social or environmental outcomes. Tools and metrics such as the social return on investment or ESG criteria can be invaluable in this assessment, ensuring that your investments are achieving the desired impact.

Case Studies

Consider the story of a private foundation that redirected its endowment to focus exclusively on impact investments. The foundation decided to invest in a range of assets, including a fund that supports small businesses in developing countries and a green bond issued by a company developing renewable energy projects. Over five years, the foundation not only saw solid financial returns but also contributed to the creation of thousands of jobs and significant growth in sustainable energy infrastructure. Another inspiring example comes from an individual investor who chose to invest in social impact bonds aimed at reducing recidivism. The program funded by the bonds provided comprehensive job training and support to recently released inmates. The success of the program led to lower repeated offense rates than the national average, and the investor earned a return linked to the cost savings generated for the government from reduced incarceration rates.

These stories exemplify how aligning your investment portfolio with your philanthropic values fosters societal advancements and generates rewarding financial outcomes. By choosing to invest philanthropically, you are part of a growing movement that views capital as a force for good, capable of driving significant social and environmental transformation alongside financial growth. As you explore these opportunities, remember that each investment is a step toward realizing a vision of a world where finance and philanthropy are not just parallel worlds but are intertwined, each enriching the other.

7.3 Ethical Banking: Choosing Financial Institutions That Align With Your Values

In today's financial landscape, where your dollar holds power beyond just purchasing, the concept of ethical banking has emerged as a beacon for those of you striving to align your financial activities with your values. Ethical banking differs significantly from conventional banking by prioritizing social responsibility and transparency. Unlike traditional banks, which primarily focus on profitability, ethical banks commit to using your money to support practices that benefit society and the environment. This might include lending to environmentally sustainable businesses, supporting nonprofit organizations, or providing loans to underserved communities. By choosing an ethical bank, you're not just selecting a place to store your money; you're deciding to make a positive impact with every deposit or investment you make.

When it comes to selecting an ethical bank, several factors come into play, each crucial in ensuring that your chosen institution aligns with your values. Start by examining their lending practices. What projects or businesses does the bank typically finance? Are these aligned with your values, be it environmental sustainability, social justice, or community development?

Also, consider the bank's investment activities. Ethical banks often avoid investing in industries that contradict sustainability goals such as fossil fuels, tobacco, or arms. Instead, they may focus on sectors like renewable energy or healthcare. Another critical factor is the bank's commitment to social and environmental issues. Look for banks that not only avoid negative impacts but actively promote positive change through community engagement and sustainable practices. This could be through educational programs, community projects, or direct funding to local initiatives.

The benefits of choosing an ethical bank extend far beyond personal satisfaction. By banking ethically, you contribute to the broader movement toward a more sustainable and equitable world. Your deposits help fund projects that might be overlooked by traditional banks, from renewable energy initiatives to small businesses in developing regions. This not only aids in the progress toward global sustainability goals but also fosters economic growth in underserved areas, potentially lifting communities out of poverty. Moreover, ethical banks are often highly transparent about their activities, giving you a clear view of where your money is going and the impact it's having. This transparency builds trust and ensures that you feel secure in the knowledge that your financial choices are contributing to positive change.

List of Ethical Banks

Here's an overview of well-regarded ethical banks that are known for their commitment to social responsibility and transparency:

1. Triodos Bank: Based in the Netherlands, Triodos is one of the world's leading sustainable banks. It finances projects and companies that add cultural value and benefit people and the environment with a clear and transparent banking model that allows customers to see exactly where their money goes.

2. Amalgamated Bank: As America's largest B-Corp-certified bank, Amalgamated offers a variety of services that support social justice, environmental sustainability, and workers' rights.

It's known for its advocacy of ethical practices and transparency.

3. GLS Bank: A pioneer in ethical banking in Germany, GLS Bank focuses on social and ecological projects that aim to tackle challenges in sectors such as renewable energy, organic agriculture, and education.

4. Bank Australia: Committed to responsible banking, Bank Australia does not invest in industries that harm the environment, such as fossil fuels, gambling, or arms. It also puts profits back into projects that help people and the planet.

Each of these banks represents a commitment to ethical banking practices, offering you platforms where your financial actions can reflect your deepest values. By choosing to bank ethically, you not only ensure your money is managed responsibly, but you also contribute to the funding of projects and businesses that are making a real difference in the world. As you consider where to bank, think of your choice as a vote for the kind of world you want to live in and a step toward aligning your financial practices with your commitment to social and environmental responsibility. This alignment not only enriches your sense of personal integrity but also contributes to the momentum toward a more ethical global financial system.

7.4 Impact Investing: Helping Others While Growing Your Wealth

Impact investing stands out as a transformative approach where your investments can directly contribute to social and environmental benefits while also targeting financial returns. This investment strategy goes beyond mere corporate responsibility; it's about actively choosing to place capital into companies, organizations, and funds that are committed to addressing some of the world's most pressing challenges. Whether it's by supporting innovative startups that aim to clean the oceans or backing companies that provide affordable housing, impact investing puts your money to work toward creating positive change in the world, aligning your portfolio with your desire to make a difference.

The scope of impact investing is vast and varied, covering numerous sectors such as renewable energy, education, healthcare, and affordable housing. Each of these sectors represents critical areas where targeted investments can lead to substantial improvements in quality of life and environmental sustainability. For instance, by investing in renewable energy projects, like solar or wind farms, you are contributing to the reduction of carbon emissions and supporting the growth of sustainable energy sources. Impact investments might also help fund technologies that enhance access to quality education in underserved communities or support educational programs that equip people with essential skills for the workforce. Similarly, impact investments in healthcare can facilitate the development of innovative medical treatments or improve healthcare accessibility, thereby enhancing community health outcomes.

When it comes to evaluating impact investments, the process involves a careful analysis of potential social and environmental impacts alongside financial returns. This dual-return approach requires a thorough assessment to understand the tangible outcomes your investment could generate. Start by examining the track record of the entity or project you're considering investing in. Look for quantifiable evidence of social or environmental impact, such as reduced pollution levels, the number of jobs created, or improvements in patient care.

Financially, while assessing the potential return on investment, consider the stability and growth prospects of the sector and the specific business model of the company or project. It's also crucial to understand the risks involved, which could range from market and regulatory risks to specific issues related to the project's scale and scope.

To bring these concepts to life, consider the case of a green technology firm that developed an innovative water purification system. Investors who funded this company not only enjoyed robust returns as the technology gained market acceptance, but they also contributed to significant environmental benefits through the reduction of waterborne diseases in developing countries. Another example is an investment fund focused on affordable housing, which provided investors with steady returns from rent revenues and addressed the critical need for housing among low-income families, thus improving their standard of living and stability.

These real-world examples illustrate the powerful impact that your investments can have when directed toward causes that not only yield financial returns but also contribute positively to society and the environment. As impact investing continues to grow in popularity, especially among younger investors eager to drive change, it offers a compelling pathway to align your financial goals with your values. By choosing to invest in projects and companies that are actively working toward making a positive impact, you're not just building wealth; you're also participating in shaping a better world.

7.5 Community-Based Financial Initiatives for Broader Impact

In the vibrant ecosystem of financial opportunities, community-based financial initiatives stand out as powerful tools for social and economic development. These initiatives, which include credit unions, community development finance institutions (CDFIs), and local currencies, are rooted in the principle of serving the community's needs directly by fostering access to financial resources and enhancing local economic growth. Unlike traditional banking institutions, these community-focused entities reinvest in the local economy, support small businesses, fund social projects, and provide financial services tailored to the unique needs of their communities.

Credit unions, for instance, are member-owned financial cooperatives that typically offer lower fees, higher savings rates, and a more personalized customer service experience than traditional banks. By focusing on members' needs rather than generating profits for shareholders, credit unions help keep financial resources within the community, strengthening local economies. Furthermore, CDFIs play a crucial role in economically disadvantaged areas. These institutions provide capital to revive struggling neighborhoods through small business loans, housing finance, and community facilities loans. Their efforts often lead to job creation, housing stability, and improved community facilities, which significantly enhance local economic health.

Local currencies are another innovative form of community-based financial initiative. These currencies, which can only be spent within a specific geographic area, aim to encourage spending within the local economy, supporting independent businesses and reducing the environmental impact of transportation. By using local currencies, consumers not only help maintain the economic vitality of their communities but also build stronger ties with local vendors, fostering a sense of community cohesion and mutual support.

The benefits of participating in these community-based financial initiatives are substantial. For individual community members, engaging with institutions like credit unions often leads to better financial conditions due to lower fees and more favorable loan rates. CDFIs provide financial backing and valuable business advice and support to small business owners, which might be inaccessible through traditional banks. The overall effect of these initiatives is a more empowered community where economic opportunities are more accessible to all members, regardless of their economic background.

Success stories from across the globe illuminate the profound impact of community-based financial initiatives. In one notable example, a CDFI in a small rural town provided crucial funding to a local start-up that brought high-speed internet to the area for the first time, dramatically improving educational and economic opportunities for local residents. In another case, a city introduced a local currency that could be earned by volunteering in community projects. This currency, accepted by local businesses, not only boosted the local economy but also increased community engagement and made residents more invested in both the economic and social well-being of their area.

These initiatives exemplify how finance can be a powerful force for good, directly contributing to the enhancement of community life. By supporting these types of organizations and participating in their services, you are investing in the health and prosperity of your own community while also enjoying the practical benefits they offer. As these community-based financial models continue to evolve and expand, they present a compelling alternative to traditional finance, one that is more closely aligned with the values of inclusivity, sustainability, and mutual benefit.

7.6 Green Investing: Opportunities in Renewable Energy and Sustainable Practices

As the global consciousness around environmental sustainability grows, so does the field of green investing. This investment avenue is not just about avoiding harm but also about actively contributing to an environmental solution, making it a compelling choice for those of you looking to make a positive impact on the world. Green investing includes a broad range of activities from investing in renewable energy companies to buying green bonds that fund environmental projects. This approach aligns particularly well with the values of younger investors who often want their financial decisions to reflect their ecological concerns.

Growth of Green Investing

In recent years, green investing has moved from a niche part of the market to a significant growth area, driven by increasing awareness of environmental issues like climate change and resource depletion. The global push toward sustainability has led to greater regulatory support for green projects and technologies, encouraging more companies and governments to turn to green finance as a means to fund their transition to sustainable operations. The financial sector has responded with a growing array of green investment opportunities, making it easier than ever for individuals to contribute to environmental goals through their investment choices. This surge is about good intentions and economics. As renewable energy becomes cheaper and more efficient, investments in this area offer promising returns, attracting ethically motivated investors and those looking for solid financial performance.

Types of Green Investments

Green investments are diverse, ranging from direct investments in renewable energy companies to green bonds and sustainable mutual funds. Renewable energy stocks are perhaps the most direct way to invest in green growth, encompassing companies involved in solar, wind, hydro, and other renewable technologies. These companies range from well-established firms expanding their renewable capacity to new startups that innovate energy storage and efficiency technologies.

Green bonds, another significant type of investment, are issued by governments and corporations to fund projects that have positive environmental impacts, such as energy efficiency upgrades or clean transportation solutions. These bonds provide a way to earn a return on your money while also funding projects that contribute to environmental sustainability. Sustainable mutual funds offer a more diversified approach, investing in a portfolio of stocks or bonds selected for their environmental credentials, allowing you to reduce risk while still supporting green initiatives.

Evaluating Green Investments

When evaluating green investments, it's crucial to look beyond the environmental hype and assess the actual sustainability impact and financial viability of the investment. Consider the specific environmental benefits touted, such as reduced carbon emissions or conservation of natural resources, and check these claims against independent assessments or certifications. Financially, while the green sector is growing, it's important to assess the stability and profitability of the investment. Look at traditional financial metrics such as earnings growth, debt levels, and cash flow stability. Also, consider the market potential of the technology or project being invested in, as well as regulatory or political risks that could impact future growth. Being well-informed will help you avoid "greenwashing," which is when companies overstate their environmental contributions to attract investors.

Future Trends in Green Investing

Looking forward, the trajectory of green investing is poised for continued expansion. Technological advancements, particularly in energy storage and smart grid technologies, are expected to further reduce costs and increase the efficiency of renewable energy, enhancing its investment appeal. Additionally, international agreements on climate change are likely to bolster regulatory support for green projects, increasing the security and attractiveness of these investments. Moreover, consumer preferences are shifting toward sustainability, influencing corporate behaviors and investment flows across sectors. As technologies develop and regulations evolve, staying informed and adaptable will be key to navigating this promising but changing landscape.

As we wrap up this exploration into green investing, remember the broader implications of your investment choices. By choosing to invest in renewable energy and sustainable practices, you are positioning yourself to benefit from the growth of green technologies and contributing to the global effort to combat climate change and protect our planet for future generations.

Your investment decisions have the power to shape the world, and with green investing, that power is a force for positive environmental change. As we move forward, continue to consider how your financial strategies can align with your values and goals, not just for personal gain but for the greater good of the community and the world.

Wrapping up and Looking Forward

In this chapter, we've explored various facets of socially responsible and ethical investing, each offering unique opportunities to align your financial investments with your personal values and societal contributions. From green investing in renewable energies to engaging with community-based financial initiatives, the options are as diverse as they are impactful. As we transition into the next chapter, we'll delve deeper into how these strategies shape the broader economic landscape and reflect a growing trend toward sustainability and ethical practices in finance. The journey toward financial independence is intertwined with the global movement toward a more equitable and sustainable future. As you continue to navigate your investment choices, consider how each decision can contribute to this larger goal, enhancing not only your financial portfolio but also the world in which we all live.

CHAPTER 8

PREPARING FOR THE FUTURE

Chapter 8:

Preparing for the Future

Welcome to a pivotal moment in your financial journey—one where foresight meets action to secure a future that resonates with freedom and fulfillment. As we navigate the often-overlooked terrain of retirement planning, especially for millennials, it's crucial to redefine what retirement means in today's dynamic world. Gone are the days of viewing retirement solely as the final chapter of work life; instead, envision it as a stage where you can fully explore your passions without financial constraints. This shift in perspective is not just refreshing but essential, as it aligns with the aspirations of a generation that values flexibility, sustainability, and well-being over mere financial accumulation.

8.1 Retirement Planning for Millennials: Starting Early to Retire Young

Importance of Early Retirement Planning

Time is your greatest ally. Starting early capitalizes on the compounding benefits, where the returns on your investments generate their own returns. Consider this: A modest monthly investment of $300 with an annual return of 5% grows to over $200,000 in 30 years. Increase the monthly investment to $500, and you're looking at a fund of $350,000. This exponential growth is the magic of compounding, where even small, consistent contributions can grow into significant sums over time. This strategy not only makes the goal of early retirement more attainable but also reduces the financial stress often associated with retirement planning. By starting early, you give yourself the flexibility to adjust your investment amounts and strategies based on changes in your career, lifestyle, and financial goals.

Setting Retirement Goals

Crafting a vision for your retirement is the first step toward making it a reality. Begin by assessing your current financial situation—your income, debts, and expenses. This assessment provides a clear starting point for what you need to save. Next, envision your ideal retirement lifestyle. Do you see yourself traveling around the world, starting a new venture, or perhaps settling into a cozy beachside community? Estimating the financial implications of these lifestyle choices can help you set specific and realistic financial targets. For instance, if your dream is to retire by 50, calculate the potential costs of living, health care, and leisure activities you anticipate during retirement. Tools like retirement calculators can offer a snapshot of how much you need to save each month to reach your retirement goals, considering factors such as inflation and expected rates of return on investments.

Retirement Savings Strategies

Navigating the path to a secure retirement is less daunting when you have a variety of strategies at your disposal. One effective approach is to maximize contributions to retirement accounts such as IRAs or employer-sponsored 401(k)s, especially if they offer matching contributions. This is essentially free money and serves as an immediate return on your investment. Additionally, diversifying your investment portfolio can protect against market volatility and increase your chances of consistent growth. This might include a mix of stocks, bonds, real estate, and other investment vehicles. Consider speaking with a financial advisor to tailor your investment strategy to your specific risk tolerance and retirement timeline, ensuring that your portfolio aligns with your long-term financial goals.

Tools and Resources for Planning

To streamline your retirement planning process, leverage tools and resources that provide insights and assistance. Retirement calculators are invaluable for projecting how your current savings and future contributions will grow over time. Financial planning software can help you manage your investments, track your progress toward your retirement goals, and adjust your strategies as needed. Additionally, consider engaging with financial planning workshops or webinars that offer professional advice and networking opportunities with other future retirees. These resources aid in your retirement planning and enhance your financial literacy, empowering you to make informed decisions that pave the way to a financially secure and fulfilling retirement.

As you integrate these insights and strategies, remember that the journey to retirement should be as rewarding as the destination. Each step you take builds a foundation not just for a secure retirement, but for a life enriched with the freedom to pursue your passions and embrace opportunities without financial burden. Your future self will thank you for the foresight and dedication you invest today. Visit https://www.bankrate.com/retirement/calculators/ or Scan the QR code below to access an example retirement planning calculator and kickstart your retirement plan today!

8.2 Understanding and Setting up IRAs and 401(k)s

Understanding IRAs and 401(k)s

Both IRAs and 401(k)s are powerful tools designed to aid in building your retirement savings, but they operate under different rules and offer distinct advantages.

IRAs provide a flexible way to save for retirement regardless of your employment status. There are several types of IRAs, including traditional IRAs and Roth IRAs, each with specific tax implications. Traditional IRAs often allow you to make pre-tax contributions, meaning the money you invest is deducted from your taxable income, potentially lowering your tax bill each year you contribute. The funds in this account grow tax-deferred, and you only pay taxes when you withdraw the money in retirement, ideally at a lower tax rate. Conversely, Roth IRAs are funded with after-tax dollars, meaning the money you contribute has already been taxed. The benefit here is that your money grows tax-free, and you can make tax-free withdrawals in retirement, providing a significant advantage if you expect to be in a higher tax bracket later on.

401(k)s are employer-sponsored plans that often come with the added benefit of matching contributions from your employer, which can dramatically increase your retirement savings. Like traditional IRAs, contributions to a traditional 401(k) plan are made pre-tax, reducing your taxable income for the year. These contributions and their earnings then grow tax-deferred until withdrawal. Some employers now offer a Roth 401(k) option, which, similar to a Roth IRA, involves after-tax contributions that grow tax-free.

Setting up IRAs and 401(k)s

The process of setting up these accounts is straightforward but requires careful consideration of your financial situation and retirement goals. To establish an IRA, you typically need to choose a financial institution that offers retirement accounts and decide between a traditional or Roth IRA based on your current and anticipated future financial circumstances. The setup involves filling out an application, choosing your investments, and setting up a funding method, such as regular transfers from a checking or savings account.

Setting up a 401(k) is slightly different, as it involves coordinating with your employer. If your employer offers a 401(k) plan, you will need to enroll in the plan, decide how much of your salary you want to contribute, and select your investments from the options provided by the plan. If your employer offers a match, ensure you contribute at least enough to receive the full matching amount, as this is essentially free money that can significantly boost your retirement savings.

Tax Implications

Understanding the tax implications of these retirement accounts is crucial for maximizing your benefits. Contributions to traditional IRAs and 401(k)s can reduce your yearly taxable income, potentially placing you in a lower tax bracket and reducing your overall tax liability. However, keep in mind the IRS sets limits on how much you can contribute to these accounts each year. For 2021, the contribution limit for individuals under 50 is $6,000 for IRAs and $19,500 for 401(k)s. Additionally, withdrawals from these accounts are subject to ordinary income tax, and early withdrawals before age 59½ may incur a 10% penalty unless specific conditions are met.

Roth IRAs and Roth 401(k)s do not provide a tax break on contributions, but they offer tax-free growth and tax-free withdrawals in retirement. There are also contribution limits for Roth accounts, and high earners may be phased out from contributing to a Roth IRA directly, though a backdoor Roth IRA conversion is a possible workaround.

Case Studies

Consider the case of Emily, a graphic designer who started contributing to a Roth IRA at age 25. She consistently invested $5,000 per year until retirement at age 65. Assuming an average annual return of 7%, her Roth IRA grew to over $1 million by retirement, all of which she can withdraw tax-free. In contrast, John, an engineer, opted for his employer's 401(k) plan, contributing $19,500 annually and receiving a 50% employer match on the first 6% of his salary. By retirement, John's 401(k) accumulated over $2 million, thanks to the generous employer match and tax-deferred growth, providing a substantial nest egg to support his retirement dreams.

By understanding and utilizing IRAs and 401(k)s effectively, you can significantly enhance your financial readiness for retirement, ensuring that your later years are characterized by freedom and stability rather than financial stress.

8.3 Estate Planning Basics: Ensuring Your Legacy

Estate planning might sound like something reserved for the wealthy or the elderly, but in reality, it's a crucial step for anyone who wants to ensure their assets are distributed according to their wishes and in a tax-efficient manner. Think of estate planning as a roadmap that not only guides your financial legacy after your passing but also offers peace of mind knowing that your loved ones will be taken care of in your absence. This process involves a range of legal documents and strategies designed to protect your assets and your family's future. Whether you own a home, have some savings, or even just possess sentimental personal items, having an estate plan in place is an essential aspect of responsible financial management.

The cornerstone of any estate plan is a will. This document lays out your wishes regarding the distribution of your assets and the care of any minor children. Without a will, state laws dictate how your assets are divided, which might not align with your wishes. Trusts are another pivotal element, offering more control over how your assets are managed and distributed. They can help bypass probate, potentially saving time and money, and provide a degree of privacy about your estate's distribution that a will cannot. Trusts can also be instrumental in managing tax liabilities and protecting your estate from legal claims.

Healthcare directives, also known as living wills, ensure that your healthcare preferences are followed if you cannot communicate them yourself. This can cover decisions about life-sustaining treatment and other medical interventions. Powers of attorney are equally important, allowing you to appoint someone to manage your affairs if you're unable to do so. This can be a general power of attorney, giving broad authority over your affairs, or a limited one, which is specific to certain acts or situations.

For those starting the estate planning process, the initial step is to take a comprehensive inventory of your assets, which includes your investments, property, and personal items of value. Deciding on beneficiaries and how you want your assets distributed among them is the next critical step. This might involve direct distributions, creating trusts, or even making charitable donations as part of your legacy. Choosing an executor or trustee who will manage your estate and ensure your wishes are carried out is also crucial. This should be someone you trust implicitly, who is organized and communicative, and ideally, financially savvy.

Consulting with estate planning professionals such as attorneys and financial advisors can ensure your documents are legally sound and align with your financial goals. These professionals can provide valuable insight into potential tax implications and legal hurdles, helping tailor your estate plan to your specific needs and changing life circumstances.

However, a common pitfall in estate planning is the "set it and forget it" mindset. It's vital to regularly review and update your estate plan, particularly after major life events like marriage, divorce, the birth of a child, or significant changes in your financial situation. Failing to update beneficiaries or adjust your plan to reflect current laws can lead to unintended consequences, such as assets going to former spouses or estranged family members. Another frequent oversight is neglecting to account for all assets in your estate plan. It's easy to remember major assets like homes or bank accounts, but smaller items or digital assets like social media accounts often get overlooked. Ensuring these are included can prevent confusion and ensure that all your assets are distributed according to your wishes.

By understanding these basics and taking proactive steps to create and maintain your estate plan, you place yourself in a position of control over your financial legacy and as a guardian of your family's future well-being.

8.4 Insurance Options for Long-Term Security

Whether you're just starting out in your career or are well on your journey, understanding the different types of insurance and integrating them into your financial plan is essential. Life insurance, long-term care insurance, and disability insurance each serve unique purposes, protecting against unforeseen events that could otherwise derail your financial goals and burden your loved ones.

Life insurance, for starters, is fundamental for anyone with dependents or significant debts. It acts as a financial buffer for your loved ones in the event of your untimely passing, providing them with a sum that can help maintain their living standards or cover outstanding debts. It's not just about the payout; it's about the certainty it provides.

Long-term care insurance is designed to cover the costs of long-term care services, which are not typically covered by regular health insurance. This type of insurance is particularly pertinent as you age, considering the potential need for assistance with daily activities due to chronic illnesses or disabilities. Disability insurance, often overlooked, replaces a portion of your income if you're unable to work due to a disability. This type of insurance ensures that you're able to continue covering your expenses and maintain your standard of living, even if you cannot earn an income temporarily or permanently.

Choosing the right insurance coverage requires a thoughtful assessment of your personal and family circumstances, financial goals, and existing coverage. Start by evaluating your current life stage and financial responsibilities. Are you the primary breadwinner? Do you have dependents relying on your income? Are there debts that need to be covered? These questions will help determine the amount and type of coverage you need. For instance, if you have young children, a term life insurance policy might be ideal to ensure their needs are met until they are financially independent. Conversely, if you're approaching retirement, long-term care insurance should be considered to protect your retirement savings from being depleted by the high costs of healthcare services.

Integrating insurance into your overall financial plan is more than just an added expense—it's a strategic move to protect your finances. Insurance policies can be structured to work in tandem with your other financial strategies, creating a cohesive protection plan. For example, a whole life insurance policy can serve a dual purpose by providing a death benefit and acting as a tax-advantaged savings vehicle. The cash value that builds up in a whole life policy can be borrowed against or withdrawn, offering a financial resource that can complement your retirement savings or serve as an emergency fund.

When it comes to selecting an insurance provider, it's crucial to choose a company that is not only financially stable but also known for its customer service and claims reliability. Research potential insurers' financial strength ratings through agencies like A.M. Best or Standard & Poor's, which rate an insurer's ability to meet financial commitments. Reviews and ratings on claims handling and customer service can also provide valuable insights into how the insurer treats its policyholders, especially when they need support the most.

Moreover, understanding the specific terms and conditions of different policies is essential. Look for clear information on what is covered and what is excluded, the terms of premium payments, and the benefits provided. A reliable insurer should offer transparency and be willing to explain the finer details of their policies. Engaging with independent insurance agents or brokers can also provide a comparative perspective, helping you navigate the complex landscape of insurance options and find the best coverage to meet your unique needs.

In essence, insurance is not just a safeguard but a cornerstone of sound financial planning. It provides security and stability, ensuring that unforeseen circumstances do not derail your financial goals or burden your loved ones. By carefully selecting the right types and amounts of insurance and integrating them into your broader financial strategy, you fortify your financial foundation, ensuring that you and your family are protected no matter what the future holds.

As you continue to adapt and grow your financial plan, revisit your insurance needs regularly to ensure they align with your evolving life circumstances, keeping your security net robust and responsive to your life's changing dynamics.

8.5 The Future of Personal Finance: Trends to Watch

Personal finance is undergoing a profound transformation, guided by advancements in AI, blockchain, and fintech innovations. These technologies are not merely enhancing but reshaping the way we interact with money, from simplifying transactions to redefining investment strategies. AI, for example, is revolutionizing financial services through personalized banking experiences and smarter wealth management. AI-driven apps can analyze your spending habits, offer tailored financial advice, and even predict future needs by learning from your financial behaviors. This means more personalized budgeting advice and investment strategies that adapt to your financial goals over time.

Blockchain technology, known for its role in cryptocurrencies, offers far more, particularly in financial security enhancement and transparency. Its ability to maintain a decentralized and tamper-proof ledger of transactions makes it an excellent tool for everything, from simplifying payments to securing sensitive financial data. Imagine a future where you can trace every cent of your investment, knowing exactly where your money goes and how it's being used. This level of transparency builds trust and empowers you to make informed decisions about where to invest your money.

Fintech innovations continue to break down barriers, making financial services more accessible and less costly. Online platforms now allow individuals to trade stocks without hefty fees, manage portfolios with minimal effort, and access financial services traditionally reserved for the wealthy. Peer-to-peer lending platforms exemplify this shift, providing a way for individuals to lend money directly to others, bypassing traditional financial institutions. This democratization of finance not only levels the playing field but also introduces a more community-focused approach to lending and borrowing.

As global economic policies evolve, the implications for personal financial planning are significant. Shifts in regulatory frameworks can impact everything from your retirement savings to your investment choices. For instance, changes in pension regulations might affect how you plan for retirement, necessitating adjustments to your savings strategy or prompting a shift toward alternative retirement plans. Similarly, international trade policies can influence market conditions, affecting your investment portfolio's performance. Staying informed about these changes and understanding their implications is crucial, allowing you to adapt your financial strategies to ensure they remain robust and aligned with your goals.

The surge in interest in sustainable and green finance reflects a broader awareness of the need for environmentally responsible investing. More investors are choosing funds that prioritize companies with strong environmental credentials or support projects contributing to sustainable development. This shift is not just about ethical responsibility but also about financial prudence. Investments in sustainability-focused companies tend to be less volatile and more resilient, often outperforming their less sustainable counterparts. As this trend continues, the opportunities for investing in green technologies and sustainable projects are likely to increase, providing new avenues for growth in your investment portfolio.

Preparing for the unknown is a fundamental aspect of personal financial planning, especially in a world where change is the only constant. Building financial resilience involves more than just saving; it requires a strategy that includes diversification, continuous learning, and flexibility. Diversifying your investments can protect against market volatility, spreading your assets across different sectors and geographies to mitigate potential losses. Engaging in continuous learning about financial trends and new investment opportunities allows you to adapt to economic changes and take advantage of emerging markets. Moreover, maintaining flexibility in your financial plans enables you to adjust your strategies in response to personal circumstances or global economic shifts, ensuring that your financial goals remain attainable regardless of what the future holds.

As technology continues to evolve and global economies shift, the landscape of personal finance will undoubtedly present new challenges and opportunities. By staying informed, embracing innovation, and planning with foresight, you can navigate this ever-changing terrain, ensuring that your financial future is not only secure but also aligned with your values and aspirations. Embrace these changes with confidence and curiosity, knowing that each step forward is a step toward a more empowered and financially savvy future.

8.6 Building a Financially Independent Life: Putting It All Together

In the tapestry of financial independence, the threads of budgeting, saving, investing, and planning weave together to create a robust and vibrant picture.

Effective budgeting acts as the keel that keeps your financial ship steady, allowing you to navigate through monthly expenses while saving for future goals. It's the practice of telling every dollar where it should go, rather than wondering where it went.

Savings build the reservoir from which you can draw in times of need or invest to multiply your wealth. Whether it's setting aside a portion of your income in a high-yield savings account or contributing to an emergency fund, the discipline of saving is fundamental to financial resilience.

Investing is where the potential for financial growth truly comes into play. By wisely investing in a diversified portfolio, you not only beat inflation but also grow your wealth over time. This could mean investing in stocks, bonds, real estate, or mutual funds—the key is to choose investments that align with your risk tolerance and financial goals. Remember, investing is not about *timing* the market but *time in* the market. Long-term investments have historically proven to be one of the most effective ways to build substantial wealth.

Planning, the final thread, supports all these strategies and ensures they work in harmony toward achieving your financial goals. It involves setting clear, actionable objectives, developing strategies to reach them, and periodically reviewing and adjusting them as your financial situation and goals evolve.

Creating a personalized financial plan is like drawing a map for your journey toward financial independence. Start by assessing your current financial situation—your income, debts, expenditures, and investments. This snapshot provides the baseline from which to set realistic and achievable financial goals. Next, allocate roles to each dollar you earn. Some will be earmarked for immediate expenses, others for short-term savings, and others still for long-term investments. Tools like digital budgeting apps or financial planning software can be immensely helpful in tracking and managing your finances. They provide visual insights into your financial health, help you stick to your budget, and adjust your spending habits as necessary.

Regular reviews of your financial plan are crucial. Life is dynamic, so your financial plan should be too. A quarterly or bi-annual review of your financial plan helps you adjust to changes in your income, lifestyle, or financial goals. These adjustments might include increasing your savings rate following a salary hike, rebalancing your investment portfolio, or cutting back on non-essential expenses if you're saving for a major goal like buying a house or starting a business. Such regular check-ins keep your financial goals on track and make the daunting task of wealth accumulation more manageable and systematic.

Moreover, a proactive approach to financial education can dramatically enhance your ability to manage your finances effectively. The world of finance is ever-evolving, with new products, technologies, and strategies emerging regularly. Keeping abreast of these developments through books, podcasts, webinars, and financial news can provide advanced insights and techniques for managing your money. More importantly, this continuous learning fosters a growth mindset, which is essential in today's fast-paced financial environment. One of my other books, "BE R.E.A.L: The Mindset to Achieve The Winning Lifestyle You Desire," is all about the power and benefits of having the ideal mindset. It offers a comprehensive, guided approach to building a growth mindset and is worth checking out.

In essence, building a financially independent life is about more than just accumulating wealth—it's about creating a sustainable financial ecosystem that supports your life's goals and dreams. It's also about making informed, confident financial decisions and adjusting your strategies to meet the challenges and opportunities that life inevitably presents. Carry forward our budgeting, saving, investing, and planning lessons. Let them guide you to a future where financial independence isn't just a goal but a reality.

Conclusion

As we wrap up our journey through, it's crucial to reflect on the transformative path we've navigated together. From laying the foundational knowledge of budgeting and understanding essential financial terms to embracing cutting-edge tools and investment strategies, this book has equipped you with the insights to not only manage your finances but thrive in a rapidly evolving economic landscape.

The importance of starting your financial education early cannot be overstated. Just like the magic of compound interest, the earlier you begin, the more profound your knowledge and wealth can grow. This isn't just about being able to afford the lifestyle you desire but about securing your future and achieving independence.

We've covered the core principles essential for anyone aiming to conquer their financial destiny: diligent budgeting, strategic saving, wise investing, and timely adoption of new technologies that streamline these processes. Furthermore, we delved into the power of personal growth, the significance of making ethically sound investments, and the necessity for meticulous long-term planning.

Remember, the journey toward financial freedom is as much about mindset as it is about technique. Cultivating a positive financial mindset can transform obstacles into opportunities and failures into stepping stones toward success. You can read more about cultivating the ideal mindset for a successful life in my book, "BE R.E.A.L: The Mindset to Achieve The Winning Lifestyle You Desire."

It's not merely about accumulating wealth but about developing a resilient and proactive attitude toward all of life's financial aspects.

I urge you not just to read this book but to live by it. Apply the strategies discussed, use the tools recommended, and continuously adapt to new information and changes in the financial world. Stay curious and informed, always ready to tweak your financial plan to better suit the changing tides of the economy and your personal circumstances.

In your financial decisions, never lose sight of your personal values. Let your financial practices reflect your ethics, contributing positively to your community and the environment. This alignment brings deeper fulfillment and a sense of purpose to your financial endeavors.

Now, take the crucial step: Begin crafting a personalized financial plan that mirrors your unique goals, circumstances, and values. Visualize not only reaching but surpassing your financial goals. Imagine the freedom, peace of mind, and myriad opportunities accompanying true financial independence.

Share your knowledge and journey with others. Promoting financial literacy isn't just about enhancing individual lives but about uplifting entire communities. Your insights could empower someone else to start their journey toward financial freedom.

As we conclude, remember that this book isn't just a guide but a launchpad for your ongoing adventure in personal finance. You are fully equipped, informed, and capable. Embrace the power you hold to mold your financial future and, by extension, your life. Let optimism and empowerment be your companions as you step forward into a future where you are the master of your financial destiny.

I always love to hear from my readers, so do leave me a review on Amazon to share your thoughts or stories of progress. If my book has benefited you or your loved ones in any way, please consider leaving me a favorable review. That way, you can help others find the help and support they need to spruce up their financial plans. I'd also love to hear your thoughts on what you'd like to see in my future books. Your willingness to leave feedback makes a world of difference and can be accomplished easily by scanning the QR code below or using this link: https://www.amazon.com/review/review-your-purchases/?asin=B0DCJXC3QP.

Thank you for trusting me to be a part of your financial journey. Here's to your success, growth, and freedom. Let's make it count!

References

Admin. (2023, November 28). *Why do you need to have an entrepreneurial mindset and understand the value of failure.* Earneaze. https://earneaze.com/why-entrepreneurial-mindset-important-you-skills/

Are you staying cyber safe? 8 tips for securing your financial accounts. (n.d.). Finra. https://www.finra.org/investors/insights/cyber-safe-financial-accounts

Ayoola, E. (2024, February 20). *The 7 best budget apps for 2021.* NerdWallet. https://www.nerdwallet.com/article/finance/best-budget-apps

CFI Team. (n.d.). *Ethical banking.* Corporate Finance Institute. https://corporatefinanceinstitute.com/resources/esg/ethical-banking/

Chen, J. (2019). *Investment crowdfunding.* Investopedia. https://www.investopedia.com/terms/i/investment-crowdfunding.asp

Clarke, A. (2024, January 31). *Blockchain meets banking: A new era of financial services.* Nasdaq. https://www.nasdaq.com/articles/blockchain-meets-banking-a-new-era-of-financial-services

Curtis, G. (2022, February 27). *6 estate planning must-haves.* Investopedia. https://www.investopedia.com/articles/pf/07/estate_plan_checklist.asp

Duggan, W. (2024, February 27). *7 best cryptocurrency investing strategies.* U.S. News Money. https://money.usnews.com/investing/articles/best-cryptocurrency-investing-strategies

Fabregas, K. (2024, March 1). *29 side hustle ideas to make extra money in 2023.* Forbes. https://www.forbes.com/advisor/business/best-side-hustle-ideas/

Goldberg, M. (2022, March 24). *How to start (and build) an emergency fund.* Bankrate. https://www.bankrate.com/banking/savings/starting-an-emergency-fund/

Gourley, D. (2019, July 19). *8 social media success stories to inspire you.* Single Grain. https://www.singlegrain.com/social-media/8-social-media-success-stories-to-inspire-you/

Guide to retirement planning for millennials. (n.d.). Smartasset. https://smartasset.com/retirement/retirement-planning-for-millennials

Guinan, K. (n.d.). *How your credit score affects a loan application.* Bankrate. https://www.bankrate.com/loans/personal-loans/how-does-credit-score-affect-loan-chances/

Haskins, J., & Crail, C. (2022, March 28). *What are the basic legal requirements for starting A small business?* Forbes Advisor. https://www.forbes.com/advisor/business/small-business-legal-requirements/

Hogan, V. (2023, April 17). *How to balance your full-time job with your side hustle.* Forbes. https://www.forbes.com/sites/ginnyhogan/2023/04/17/how-to-balance-your-full-time-job-with-your-side-hustle/

Impact investment examples. (n.d.). Sopact. https://www.sopact.com/guides/impact-investment-examples

The Investopedia Team. (2020). *A real estate investing guide.* Investopedia. https://www.investopedia.com/mortgage/real-estate-investing-guide/

Mitchell, O. S., & Lusardi, A. (2015). Financial literacy and economic outcomes: Evidence and policy implications. *The Journal of*

Retirement, 3(1), 107–114. https://doi.org/10.3905/jor.2015.3.1.107

Napoletano, E. (2021, January 21). *Environmental, social and governance: What is ESG investing?* Forbes Advisor. https://www.forbes.com/advisor/investing/esg-investing/

Océane. (2024, January 1). *How to invest in art for beginners: Why art is a good investment in 2024.* Artelier. https://www.artelier.com/post/how-to-invest-in-art-for-beginners-why-art-is-a-good-investment-in-2024

Perry, E. (2024, April 12). *How to develop an abundance mindset and break free from scarcity.* BetterUp. https://www.betterup.com/blog/abundance-mindset

Polakoff, K. (2024, April 9). *10 benefits of automating the finance function.* Cohnreznick. https://www.cohnreznick.com/insights/10-benefits-automating-finance-function

Schreier, H. (2021, February 25). *Financial planning for young adults: Income tax tips.* Forbes. https://www.forbes.com/sites/halseyschreier/2021/02/25/financial-planning-for-young-adults-income-tax-tips/

The top 10 student loan tips for recent graduates. (n.d.). The Institute for College Access & Success. https://ticas.org/for-students-parents/the-top-10-student-loan-tips-for-recent-graduates/

Trentmann, N. (2022, September 6). Zero-based budgeting gains clout as a way for companies to find savings. *Wall Street Journal.* https://www.wsj.com/articles/zero-based-budgeting-gains-clout-as-a-way-for-companies-to-find-savings-11662463800

2023 Sustainable Investing Trends. (2023, February 1). Morgan Stanley. https://www.morganstanley.com/ideas/sustainable-investing-trends-outlook-2023

University of Pennsylvania. (n.d.). *Popular budgeting strategies.* Penn Student Registration & Financial Services.

https://srfs.upenn.edu/financial-wellness/browse-topics/budgeting/popular-budgeting-strategies

Valley. (2024, January 17). *How financial health impacts your mental and physical health*. Learning Center – Valley Bank. https://insights.valley.com/managing-your-money/article/how-financial-health-impacts-your-mental-and-physical-health/

Walker, W. (2023, August 18). *Success strategies: Insights from the Columbus financial coach*. Daily Dump Show. https://dailydumpshow.com/success-strategies-insights-from-the-columbus-financial-coach/

What is a financial mentor, and why do I need one? (2024, January 8). MentorCruise. https://mentorcruise.com/blog/what-is-a-financial-mentor-and-why-do-i-need-one/

YEC. (2023, June 22). *Council post: The rise of young entrepreneurs: How millennials and gen-z are shaping the business landscape*. Forbes. https://www.forbes.com/sites/theyec/2023/06/22/the-rise-of-young-entrepreneurs-how-millennials-and-gen-z-are-shaping-the-business-landscape/

Yochim, D. (2024, February 21). *IRA vs. 401(k): How to choose*. NerdWallet. https://www.nerdwallet.com/article/investing/ira-vs-401k-retirement-accounts

Your Coffee Break. (2023, June 7). *The personal finance trends you should know about*. Her Agenda. https://heragenda.com/p/major-personal-finance-trends-for-2023/

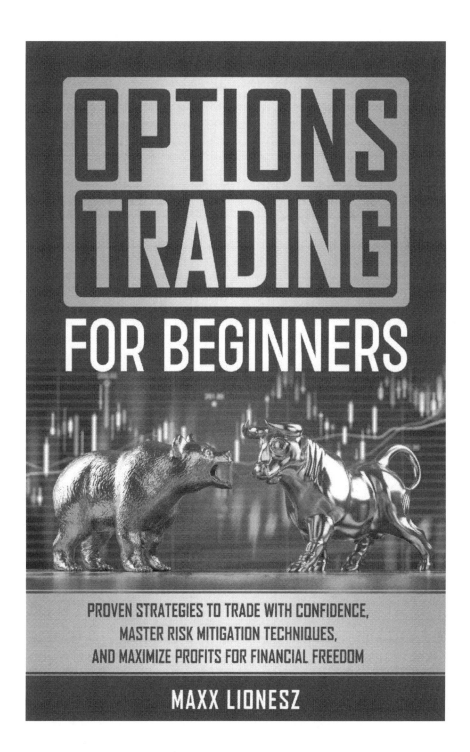

OPTIONS TRADING

FOR BEGINNERS

PROVEN STRATEGIES TO TRADE WITH CONFIDENCE,
MASTER RISK MITIGATION TECHNIQUES,
AND MAXIMIZE PROFITS FOR FINANCIAL FREEDOM

MAXX LIONESZ

INTRODUCTION

Introduction

Options trading can seem like a maze filled with jargon and complex strategies. But think about this: My journey into options trading started much like yours. I faced the same hurdles, the same confusion, and the same fear of losing money. Yet, through persistence and learning, I found strategies that worked. I experienced both failures and successes, each teaching me valuable lessons. These experiences shaped my approach to the market and fueled my passion for helping others navigate this complex field.

The primary goal of this book is simple: to provide you with the knowledge and strategies needed to trade options confidently, manage risk effectively, and maximize profits. We aim to demystify options trading, breaking down complex concepts into easy-to-understand language. By the end of this book, you'll have a solid foundation and actionable strategies to start trading with confidence.

Why focus on options trading? The potential for generating income and managing investment risk is unparalleled, and options are growing to be recognized as valuable tools for building financial independence. Whether you're looking to supplement your income or secure your financial future, options trading offers a path worth exploring.

This book is built on core principles designed to help you succeed:

1. **Ease of understanding:** We break down complex trading concepts into simple, understandable language.

2. **Actionable strategies:** You'll find clear, step-by-step guidance to ensure you're not overwhelmed.

3. **Comprehensive coverage:** We've got you covered from basics to advanced strategies.

4. **Insights into trading psychology:** Learn the psychological aspects that can make or break your trading success.

5. **Visual aids:** Diagrams and charts will help illustrate key concepts.

Here's a brief overview of what you can expect from this book:

- **Chapter 1: Laying the Foundation:** Introduces the basics of options trading, including key concepts like call and put options, strike prices, expiration dates, and the significance of in-the-money vs. out-of-the-money options. It explores the operation of options markets, the key factors influencing options prices, and essential concepts like the Greeks and volatility.

- **Chapter 2: Basic Strategies:** Covers fundamental options and trading strategies such as buying calls and puts, covered calls, protective puts, and cash-secured puts.

- **Chapter 3: Intermediate Strategies:** Introduces more advanced strategies including vertical spreads, butterfly spreads, iron condors, and strategies for profiting from market volatility.

- **Chapter 4: Risk Management:** Focuses on understanding and calculating risk in options trading, using stop-loss orders, diversifying portfolios, and hedging techniques to manage risk effectively.

- **Chapter 5: Trading Psychology:** Discusses the psychological aspects of trading, including overcoming fear and greed, building emotional resilience, and maintaining discipline in trading routines.

- **Chapter 6: Recurring Income:** Explores strategies for generating consistent income through weekly and monthly options, leveraging short-term volatility, and understanding the role of time decay.

- **Chapter 7: Technical Analysis:** Introduces the basics of technical and fundamental analysis, including chart patterns, indicators, and the use of economic indicators in options trading.

- **Chapter 8: Tools and Platforms:** Guides readers in choosing the right trading platforms, utilizing trading software effectively, and setting up a workspace for successful trading.

- **Chapter 9: Learning Exercises:** Provides interactive tools and exercises for testing knowledge, practicing real-world trading, and using simulation tools to improve trading skills.

- **Chapter 10: Learning and Improvement:** Emphasizes the importance of continuous learning, keeping up with market trends, utilizing trading simulations, and accessing ongoing education and trading communities.

By the end of this book, you'll gain:

- **A strong understanding of options trading:** You'll know how to use both basic and intermediate strategies to trade confidently.

- **Actionable strategies:** You'll have actionable strategies that you can start implementing right away.

- **Risk management insights:** You'll learn how to protect your investments and manage risk effectively.

- **Knowledge of key market factors:** You'll understand how to use market conditions and analysis to improve your trading results.

- **Practical experience:** You'll benefit from real-life examples and exercises, helping you apply what you've learned in actual trading situations.

I encourage you to actively engage with the content. Take notes, apply the strategies discussed, and don't hesitate to revisit chapters as needed. As you embark on this journey, expect positive changes. By mastering options trading, you'll gain financial freedom, increased confidence, and a better understanding of market dynamics. The road may be challenging, but the rewards are well worth it. So, let's get started. Your path to financial freedom begins here.

Before diving deeper, let's cover some basic terminology. Understanding these terms will be essential as we progress.

Glossary of Key Terms

This glossary covers key terms and concepts encountered throughout your book.

At-the-Money (ATM): An option is considered at-the-money if the current price of the underlying asset is equal to the option's strike price.

Bear Market: A market condition characterized by falling prices, typically defined as a decline of 20% or more in a broad market index.

Bear Put Spread: An options strategy that involves buying a put option and selling another put option with a lower strike price on the same underlying asset, both with the same expiration date. It is used to profit from a decline in the underlying asset's price.

Bid-Ask Spread: The difference between the highest price a buyer is willing to pay for an asset (bid) and the lowest price a seller is willing to accept (ask). This spread is a key measure of market liquidity.

Bull Market: A market condition characterized by rising prices, typically defined as an increase of 20% or more in a broad market index.

Bull Call Spread: An options strategy that involves buying a call option and selling another call option with a higher strike price on the same underlying asset, both with the same expiration date. It is used to profit from an increase in the underlying asset's price.

Call Option: A financial contract that gives the holder the right, but not the obligation, to buy an underlying asset at a specified price (strike price) within a certain period.

Covered Call: An options strategy where the investor holds a long position in a stock and sells call options on that same stock to generate income from the premiums.

Delta: A measure of how much the price of an option is expected to move for every one-point move in the price of the underlying asset. It is one of the key "Greeks" used to assess options risk.

Derivative: A financial security whose value is derived from an underlying asset, such as a stock, bond, commodity, or index.

Expiration Date: The last date on which an options contract can be exercised. After this date, the option expires and becomes worthless.

Gamma: A measure of the rate of change of Delta in response to changes in the price of the underlying asset. It is used to assess the risk of an options position.

Greeks: Financial variables used to assess different levels of risk. The most common Greeks include delta, gamma, theta, and vega.

Hedge: An investment made to reduce the risk of adverse price movements in an asset. Options are commonly used as hedging instruments.

Implied Volatility (IV): The market's forecast of a likely movement in an asset's price, reflected in the price of its options. Higher implied volatility indicates greater expected price movement.

In-the-Money (ITM): An option that has intrinsic value. For a call option, it is in-the-money if the current price of the underlying asset is above the strike price. For a put option, it is in-the-money if the current price is below the strike price.

Iron Condor: An options strategy that involves selling a call spread and a put spread on the same underlying asset with the same expiration date but different strike prices. It is used to profit from low volatility in the underlying asset.

Margin: Borrowed money used to increase the potential return on an investment. In options trading, margin requirements must be met to cover potential losses.

Out-of-the-Money (OTM): An option that has no intrinsic value. For a call option, it is out-of-the-money if the current price of the underlying asset is below the strike price. For a put option, it is out-of-the-money if the current price is above the strike price.

Premium: The price paid by the buyer of an option to the seller for the rights that the option contract confers. The premium reflects the option's intrinsic and extrinsic value.

Protective Put: An options strategy where an investor buys a put option on a stock they already own to protect against potential losses if the stock's price declines.

Put Option: A financial contract that gives the holder the right, but not the obligation, to sell an underlying asset at a specified price (strike price) within a certain period.

Straddle: An options strategy that involves buying a call and a put option with the same strike price and expiration date. It profits from large price movements in either direction.

Strangle: An options strategy that involves buying a call and a put option with different strike prices but the same expiration date. It profits from large price movements in either direction and is typically cheaper than a straddle.

Strike Price: The price at which the holder of an option can buy (call option) or sell (put option) the underlying asset.

Theta: A measure of the rate at which an option's value declines over time, also known as time decay. As the expiration date approaches, the theta value increases, reducing the option's value.

Vega: A measure of an option's sensitivity to changes in the volatility of the underlying asset. Higher vega indicates greater sensitivity to changes in volatility.

Vertical Spread: An options strategy that involves buying and selling two options of the same type (calls or puts) with different strike prices but the same expiration date.

Volatility: The degree of variation in the price of a financial instrument over time, often measured by standard deviation. High volatility indicates large price swings, while low volatility indicates more stable prices.

Weekly Options: Options contracts that expire on a weekly basis, typically on Fridays. They are useful for short-term trading strategies.

CHAPTER 1

LAYING THE
FOUNDATION

Chapter 1:

Laying the Foundation

In the world of finance, there's always a story that captures the imagination and inspires a new generation of traders. You might wonder what exactly options trading is and why it holds such promise. Unlike stocks or bonds, options allow for more strategic flexibility. They provide tools for hedging against market risks and speculating on price movements with relatively lower capital requirements.

In modern times, the establishment of formal options exchanges in the 1970s, such as the Chicago Board Options Exchange (CBOE), marked a significant milestone. This development standardized contracts, making options trading more accessible and structured for everyday investors.

1.1 Introduction to Options Trading

The history of options trading is rich and varied. In ancient Greece and Rome, merchants used similar contracts to secure prices for future deliveries of goods. This concept evolved over centuries, with significant developments in the 17th century when Dutch traders used options to speculate on tulip bulbs during the infamous tulip mania. The modern era of options trading began in the 1970s with the establishment of the Chicago Board Options Exchange (CBOE). This regulatory milestone made options trading more accessible to the public by standardizing contracts and improving transparency.

Understanding the basic terminology is essential for navigating the options market. An options contract is the agreement between two parties, detailing the terms of the trade.

The underlying asset is the financial asset upon which the option is based, such as a stock or index. The premium is the price you pay to acquire the option, reflecting its market value. These fundamental terms will recur throughout this book, forming the backbone of your options trading knowledge.

As we progress, we'll build on these basics, introducing more complex strategies and concepts. But for now, grasping these foundational elements is crucial. Options trading offers a unique blend of opportunities and challenges. By understanding its core principles and engaging with the material actively, you'll be well-equipped to navigate this dynamic market.

Understanding Call and Put Options

When you first step into options trading, the concepts of call and put options can seem a bit daunting. But let's break them down to their basics. Throughout the book, we will repeat some of the basic concepts to reinforce your learning and understanding. After all, a little repetition is great for your memory and recall.

A call option gives you the right, but not the obligation, to buy an underlying asset at a specified price within a certain timeframe. Think of it as a reservation. For example, imagine reserving a table at a popular restaurant: You secure the right to dine at a specific time, but you're not obligated to show up. If the restaurant becomes incredibly popular, your reservation gains value. In options trading, if the asset's price rises above the specified price (strike price), your call option becomes more valuable.

On the flip side, a put option provides you the right, but not the obligation, to sell an underlying asset at a specified price within a certain period. This is like having the right to return a product to a store for a refund, regardless of whether the product's value has dropped. If you think an asset's price will fall, a put option can be beneficial. It allows you to sell the asset at a higher price than the market value, thus protecting your investment or even profiting from the decline.

Now, let's differentiate between buying and selling options. When you buy a call option, you're betting that the asset's price will go up. Your risk is limited to the premium you paid for the option, but your potential reward is theoretically unlimited. Conversely, when you sell a call option, you are obligated to sell the asset if the buyer decides to exercise the option. This means your potential loss could be substantial if the asset's price skyrockets. Similarly, buying a put option involves paying a premium for the right to sell, with the risk limited to that premium, while selling a put option obligates you to buy the asset if the buyer exercises the option, exposing you to potentially significant losses if the asset's price plummets.

Consider a real-life scenario to make this more relatable. Suppose you believe a tech stock will perform exceptionally well due to an upcoming product launch. You decide to buy a call option. If the stock price rises significantly after the product launch, your call option increases in value, and you can either sell the option for a profit or exercise it to buy the stock at the lower strike price. On the other hand, if you anticipate that a retail stock will suffer due to poor holiday sales, you might buy a put option. As the stock price drops, the value of your put option increases, allowing you to sell the stock at a higher price than the current market value.

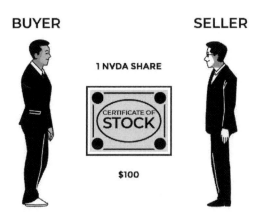

An options contract typically represents 100 shares of the underlying asset. This standardization simplifies trading and ensures consistency across the market. When you purchase an option, you're essentially buying the right to control 100 shares, which amplifies the potential impact of price movements, both positively and negatively.

To contrast call and put options further, let's discuss their rights and obligations. A call option holder has the right to buy, while the seller has the obligation to sell if the option is exercised. Conversely, a put option holder has the right to sell, and the seller has the obligation to buy if exercised. This dynamic creates different risk profiles. Call options are generally profitable in bullish markets, where asset prices are expected to rise. Put options, however, are advantageous in bearish markets, where asset prices are anticipated to fall.

Imagine you've bought a call option on a tech stock, expecting a solid quarterly earnings report. If the report is favorable, the stock price rises, and your call option becomes profitable. Alternatively, consider buying a put option on a retail stock facing declining sales. As the stock price falls, your put option's value increases, providing a profitable exit strategy.

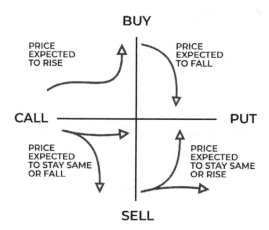

Understanding these fundamental concepts of call and put options is crucial. They form the foundation upon which more advanced strategies are built. By grasping the basics, you'll be better equipped to navigate the complexities of the options market and make informed trading decisions.

1.2 Strike Prices, Expiration Dates, and Premiums

Understanding the role of strike prices and expiration dates is fundamental to mastering options trading. The strike price is the predetermined price at which you can buy or sell the underlying asset, like a marker that sets the playing field. Think of it as the price tag you lock in when you purchase an option. If you're buying a call option, you're hoping the market price will exceed this strike price; with a put option, you want the market price to fall below it. The strike price directly influences the cost of the option, known as the premium. For instance, options with strike prices closer to the current market price usually have higher premiums because they're more likely to be exercised profitably.

Choosing the right strike price is a strategic decision. It hinges on your market outlook. If you're bullish and expect a significant price increase, you might choose a strike price slightly above the current market price for a call option. This approach balances risk and reward, often resulting in a lower premium. Conversely, if you're bearish, you'll select a strike price below the current market price for a put option, again aiming for a sweet spot between affordability and profit potential.

Expiration dates are equally crucial. They mark the deadline by which you must exercise the option. Options come with various expiration timelines, including weekly, monthly, and quarterly. Weekly options offer frequent trading opportunities but come with rapid time decay. Monthly and quarterly options provide more extended periods to realize profits but can be more expensive. The concept of time decay, or *theta*, is essential here. As the expiration date approaches, the time value of the option decreases, impacting its premium.

Intrinsic and extrinsic values are critical components of an option's pricing. The intrinsic value is straightforward: It's the difference between the underlying asset's current price and the strike price, but only if this difference is positive. For instance, if you have a call option with a strike price of $50 and the underlying asset is trading at $55, the intrinsic value is $5. On the flip side, extrinsic value encompasses the time value and volatility. This is the "what if" premium—what if the market moves in your favor before expiration? It's a speculative element, reflecting the potential for movement in the underlying asset's price.

Example Scenario: Choosing Strike Prices and Expiration Dates

Considerations for selecting strike prices involve assessing your risk tolerance and market outlook. If you're conservative, you might opt for in-the-money (ITM) options, where the strike price is advantageous relative to the market price. These options have higher premiums but offer a higher probability of profit. For example, if you buy a call option with a strike price of $45 on a stock currently trading at $50, you're already in a profitable position. However, if you're more speculative, you might choose out-of-the-money (OTM) options, with less favorable strike prices but cheaper premiums. These have higher potential returns but come with greater risk.

Factors influencing expiration date selection include your trading strategy and market conditions. A trader expecting a quick price movement due to an earnings report might choose a near-term expiration to capitalize on the event. For instance, buying a call option with a one-week expiration on a tech stock expecting a strong earnings beat could yield significant profits if the stock price jumps. Conversely, if you're betting on a longer-term trend, selecting a put option with a three-month expiration on a retail stock facing declining sales allows more time for the price to move in your favor.

Understanding the interplay between strike prices, expiration dates, and premiums is crucial for effective options trading. By carefully choosing these parameters based on your market outlook and risk tolerance, you can optimize your strategies for better outcomes.

In-the-Money vs. Out-of-the-Money Options

When it comes to options trading, understanding the concepts of in-the-money (ITM) and out-of-the-money (OTM) options is crucial. These terms define the intrinsic value of options, which plays a significant role in your trading strategy and potential profits. An option is considered ITM when it has intrinsic value. For a call option, this means the underlying asset's price is above the strike price. For a put option, it means the asset's price is below the strike price. In contrast, OTM options have no intrinsic value. A call option is OTM when the underlying asset's price is below the strike price, and a put option is OTM when the asset's price is above the strike price.

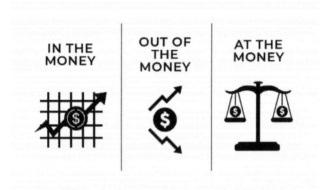

The implications of ITM and OTM statuses are profound. ITM options typically have higher premiums due to their intrinsic value, but they also offer a higher probability of profit. For instance, an ITM call option nearing expiration may be exercised to buy the underlying asset at a price lower than the current market value, yielding an immediate profit. Conversely, OTM options are cheaper but carry a higher risk. They rely entirely on future price movements to become profitable. For example, an OTM put option only becomes valuable if the underlying asset's price drops below the strike price before expiration.

Let's bring this to life with a real-world scenario. Suppose you hold an ITM call option on a tech stock that is trading at $100 with a strike price of $90. As the expiration date approaches, the option's intrinsic value is $10 per share, making it a strong candidate for exercise. In another example, consider an OTM put option on a retail stock trading at $50 with a strike price of $40. The put option is currently out-of-the-money, but if the retail sector underperforms and the stock price drops to $35, the option gains intrinsic value and becomes profitable.

Volatility plays a pivotal role in determining whether options move ITM or OTM. High market volatility can significantly impact the likelihood of an option becoming profitable. In volatile markets, even OTM options can quickly move ITM, offering substantial returns. Conversely, ITM options might retain their value in low-volatility environments, but OTM options may struggle to gain traction. Therefore, strategies must adapt to current volatility levels. Strategies like straddles or strangles can be effective in high-volatility scenarios, while in low-volatility scenarios, strategies like iron condors may be more appropriate.

Consider a scenario where you own an ITM call option nearing expiration. The underlying asset is a tech stock trading well above the strike price. As the expiration date approaches, you must decide whether to exercise the option or sell it. Given the significant intrinsic value, exercising the option to buy the stock at the lower strike price and either holding or selling it immediately can be highly profitable. On the flip side, imagine holding an OTM put option on a stock recently facing negative news. The stock's price starts to decline rapidly. If the price falls below the strike price before expiration, your OTM put option transitions to ITM, offering a lucrative opportunity.

In conclusion, the distinction between ITM and OTM options is fundamental to your trading strategy. With their intrinsic value, ITM options offer higher premiums and a greater likelihood of profit but come at a higher cost. OTM options, while cheaper, are more speculative and depend on significant price movements to become profitable. Volatility further complicates these dynamics, influencing the probability of options moving ITM or OTM. By understanding these concepts and their implications, you can make informed decisions, optimize your strategies, and navigate the complexities of the options market with confidence.

1.3 How Options Markets Operate

Imagine the bustling floor of the New York Stock Exchange—the cacophony of voices, the rapid movement of traders, and the constant flow of information. Now, picture a similar environment, but it's entirely digital, with participants from around the globe executing trades with the click of a mouse. This is the world of options trading, a dynamic market with players of all types. Understanding how this market operates is the first step in mastering options trading.

The options market is a complex ecosystem with various participants, each playing a unique role in ensuring its smooth operation. As a retail trader, you are one of the many individuals who buy and sell options to achieve personal financial goals. You might be looking to supplement your income, diversify your investment portfolio, or hedge against potential losses in your stock holdings. Retail traders like you bring liquidity and diversity to the market, making it more dynamic and accessible.

Institutional investors, such as hedge funds, pension funds, and mutual funds, trade options on a much larger scale. These entities often employ sophisticated strategies and have access to vast resources, allowing them to influence market trends and prices. Their participation ensures substantial liquidity and stability in the market. They use options to manage large portfolios, hedge risks, and capitalize on market inefficiencies.

Market makers are another crucial component of the options market. These are specialized traders or firms that continuously buy and sell options to provide liquidity. Their primary function is to ensure that a counterparty is always available for any trade, thus facilitating smooth transactions. Market makers manage risk by using delta hedging, a strategy that involves balancing their positions in the underlying asset to offset potential losses from options trades. By doing so, they maintain an equilibrium in the market, making it more efficient and less volatile.

Brokers play an essential role in connecting traders to the market. They act as intermediaries, facilitating trades between buyers and sellers. Brokers provide the platforms and tools necessary for executing trades, such as trading software, analytical tools, and real-time market data. They offer various services, including research reports, educational resources, and customer support, to help traders make informed decisions. The fees and commissions charged by brokers can vary, so it's essential to choose one that aligns with your trading needs and budget.

The structure of the options market includes both regulated exchanges and over-the-counter (OTC) markets. Major options exchanges, such as the Chicago Board Options Exchange (CBOE), provide a centralized platform where standardized options contracts are traded. These exchanges offer transparency, liquidity, and regulatory oversight, ensuring a fair and orderly market. On the other hand, OTC options markets involve direct transactions between parties, often customized to meet specific needs. While OTC markets offer flexibility, they come with higher counterparty risk due to the lack of standardization and regulation.

Electronic trading platforms have revolutionized the options market by making it more accessible and efficient. These platforms enable traders to execute orders, monitor positions, and analyze market trends in real time. They provide advanced tools such as algorithmic trading, automated strategies, and risk management features, catering to both novice and experienced traders. The rise of electronic trading has democratized access to the options market, allowing anyone with an internet connection and a brokerage account to participate.

Understanding the various order types and their execution is vital for successful options trading. Market orders are executed immediately at the current market price, ensuring quick entry or exit but without price control. Limit orders, on the other hand, allow you to specify the price at which you want to buy or sell, providing more control but with no guarantee of execution if the market doesn't reach your desired price. Stop orders become market orders once a specified price is reached, helping to limit losses or protect profits. Stop-limit orders combine the features of stop and limit orders, triggering a limit order once the stop price is reached and offering precise control over trade execution.

For example, placing a market order for a call option involves selecting the underlying asset, specifying the number of contracts, and executing the trade at the prevailing market price. This ensures immediate entry into the position but exposes you to the risk of price fluctuations. In contrast, a limit order for the same call option allows you to set a specific purchase price, ensuring you only buy at that price or better, though it may take longer to execute.

The regulatory framework that governs options trading ensures market integrity and protects investors. Regulatory bodies such as the Securities and Exchange Commission (SEC), the Financial Industry Regulatory Authority (FINRA), and the Options Clearing Corporation (OCC) oversee the market, enforcing rules and regulations to maintain transparency and fairness. These organizations set standards for market conduct, monitor trading activities, and ensure compliance with financial laws. Traders must adhere to these regulations, including reporting requirements, margin rules, and trading limits, to participate in the market responsibly.

Understanding these essential principles and market mechanics is crucial for making informed decisions in the options market. By grasping the roles of market participants, the structure of the market, order types, and the regulatory environment, you'll be better equipped to make informed trading decisions and manage your investments with confidence.

Key Factors Influencing Options Prices

Understanding the factors that influence options prices is crucial for making informed trading decisions. One of the most significant factors is the price of the underlying asset. The relationship between the asset price and the option's premium is direct and straightforward. For a call option, as the price of the underlying asset increases, the premium of the call option also rises. Conversely, for a put option, as the price of the underlying asset decreases, the premium of the put option increases. For instance, if a tech stock is trading at $100 and you hold a call option with a strike price of $90, an increase in the stock price to $110 will significantly boost the value of your call option. This direct relationship makes monitoring the underlying asset's price crucial for any options trader.

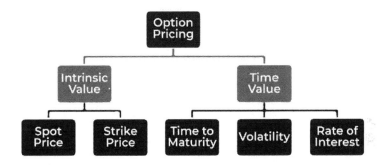

Strike prices and expiration dates are equally vital in determining an option's value. The proximity of the strike price to the current asset price plays a critical role. Options with strike prices closer to the asset's current price (at the money) generally have higher premiums because they have a greater chance of being exercised profitably. Additionally, the time remaining until expiration impacts the option's value. Options with longer expiration dates tend to have higher premiums due to the potential for the underlying asset's price to move favorably over a more extended period. For instance, an option with a three-month expiration might be more valuable than a one-week option because it allows more time for the price to reach the strike price. This interplay between strike price, expiration date, and option value requires careful consideration when selecting options to trade.

Interest rates and dividends also influence options prices. Rising interest rates tend to increase the cost of holding options, making call options more expensive and put options cheaper. This is because higher interest rates raise the opportunity cost of holding cash, which is factored into the option's premium. On the other hand, expected dividends can decrease the price of call options and increase the price of put options. This is because dividends reduce the underlying asset's price on the ex-dividend date, impacting the option's intrinsic value. For example, if you hold a call option on a dividend-paying stock, the expected dividend will be factored into the option's price, reducing its premium. Understanding these nuances helps you anticipate changes in option prices due to shifts in interest rates and dividend expectations.

Market sentiment and news events also play a pivotal role in options pricing. Investor sentiment, driven by market trends and news, can cause significant price fluctuations. Positive news, such as robust earnings reports or favorable economic data, can drive up the price of call options as investors anticipate higher asset prices. Conversely, negative news, such as geopolitical tensions or economic downturns, can increase the value of put options as investors expect asset prices to fall. For instance, during earnings season, options prices can be highly volatile, reflecting the market's expectations and reactions to earnings announcements. A company reporting better-than-expected earnings might see a surge in its stock price, increasing the premiums on call options. Conversely, disappointing earnings can lead to a spike in put option premiums as investors rush to hedge against potential losses.

Case Study: Options Price Fluctuations During Earnings Season

Consider a scenario where a major tech company is set to release its quarterly earnings. Leading up to the announcement, investor sentiment is optimistic, driving up the stock price and, consequently, the premiums on call options. As the earnings release approaches, the market becomes increasingly volatile, reflecting the uncertainty and speculation. Upon release, the company reports record earnings, exceeding market expectations. This positive news causes the stock price to surge further, significantly increasing the value of pre-existing call options. Traders who anticipated this outcome and purchased call options beforehand see substantial gains. Conversely, put options lose value as the stock price rises, highlighting the impact of market sentiment and news events on options pricing.

By understanding these key factors—underlying asset price, strike price, expiration date, interest rates, dividends, market sentiment, and news events—you can better anticipate changes in options prices and make more informed trading decisions. This knowledge allows you to navigate the complexities of the options market with greater confidence and precision.

1.4 The Greeks Explained

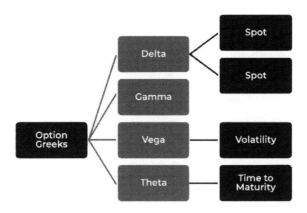

Options trading, while exciting, carries inherent risks. To anticipate and manage these risks, traders can use the Greeks, a set of measures designed to assess different aspects of risk exposure. Delta, one of the most fundamental Greeks, measures an option's sensitivity to changes in the price of the underlying asset. Think of delta as a way to gauge how much the price of an option will move for every one-point move in the underlying asset. For call options, delta is positive, indicating that the option's price will increase as the underlying asset's price rises. Conversely, for put options, delta is negative, meaning the option's price will increase as the underlying asset's price falls. For example, if you hold a call option with a delta of 0.6, and the underlying stock increases by $1, the option's price is expected to rise by $0.60. Understanding delta helps you assess directional exposure and make more informed trading decisions.

Gamma, closely related to delta, measures the rate of change of delta as the underlying asset's price changes. While delta tells you how much an option's price will change, gamma tells you how much delta itself will change with a one-point move in the underlying asset. High gamma options are particularly sensitive to price changes, leading to rapid shifts in delta. This sensitivity makes gamma crucial for managing delta risk. For instance, if you hold a high gamma call option, a slight movement in the underlying asset can significantly alter your delta, requiring you to adjust your position to maintain your desired level of risk. High gamma options can amplify profits but also increase the need for frequent adjustments to your portfolio.

Theta, another critical Greek, measures the impact of time decay on an option's price. As options approach their expiration date, their time value decreases, a phenomenon quantified by theta. This decay accelerates as expiration nears, impacting the option's premium. For example, suppose you hold a long-term call option. As time passes, the option's theta will gradually erode its value, even if the underlying asset's price remains unchanged. To mitigate theta decay, you might consider strategies such as writing (selling) options, which benefit from time decay. Selling shorter-term options can capitalize on this effect, as their value erodes more rapidly, allowing you to collect premiums more quickly.

Vega measures an option's sensitivity to changes in volatility. In volatile markets, options premiums tend to increase, reflecting the higher potential for significant price movements. Vega quantifies this sensitivity, indicating how much an option's price will change with a 1% change in implied volatility. For instance, if you hold an option with a vega of 0.10, a 1% increase in volatility will raise the option's price by $0.10. Understanding vega is essential for assessing and capitalizing on volatility spikes. In periods of high volatility, you might focus on strategies that benefit from increased premiums, such as buying options, while in low-volatility environments, selling options might be more advantageous due to lower premiums and reduced risk of significant price swings.

Let's consider an example to illustrate these concepts. Imagine you hold a portfolio of options on a tech stock. The stock is currently trading at $100, and you own a call option with a delta of 0.50, a gamma of 0.05, a theta of -0.02, and a vega of 0.12. If the stock price increases by $1, your call option's price is expected to rise by $0.50, reflecting its delta. However, this price change also affects delta, increasing it by 0.05 (gamma), making your option more sensitive to future price movements. As time passes, the option's value will decrease by $0.02 per day due to theta, reflecting time decay. If volatility spikes by 1%, the option's price will increase by $0.12, reflecting its vega.

Understanding the Greeks—delta, gamma, theta, and vega—provides a comprehensive framework for managing your options positions. By grasping how these factors influence options pricing and risk, you can make more informed decisions, optimize your strategies, and navigate the complexities of the options market with greater confidence and precision.

Volatility and Its Impact on Options Trading

Volatility is a crucial concept in options trading that reflects the degree of variation in the price of the underlying asset. It's essentially a measure of how much an asset's price is expected to fluctuate over a given period. There are two main types of volatility to consider: historical volatility and implied volatility. Historical volatility is based on past price movements and gives you an idea of how much the asset's price has fluctuated in the past. Implied volatility, on the other hand, is derived from the current prices of options and indicates the market's expectations for future volatility. Both play significant roles in options pricing models, influencing premiums and helping traders gauge potential risks and rewards.

To measure and analyze volatility, several methods are commonly used. Standard deviation is a fundamental statistical measure that quantifies the amount of variation or dispersion of a set of values. In the context of options trading, it helps you understand how much the price of the underlying asset is likely to move. Another valuable tool is the Volatility Index (VIX), often referred to as the "fear gauge." The VIX measures the market's expectation of volatility over the next 30 days based on S&P 500 index options. For example, a high VIX value indicates that traders expect significant price swings, often associated with market uncertainty or fear. Conversely, a low VIX suggests that traders expect stable market conditions. Interpreting VIX levels can provide insights into market sentiment and help you adjust your trading strategies accordingly.

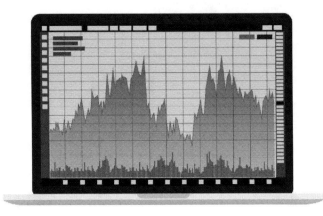

Different volatility conditions call for specific trading strategies. In high-volatility environments, strategies like straddles and strangles can be particularly effective. A straddle involves buying both a call and a put option with the same strike price and expiration date, allowing you to profit from significant price movements in either direction. Similarly, a strangle involves buying a call and a put option with different strike prices but the same expiration date, offering a less expensive alternative to the straddle. For instance, during earnings season, when companies release their quarterly results, volatility tends to spike. Implementing a straddle strategy can help you capitalize on the expected price swings, regardless of the direction.

In contrast, low-volatility environments are better suited for strategies that benefit from stable price movements, such as iron condors. An iron condor involves selling an out-of-the-money call and put option while simultaneously buying a further out-of-the-money call and put option. This strategy allows you to profit from the lack of significant price movement as the options decay in value over time. For example, if you expect a stock to trade within a specific range, an iron condor can help you generate consistent income through premiums while limiting your risk exposure.

Changes in volatility have a direct impact on options premiums. There is a positive correlation between volatility and options premiums, meaning that as volatility increases, so do the premiums. This is because higher volatility increases the likelihood of the underlying asset's price moving significantly, making the options more valuable. For example, during periods of market turbulence, such as political instability or economic uncertainty, options premiums tend to rise due to the increased risk of substantial price fluctuations. Understanding this relationship can help you adjust your trading strategies to take advantage of volatility-driven price changes.

Example: Pricing Adjustments During Market Turbulence

Imagine you hold call and put options on a major tech stock during a period of heightened political tension. The increased uncertainty leads to a spike in implied volatility, causing the premiums on both call and put options to rise. If you anticipate that the volatility will persist, you might consider selling these options to capitalize on the higher premiums. Conversely, if you expect the market to stabilize soon, buying options at the elevated premiums might not be advisable, as the premiums are likely to decrease once the volatility subsides.

Understanding volatility and its impact on options trading is essential for making informed decisions. By leveraging different strategies based on the current volatility conditions, you can optimize your trading approach and enhance your potential for profit. Whether you're navigating high-volatility environments with straddles and strangles or capitalizing on low-volatility periods with iron condors, a solid grasp of volatility dynamics will significantly improve your trading performance.

Chapter Recap - True/False Quiz:

1. True or False: The primary goal of options trading is to minimize risk and maximize profit.

2. True or False: A call option gives you the right to sell an underlying asset at a specified price within a certain timeframe.

3. True or False: The strike price is the predetermined price at which you can buy or sell the underlying asset.

4. True or False: In-the-money options have intrinsic value.

5. True or False: Market makers are responsible for providing liquidity in the options market.

True and False Answers:

1.) True 2.) False 3.) True 4.) True 5.) True

BASIC STRATEGIES

BUYING CALLS

PUTS CALLS

COVERED CALLS

PROTECTIVE PUTS

Chapter 2:

Basic Strategies

In the fast-paced world of options trading, starting with simple, effective strategies can make all the difference. Imagine you're at a bustling farmer's market with countless stalls, each offering a variety of goods. Navigating the options can be overwhelming, but it becomes much easier once you know what you're looking for. Similarly, options trading can seem complex at first, but by starting with the basics, you can build a solid foundation for more advanced strategies.

2.1 Buying Calls and Puts

Understanding the basics of buying calls is like getting your foot in the door of options trading. When you buy a call option, you acquire the right, but not the obligation, to purchase an underlying asset at a specified strike price before the option expires. This means you can buy the asset at the strike price, regardless of its current market price. This strategy is straightforward and particularly advantageous in a bullish market, where you expect the asset's price to rise. For example, suppose you believe a tech stock will soar due to an upcoming product launch. By buying a call option with a strike price of $50 and an expiration date three months away, you position yourself to profit if the stock price climbs above $50. If the stock shoots up to $70, you can exercise your option to buy at $50, securing a profit.

On the flip side, understanding the basics of buying puts is equally essential. A put option gives you the right, but not the obligation, to sell an underlying asset at a specified strike price before the option expires. This strategy shines in a bearish market, where you expect the asset's price to decline. Imagine you're keeping an eye on a retail stock that's been struggling due to poor sales. You decide to buy a put option with a strike price of $30, set to expire in two months. If the stock's price falls to $20, your put option allows you to sell at $30, locking in a profit. This makes buying puts a powerful tool for hedging against potential downturns in your portfolio.

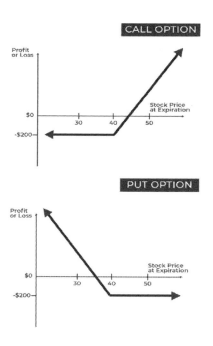

To get started with buying options, follow these steps. First, select the right underlying asset. This involves researching and identifying stocks or indices with strong potential for price movements. Next, choose the appropriate strike price and expiration date. For a call option, pick a strike price slightly above the current market price if you're bullish. For a put option, select a strike price slightly below the current market price if you're bearish. The expiration date should align with your market outlook—short-term for quick gains or long-term for extended trends. Once you've made your selections, place the order on your trading platform. This typically involves entering the asset's ticker symbol, specifying the option type (call or put), selecting the strike price and expiration date, and confirming the trade.

Evaluating potential outcomes is crucial for any options trade. When buying calls, your profit potential is theoretically unlimited, as the asset's price can rise indefinitely. However, your risk is limited to the premium paid for the option. For instance, if you paid $200 for a call option and the asset's price rises significantly, your gains can be substantial. Conversely, if the price remains stagnant or falls, you risk losing the entire premium. Similarly, when buying puts, your profit potential is substantial if the asset's price plummets, but your risk is again limited to the premium paid. For example, if you paid $150 for a put option, and the asset's price drops sharply, you can achieve significant profits. However, if the price remains stable or rises, you risk losing the premium.

Example: Calculating Potential Profits and Losses

Let's say you buy a call option on a tech stock with a strike price of $100, paying a premium of $5 per share. If the stock price rises to $120 before the option expires, your profit calculation would be as follows:

- Stock price at expiration: $120

- Strike price: $100

- Intrinsic value: $120 - $100 = $20

- Premium paid: $5

- Net profit: $20 - $5 = $15 per share

If the option represents 100 shares, your total profit would be $15 x 100 = $1,500. Conversely, if the stock price remains below $100, you would lose the $5 premium per share.

Understanding these basics of buying calls and puts provides a solid foundation for your options trading journey. By mastering these fundamental strategies, you can navigate the market with confidence and build a strong base for more advanced techniques.

2.2 Generating Income With Your Stocks

If you're looking to generate extra income from your stock holdings, the covered call strategy is a popular and effective choice. At its core, a covered call involves selling call options against stocks you already own. This means you collect premiums from the sale of these options, providing a steady income stream. Imagine you own shares in a stable, dividend-paying stock. By selling call options against these shares, you can earn additional income on top of the dividends. For example, if you hold 100 shares of a blue-chip company, selling call options with a strike price slightly above the current market price allows you to collect premiums while still benefiting from potential capital appreciation.

To write covered calls, start by selecting the underlying stock. Choose a stock you already own and are comfortable holding for the long term. Next, determine the strike price and expiration date. The strike price should be slightly above the current market price, allowing for some capital appreciation while ensuring the option gets sold. The expiration date depends on your income needs and market outlook. Monthly expirations are common as they provide a balance between income generation and flexibility. Once you've made these decisions, place the sell order on your trading platform. Enter the stock's ticker symbol, select the option type (call), set the strike price and expiration date, and confirm the trade. This process is straightforward but requires attention to detail to ensure accuracy.

Covered calls come with their own set of risks and rewards. The primary reward is the income generated from premiums. This income can be substantial, especially if you consistently sell covered calls on high-quality stocks. However, it involves a trade-off. By selling call options, you cap your upside potential. If the stock's price rises significantly above the strike price, you'll be obligated to sell your shares at the strike price, missing out on further gains. For example, if you sell a covered call with a strike price of $60 and the stock soars to $70, you're required to sell at $60, potentially foregoing $10 per share in profits. On the flip side, if the stock price drops or remains stagnant, you still keep the premium, providing a cushion against potential losses.

Managing covered call positions involves several strategies to maximize returns and minimize risks. One common approach is rolling up and out, which means buying back the original call option and selling a new one with a higher strike price and later expiration date. This allows you to capture more premium while adjusting to changing market conditions. For instance, if your stock's price rises and approaches the strike price, rolling the option up and out can help you avoid assignment and continue generating income. Another strategy is closing positions early if necessary. If the stock's price moves unfavorably or you anticipate a significant event affecting the stock, buying back the call option can limit potential losses.

Consider a scenario where you hold shares of a pharmaceutical company and have sold a covered call with a strike price of $50. As the stock price rises to $48, you might decide to roll the option up and out to a new strike price of $55 with a later expiration. This adjustment allows you to avoid assignment at $50 while capturing additional premium and potential gains if the stock continues to rise. Alternatively, if the stock price drops to $45 and you foresee further decline, you might choose to close the position by buying back the call option, thus limiting your exposure to further losses.

Covered calls offer a balanced strategy for generating income while managing risk. By understanding the dynamics of strike prices, expiration dates, and potential adjustments, you can effectively use covered calls to enhance your investment returns. This approach allows you to monetize your stock holdings, providing a steady income stream while still participating in potential capital appreciation.

Case Study: Successful Covered Call Trades

Imagine stepping into a bustling café in downtown Manhattan. At a corner table, you overhear a conversation between two traders discussing their recent successes with options trading. One mentions how a simple yet effective strategy allowed him to generate steady income from his stock portfolio. This strategy is the covered call, a favorite among traders for its dual benefits of income generation and risk mitigation.

A covered call strategy involves owning a stock and selling call options against that stock. This approach enables you to earn premiums from the sold options while still holding the underlying stock. The primary purpose of a covered call is to generate additional income from your stock holdings. It also provides a cushion against potential declines in the stock price, as the premium received can offset some of the losses. This strategy is particularly effective in stable or slightly bullish markets where significant price movements are not expected.

Let's dive into a real-life example to illustrate the effectiveness of covered calls. Meet John, a financial analyst who decided to use this strategy with a blue-chip stock known for its stability and reliable dividends. John chose to implement covered calls with shares of a major pharmaceutical company, a sector he understood well due to his professional background. The stock, trading at $100 per share, was a solid candidate for this strategy due to its low volatility and strong fundamentals.

John's initial setup involved selecting the strike price and expiration date for the call options. He decided to sell call options with a strike price of $105, slightly above the current market price. This choice allowed him to benefit from potential price appreciation while still ensuring the options would likely get sold. He chose an expiration date one month out, aligning with his goal of generating regular monthly income. By writing these call options against his owned stock, John positioned himself to earn premiums regardless of minor price fluctuations.

Executing the covered call trade was straightforward. John accessed his trading platform, entered the stock's ticker symbol, selected the option type (call), set the strike price at $105, and chose the expiration date one month away. He confirmed the trade, effectively selling call options against his owned shares. This process allowed him to collect the premium immediately, providing an instant boost to his income.

The outcome of John's trade was favorable. At the end of the month, the stock's price remained around $102, below the $105 strike price. As a result, the call options he sold expired worthless, meaning he kept the premium without having to sell his shares. John earned a premium of $2 per share, translating to $200 for every 100 shares he owned. This additional income enhanced his overall portfolio performance, providing a steady cash flow while maintaining his long-term investment in the pharmaceutical company.

Outcome and Analysis

John's successful covered call trade generated a total income of $200 from the premium. This income reduced his effective cost basis for the stock, offering a cushion against potential price declines. For example, if the stock price had dropped to $98, the premium received would have offset some of the losses, reducing the impact on his portfolio. Additionally, by holding onto the shares, John continued to benefit from the stock's dividends, further boosting his overall returns.

The lessons learned from this trade highlight the importance of selecting the right stock and strike price. Choosing a stable, low-volatility stock increases the likelihood of a successful covered call trade. Setting the strike price slightly above the current market price allows for potential price appreciation while ensuring the options are likely to get sold. Regularly implementing this strategy can generate consistent income, enhancing portfolio performance without the need for significant price movements.

By understanding and applying the covered call strategy, you can effectively boost your income while managing risk. This approach offers a balanced way to participate in the market, making it a valuable tool for both novice and experienced traders. Whether you're looking to supplement your income or enhance your investment returns, covered calls provide a resourceful and accessible strategy for achieving your financial goals.

2.3 Safeguarding Your Investments

Navigating the ups and downs of the stock market can be nerve-wracking. Imagine owning a tech stock that has shown consistent growth, but you're worried about potential volatility due to an upcoming earnings report. This is where protective puts come into play. A protective put is a risk management strategy where you buy put options to safeguard your owned stocks. Think of it as an insurance policy for your investments. If the market takes a downturn, the protective put allows you to sell your stock at the strike price, thus limiting your losses.

When you anticipate market downturns or periods of high volatility, protective puts can be particularly beneficial. For instance, if you own shares in a major tech company whose next earnings report is surrounded by uncertainty, buying protective puts can provide peace of mind. Should the stock price plummet, the put option allows you to sell at a predetermined price, mitigating potential losses. This strategy is straightforward yet powerful, offering a safety net in turbulent times.

To buy protective puts, start by selecting the underlying stock you want to protect. This should be a stock you already own and want to hedge against potential losses. Next, choose the strike price and expiration date for the put option. The strike price should be close to the current market price to provide effective protection, while the expiration date should align with the period of anticipated volatility. For instance, if you expect market turbulence over the next quarter, select an expiration date that covers this period. Once you've made these decisions, place the buy order on your trading platform. Enter the stock's ticker symbol, select the option type (put), set the strike price and expiration date, and confirm the trade.

Evaluating the costs and benefits of protective puts is crucial. The primary cost is the premium paid for the put options, which can vary based on the strike price and expiration date. While this premium represents an additional expense, it buys you significant protection. For example, if you pay $2 per share for a put option on a stock trading at $50, you're effectively paying $200 for protection on 100 shares. Scenarios analysis helps in understanding the potential outcomes. If the stock price drops to $40, your put option allows you to sell at $50, significantly reducing your losses. If the stock price remains stable or increases, your maximum loss is limited to the premium paid. This trade-off between cost and protection makes protective puts a valuable tool for risk management.

Integrating protective puts into your investment portfolio involves a balanced approach to risk management. Diversifying protective puts across multiple holdings can spread the risk and provide comprehensive protection. For instance, if you have a diversified portfolio with tech, healthcare, and financial stocks, buying protective puts for each sector can shield you from sector-specific downturns. Adjusting positions based on market conditions is also key. If market volatility decreases and the risk subsides, you might choose to let the put options expire or sell them to recoup some of the premium. Conversely, if volatility persists, you can roll the options forward to extend protection.

Consider balancing protective puts with other risk management strategies to create a robust defense. For instance, combining protective puts with covered calls can generate additional income while protecting your downside. This dual approach allows you to monetize your stock holdings through premiums from covered calls while hedging against potential losses with protective puts. The flexibility and adaptability of protective puts make them an integral part of a well-rounded investment strategy. By incorporating these techniques, you can maneuver market uncertainties with greater confidence and safeguard your investments against unforeseen downturns.

2.4 Earning Premiums on Your Cash

Cash-secured puts provide a conservative yet effective strategy for generating income while preparing to purchase stocks at a desirable price. Essentially, this strategy involves selling put options on a stock and setting aside enough cash to buy the stock if the option is exercised. This approach allows you to earn premiums while maintaining the financial readiness to buy the stock if its price falls to the strike price. Think of it as earning rent on your cash while waiting for a favorable buying opportunity.

Here's an example: Suppose you're interested in a blue-chip stock currently trading at $100 per share. You're willing to purchase it at $90, believing it's a fair price. By selling a put option with a strike price of $90, you collect a premium from the buyer. If the stock's price drops to $90 or below, you are obligated to buy it, but at a price you were already comfortable with. If the stock remains above $90, you keep the premium and can write another put option, continuing to earn income.

To write cash-secured puts, start by selecting the underlying stock. Choose a stock you wouldn't mind owning at the strike price. Next, determine the strike price and expiration date. The strike price should be a price at which you're willing to buy the stock, while the expiration date should align with your investment horizon. Once these decisions are made, set aside enough cash to cover the purchase if the option is exercised. This ensures you have the financial capacity to buy the stock if needed. Finally, place the sell order on your trading platform by entering the stock's ticker symbol, selecting the option type (put), setting the strike price and expiration date, and confirming the trade.

Cash-secured puts come with a balance of risks and rewards. The primary reward is the income generated from the premiums. This income can be significant, especially if you consistently sell puts on high-quality stocks. However, it comes with a trade-off: You are obligated to buy the stock at the strike price if the option is exercised. If the stock's price falls significantly below the strike price, you might end up purchasing it at a higher-than-market price. For example, if you sell a put with a strike price of $90 and the stock drops to $80, you must buy at $90, incurring a potential loss. Nevertheless, the premium received can offset some of this loss, making the strategy still worthwhile.

Managing cash-secured put positions involves several strategies to optimize returns and mitigate risks. One common approach is rolling down and out, where you buy back the original put option and sell a new one with a lower strike price and later expiration date. This adjustment helps you capture more premium while aligning with the current market conditions. For instance, if the stock's price drops and approaches the strike price, rolling the option down and out to a new strike price of $85 with a later expiration can help you avoid assignment and continue earning income. Another strategy is closing positions early if necessary. If the stock's price moves unfavorably or you anticipate significant events affecting the stock, buying back the put option can limit potential losses.

Consider a scenario where you sell a cash-secured put on a consumer goods stock with a strike price of $50. As the stock price drops to $48, you might decide to roll the option down and out to a new strike price of $45 with a later expiration. This adjustment allows you to avoid assignment at $50 while capturing additional premium and potential gains if the stock stabilizes. Alternatively, if the stock price continues to decline to $40 and you foresee further drops, closing the position by buying back the put option can limit exposure to further losses.

In summary, cash-secured puts offer a conservative strategy for earning income while preparing to buy stocks at desirable prices. By understanding the dynamics of strike prices, expiration dates, and potential adjustments, you can effectively use cash-secured puts to enhance your investment returns and manage risks. This approach provides a steady income stream while maintaining the flexibility to purchase stocks at favorable prices, making it a valuable tool in your investment arsenal.

As we wrap up this chapter, remember that these basic strategies form the building blocks of options trading. From buying calls and puts to writing covered calls and using protective puts, each approach offers unique benefits and risks. Mastering these techniques will provide you with a solid foundation for more advanced strategies, setting you on the path to successful options trading. Next, we'll explore intermediate strategies that build on these basics, helping you further refine your trading skills.

Chapter Recap - True/False Quiz:

1. True or False: Buying a put option is beneficial in a bullish market.

2. True or False: A covered call strategy involves selling call options on stocks that you do not own.

3. True or False: Protective puts are used to safeguard investments against potential losses.

4. True or False: Cash-secured puts require you to have enough cash to buy the stock if the option is exercised.

5. True or False: The primary purpose of buying calls is to profit from a decrease in the underlying asset's price.

True and False Answers:

1.) False 2.) False 3.) True 4.) True 5.) False

CHAPTER 3

INTERMEDIATE STRATEGIES

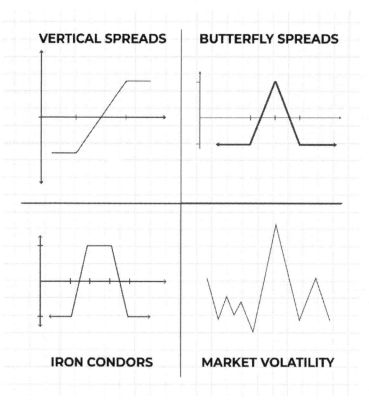

VERTICAL SPREADS	BUTTERFLY SPREADS
IRON CONDORS	MARKET VOLATILITY

Chapter 3:

Intermediate Strategies

Imagine standing on the edge of a cliff, looking out at a vast landscape. The view is breathtaking, but the tools you bring with you will determine how you navigate the terrain once you descend. In options trading, vertical spreads are like those essential tools, offering a way to manage risk while capturing potential profits. These strategies are particularly useful for traders who want to take a more calculated approach, reducing exposure while still benefiting from market movements.

3.1 Combining Calls and Puts for Better Returns

Vertical spreads are strategies that allow you to simultaneously buy and sell options of the same type (calls or puts) with different strike prices but the same expiration date. The goal is to reduce risk while still capturing price movements. Think of it as a way to hedge your bets. By setting up a vertical spread, you can limit your potential losses and gains, creating a more predictable outcome. For example, setting up a Bull Call Spread on a growth stock can be an effective way to profit from an upward movement while capping your risk.

There are two main types of vertical spreads: Bull Call Spreads and Bear Put Spreads. The Bull Call Spread is a strategy used when you expect the price of the underlying asset to rise. It involves buying a call option at a lower strike price and selling another call option at a higher strike price, both with the same expiration date. This strategy allows you to profit from the upward movement of the stock while limiting your risk to the net cost of the spread. For instance, if you expect a tech stock to rise, you can set up a Bull Call Spread by buying a call option with a strike price of $50 and selling a call option with a strike price of $60.

On the other hand, the Bear Put Spread is used when you anticipate a decline in the underlying asset's price. This strategy involves buying a put option at a higher strike price and selling another put option at a lower strike price, both with the same expiration date. The Bear Put Spread allows you to profit from a downward movement while limiting your risk. For example, if you expect a retail stock to decline, you can set up a Bear Put Spread by buying a put option with a strike price of $40 and selling a put option with a strike price of $30.

Setting up vertical spreads involves several steps. To start, select the underlying asset you want to trade. This could be a stock, ETF, or index that you have researched and believe will move in a specific direction. Next, choose the strike prices for the options in your spread. For a Bull Call Spread, select a lower strike price for the call you buy and a higher strike price for the call you sell. For a Bear Put Spread, do the opposite. Both options should have the same expiration date. Finally, place the orders on your trading platform, ensuring you enter the correct details for each leg of the spread.

Risk and reward analysis is crucial in vertical spreads. The maximum profit for a vertical spread is limited to the difference between the strike prices minus the net cost of the spread. For example, if you set up a Bull Call Spread with a $10 difference between strike prices and a net cost of $3, your maximum profit is $7 per share. The maximum loss is limited to the net cost of the spread. For instance, if the underlying asset doesn't move as expected, your loss is capped at the $3 per share you paid for the spread.

Case Study: Calculating Potential Profits and Losses for a Bear Put Spread

Imagine you set up a Bear Put Spread on a retail stock currently trading at $45. You buy a put option with a strike price of $50 for $5 and sell a put option with a strike price of $40 for $2. The net cost of the spread is $3 per share. If the stock drops to $35, your profit calculation would be as follows:

- Stock price at expiration: $35

- Strike price of bought put: $50

- Strike price of sold put: $40

- Intrinsic value of spread: $10 ($50 - $40)

- Net cost of spread: $3

- Net profit: $7 per share ($10 - $3)

By understanding vertical spreads, you can create strategies that offer better risk management while still capturing price movements. This approach provides a balanced way to participate in the market, making it an essential tool for intermediate traders ready to move beyond the basics.

The Butterfly Spread: Maximizing Profits in a Stable Market

In options trading, the butterfly spread stands out as a sophisticated strategy designed to capitalize on minimal price movement in the underlying asset. A butterfly spread combines both a bull spread and a bear spread with the same expiration date, creating a unique structure that profits most when the underlying asset's price remains relatively stable. Imagine a butterfly fluttering in place—this strategy thrives on the stillness of the market, allowing you to maximize profits when the asset's price hovers around a specific point. For instance, setting up a butterfly spread on a large-cap stock can be an effective way to capture gains in a stable market environment.

Creating a butterfly spread involves several key steps. First, select the underlying asset you believe will remain relatively stable. This could be a stock known for its low volatility or an index that typically doesn't experience significant price swings. Next, choose the strike prices for the options in your spread. A standard butterfly spread involves buying one option at a lower strike price, selling two options at a middle strike price, and buying one option at a higher strike price. All options should have the same expiration date. For example, if you set up a butterfly spread on a stock trading at $100, you might buy one call option at a strike price of $90, sell two call options at a strike price of $100, and buy one call option at a strike price of $110. Finally, place the orders on your trading platform, ensuring you enter the correct details for each leg of the spread.

Risk and reward analysis is crucial in understanding the butterfly spread strategy. The maximum profit is achieved if the underlying asset is at the middle strike price at expiration. In the previous example, if the stock's price is exactly $100 at expiration, you realize the highest possible gain. The profit is calculated as the difference between the middle strike price and the lower strike price, minus the initial investment. Conversely, the maximum loss is limited to the initial investment, which is the net cost of setting up the spread. For instance, if you paid $2 per share to establish the butterfly spread, your maximum loss is capped at $2 per share, regardless of how the stock price moves.

Managing and adjusting a butterfly spread requires a keen eye on market conditions. As the underlying asset's price moves, you might need to roll the spreads closer or farther from the current price to optimize your position. Rolling involves closing the existing positions and opening new ones with different strike prices or expiration dates. For example, if the stock price moves to $105, you might adjust the spread by rolling the middle strike price to $105 to align with the new market conditions. Another strategy is closing one side of the spread if necessary. If the market starts trending strongly in one direction, you can close the losing side to limit potential losses while keeping the winning side open.

Example: Adjusting a Butterfly Spread Position During Price Moves

Let's say you set up a butterfly spread on a stable tech stock with the following structure: buy one call option at $95, sell two call options at $100, and buy one call option at $105. The stock price unexpectedly rises to $103. To adjust, you might roll the middle strike price to $103, creating a new spread with strike prices of $93, $103, and $113. This adjustment helps you align with the current market conditions and potentially capture more profit.

In summary, the butterfly spread is an excellent strategy for maximizing profits in stable markets. By understanding the intricacies of setting up, managing, and adjusting the spread, you can navigate market fluctuations with greater precision. This approach allows you to capitalize on minimal price movements, providing a balanced way to participate in the market. With its unique structure and limited risk, the butterfly spread is a valuable addition to your options trading toolkit.

3.2 Earning Consistent Income

The iron condor strategy is a favorite among traders looking to generate consistent income while minimizing risk. This strategy involves combining two vertical spreads—one call spread and one put spread—with the same expiration date but different strike prices. The goal is to profit from low volatility, making it ideal for markets that are expected to remain stable. Imagine setting up an iron condor on an index ETF that has historically shown minimal price fluctuations. This approach allows you to capture premiums from both sides of the market, creating a balanced and relatively low-risk trading position.

To set up an iron condor, start by selecting the underlying asset. Choose one that you believe will remain within a specific price range until the options expire. Next, choose the strike prices for both the call spread and the put spread. For the call spread, select a lower strike price for the call you sell and a higher strike price for the call you buy.

For the put spread, do the opposite: select a higher strike price for the put you sell and a lower strike price for the put you buy. All options should have the same expiration date. For example, if you're setting up an iron condor on an index ETF trading at $100, you might sell a call at $110, buy a call at $115, sell a put at $90, and buy a put at $85. Finally, place the orders on your trading platform, ensuring you accurately enter the details for each leg of the spread.

The iron condor strategy provides a clear risk and reward profile. The maximum profit is limited to the total premiums received from selling the call and put spreads. For instance, if you receive $2 per share from selling the call spread and $2 per share from selling the put spread, your total premium is $4 per share. The maximum loss is limited to the difference between the strike prices of the spreads minus the premiums received. In our example, if the difference between the strike prices is $5 and the total premium received is $4, your maximum loss would be $1 per share. This clear definition of risk and reward makes the iron condor a popular choice for traders seeking consistent income with controlled risk.

Adjusting an iron condor as market conditions change is essential for maximizing its effectiveness. One common adjustment is rolling the spreads up or down. This involves closing the existing spread and opening a new one with different strike prices. For example, if the underlying asset's price starts trending upward and approaches the upper strike price of your call spread, you might roll the call spread up to higher strike prices to maintain a balanced position. Conversely, if the asset's price trends downward, rolling the put spread down can help you avoid potential losses. Another strategy is closing one side of the spread if necessary. If the market shows strong movement in one direction, closing the losing side can limit your losses while keeping the profitable side open.

Example: Adjusting an Iron Condor Position as Volatility Increases

Let's say you set up an iron condor on a stable tech stock with the following structure: sell a call at $120, buy a call at $125, sell a put at

$110, and buy a put at $105. If volatility increases and the stock price starts rising toward $120, you might adjust by rolling the call spread up to $125 and $130. This adjustment helps you stay ahead of the market movement while maintaining the potential for profit.

As this example demonstrates, the iron condor strategy is an excellent way to earn consistent income in stable markets. By understanding how to set up, manage, and adjust this strategy, you can navigate market conditions with greater confidence. This approach allows you to capture premiums from both sides of the market, providing a balanced way to participate in options trading. With its defined risk and reward profile, the iron condor is a valuable addition to your trading toolkit.

Analyzing a Winning Iron Condor Trade

The iron condor strategy is a favorite among options traders looking to generate consistent income in range-bound markets. This strategy involves selling an out-of-the-money call spread and an out-of-the-money put spread on the same underlying asset, with the same expiration date. The primary objective is to capture premiums from both sides of the market, profiting when the underlying asset stays within a specific price range. This approach is particularly effective in low-volatility environments, where significant price movements are not expected.

Consider an example involving a successful iron condor trade on an index ETF, known for its stability and predictable price range. The trader, Alex, chose this underlying asset due to its historical tendency to remain within a narrow trading band. This predictability made the index ETF an ideal candidate for the iron condor strategy. Alex's initial setup involved selecting strike prices for both the call and put spreads. He chose to sell a call at $110 and buy a call at $115, while also selling a put at $90 and buying a put at $85. All options had the same expiration date, one month out. This setup allowed Alex to capture premiums from both the call and put spreads while limiting his risk to the difference between the strike prices.

Executing the iron condor trade involved placing four separate options trades on his trading platform. Alex began by entering the ticker symbol for the index ETF and selecting the options tab. He then proceeded to sell the call option at $110 and buy the call option at $115. After confirming these trades, he moved on to the put side, selling the put option at $90 and buying the put option at $85. Each leg of the trade was carefully entered and confirmed, ensuring accuracy and alignment with his strategy. The total premium received from these trades was $4 per share, providing immediate income while establishing a balanced position.

As the month progressed, the index ETF remained within the expected price range, fluctuating between $95 and $105. This stability worked in Alex's favor, as both the call and put spreads stayed out-of-the-money, allowing the options to decay in value. At expiration, all options expired worthless, meaning Alex kept the entire premium received at the outset. The net premium received amounted to $400 for every 100 shares, representing a significant return on his initial setup.

Net Premium Received and Potential Profit

In Alex's trade, the total premium received from selling the call and put spreads was $4 per share. Given the iron condor structure, the maximum risk was limited to the difference between the strike prices of each spread, minus the total premium received. In this case, the difference was $5 per share for each spread, resulting in a maximum potential loss of $1 per share ($5 - $4). However, since the underlying asset remained within the price range, Alex's actual profit was the entire $4 per share, translating to $400 per 100 shares.

The impact of market movements on the iron condor position was minimal due to the low volatility environment. The underlying asset's price remained within the anticipated range, ensuring that both the call and put spreads stayed out-of-the-money. This stability underscored the importance of selecting the right underlying asset and strike prices, aligning with market conditions to optimize the strategy's effectiveness.

The lessons learned from this trade highlight the importance of thorough market analysis and careful selection of strike prices. Choosing an asset with predictable price movements and aligning strike prices with expected ranges significantly increases the likelihood of success. Regularly monitoring market conditions and being prepared to adjust the position if necessary are also crucial for optimizing iron condor trades. This strategy's ability to generate consistent income while limiting risk makes it a valuable tool for traders seeking steady returns in stable market environments.

3.3 Profiting From Market Volatility

When it comes to capitalizing on market volatility, straddles and strangles are two powerful strategies that can help you profit from significant price movements in either direction. A straddle involves buying both a call and a put option with the same strike price and expiration date. This setup allows you to profit regardless of whether the underlying asset's price goes up or down. On the other hand, a strangle also involves buying both a call and a put option but with different strike prices and the same expiration date. Strangles are often cheaper than straddles, as the options are bought further out-of-the-money. Imagine setting up a straddle on a stock before an earnings announcement, expecting a large price swing but uncertain of the direction. This approach lets you benefit from volatility itself, rather than having to predict the direction of the price movement.

Creating a straddle or strangle involves a few straightforward steps. First, select the underlying asset that you believe will experience significant volatility. This could be a stock, index, or ETF known for large price swings during specific events like earnings announcements or economic reports. For a straddle, choose a strike price close to the current market price and buy both a call and a put option with the same expiration date. For a strangle, select a call option with a strike price above the current market price and a put option with a strike price below the current market price, again with the same expiration date. Place the orders on your trading platform, ensuring accurate entry for each leg of the trade.

The risk and reward profile of straddles and strangles is unique. The maximum profit for both strategies is theoretically unlimited, depending on how far the underlying asset's price moves. For instance, if a tech stock experiences a massive price swing after an earnings announcement, the value of both the call and put options in a straddle can increase significantly. Conversely, the maximum loss is limited to the total premiums paid for the options. For example, if you pay $5 per share for the call and put options in a straddle, your maximum loss is capped at $10 per share, regardless of the price movement. This clear definition of risk and reward makes straddles and strangles appealing for traders seeking to profit from volatility.

Managing straddle and strangle positions requires careful attention to market conditions. One common approach is to close one side of the position if the underlying asset's price moves significantly in one direction. For instance, if you set up a strangle on a volatile stock and the price rises sharply, you might close the put option to lock in gains while keeping the call option open to capture further upside. Another strategy is rolling the options to different strike prices or expiration dates. Rolling involves closing the existing positions and opening new ones with adjusted parameters to align with the current market conditions.

Example: Adjusting a Strangle Position During Price Moves

Imagine you set up a strangle on a biotech stock with the following structure: buy a call option with a strike price of $110 and a put option with a strike price of $90, both expiring in one month. If the stock price unexpectedly rises to $120, you might decide to close the put option to lock in gains and roll the call option to a higher strike price, such as $130, to capture additional profit potential. This adjustment helps you stay ahead of market movements while managing risk effectively.

Straddles and strangles offer versatile strategies for profiting from market volatility. By understanding how to set up, manage, and adjust these positions, you can navigate unpredictable market conditions with greater confidence. These approaches allow you to capitalize on significant price movements, providing a balanced way to participate in options trading. With their unique risk and reward profiles, straddles and strangles are valuable additions to your trading toolkit.

By now, you should have a solid grasp of intermediate options strategies that can help you navigate different market conditions. From vertical spreads to straddles and strangles, these techniques offer a variety of ways to manage risk and capture potential profits. As you continue your journey in options trading, these strategies will serve as essential tools in your arsenal.

Next, we will delve into advanced strategies, building on the foundation you've established to tackle more complex trades. Get ready to take your options trading skills to the next level!

3.4 Applying Advanced Strategies in Real Markets

When you start feeling comfortable with basic and intermediate options strategies, it's time to explore more advanced techniques. These strategies, such as butterfly spreads, calendar spreads, and diagonal spreads, offer nuanced ways to navigate different market conditions. Understanding and applying these advanced techniques can significantly enhance your trading prowess and provide a deeper layer of risk management and potential profit.

Consider the butterfly spread, a strategy designed to profit from minimal price movement in the underlying asset. Let's imagine Sarah, a seasoned trader, who decided to use a butterfly spread on a stable ETF. She selected this ETF due to its historical tendency to remain within a narrow trading range. Sarah's setup involved buying a call option at $50, selling two call options at $55, and buying another call option at $60, all with the same expiration date. Her rationale was based on the ETF's stable price behavior, making it a prime candidate for this strategy.

Executing the trade, Sarah placed orders for the four options on her trading platform. She carefully entered the details for each leg of the spread, ensuring accuracy. As the expiration date approached, the ETF's price hovered around $55, the middle strike price. This stability allowed Sarah to realize maximum profit from the butterfly spread. She captured the difference between the middle strike price and the lower strike price, minus the initial investment. The success of this trade reinforced the importance of selecting the right asset and strike prices for a butterfly spread.

Next, let's consider a calendar spread, another advanced strategy. This involves buying and selling options with the same strike price but different expiration dates. Meet David, an experienced trader who used a calendar spread on a tech stock. He chose this stock due to its predictable price movements and upcoming earnings report. David's setup involved buying a call option with a three-month expiration and selling a call option with a one-month expiration, both at a strike price of $100.

To execute the calendar spread, David entered the orders on his trading platform, ensuring the correct strike price and varying expiration dates. As the one-month option approached expiration, the stock price remained around $100, resulting in the sold option expiring worthless. The longer-term option retained its value, allowing David to profit from the time decay of the sold option. This trade highlighted the effectiveness of calendar spreads in capitalizing on time decay, especially in stable or moderately volatile markets.

Lastly, let's explore the diagonal spread, which combines elements of both vertical and calendar spreads. This strategy involves buying and selling options with different strike prices and expiration dates. Consider Emma, a trader who used a diagonal spread on a consumer goods stock. She chose this stock due to its seasonal price fluctuations. Emma's setup involved buying a call option with a $50 strike price and a six-month expiration while selling a call option with a $55 strike price and a three-month expiration.

Executing the diagonal spread, Emma carefully entered the details on her trading platform, ensuring the correct strike prices and expiration dates. As the three-month option approached expiration, the stock price neared $55, resulting in the sold option expiring with minimal intrinsic value. The longer-term option appreciated due to the stock's seasonal price increase, allowing Emma to profit from both time decay and price movement. This trade underscored the benefits of diagonal spreads in capturing gains from both volatility and time decay.

Incorporating these advanced strategies into your trading toolkit can provide new avenues for profit and risk management. The butterfly spread offers stability in range-bound markets, the calendar spread capitalizes on time decay, and the diagonal spread combines the best of both worlds. By understanding and applying these techniques, you can navigate complex market conditions with greater confidence and precision. Next, we will look at essential tools and platforms, guiding you to choose the right resources for your trading needs.

Chapter Recap - True/False Quiz:

1. True or False: A vertical spread involves buying and selling options with the same expiration date but different strike prices.

2. True or False: The butterfly spread strategy is most effective in volatile markets.

3. True or False: The iron condor strategy involves combining two vertical spreads to profit from low volatility.

4. True or False: In a bear put Spread, you profit when the underlying asset's price rises.

5. True or False: Straddles are used to profit from significant price movements in either direction.

True and False Answers:

1.) True 2.) False 3.) True 4.) False 5.) True

RISK MANAGEMENT

Chapter 4:

Risk Management

Picture this: You're at a high-stakes poker table in a Las Vegas casino. The lights are dim, the air thick with tension. Every player is calculating their risks, weighing their odds, and making strategic decisions. Options trading is not much different. To succeed, you need to understand and manage risk effectively.

4.1 Understanding and Calculating Risk in Options Trading

Risk in options trading refers to the potential for losing money. It's the flip side of the coin that traders must always consider. You must be aware of several types of risk: market risk, credit risk, and liquidity risk. Market risk is the possibility that the entire market or a specific asset class will move against your position. This is influenced by factors like economic data, geopolitical events, and market sentiment. For instance, a sudden economic downturn can cause a broad market decline, impacting all stocks and options.

Credit risk refers to the possibility that the counterparty in a financial transaction will not fulfill their obligations. In the context of options, this is usually mitigated by clearinghouses that guarantee the performance of options contracts. Liquidity risk, on the other hand, is the risk that you won't be able to buy or sell an asset without significantly impacting its price. This can be particularly relevant in options with low trading volumes.

To quantify these risks, traders use several methods. The Greeks—delta, gamma, theta, vega, and rho—are essential tools. Delta measures an option's sensitivity to changes in the price of the underlying asset. For example, a delta of 0.5 means the option will move $0.50 for every $1.00 move in the underlying asset. Gamma measures the rate of change in delta, providing insight into how delta will shift as the underlying asset's price changes. Theta represents time decay, indicating how much an option's price will decrease as it approaches expiration. Vega measures sensitivity to volatility, showing how much the option's price will change with a 1% change in implied volatility. Rho measures sensitivity to interest rate changes, which can impact the cost of holding options.

Value at risk (VaR) is another method used to calculate risk. It estimates the maximum potential loss over a specified period with a given confidence level. For instance, a one-day VaR of $1,000 at a 95% confidence level means there is a 95% chance that the loss will not exceed $1,000 in a single day. Maximum drawdown, on the other hand, measures the largest peak-to-trough decline in the value of a portfolio, providing insight into the potential for significant losses over time.

The risk-reward ratio is a crucial concept in guiding trading decisions. It compares the potential profit of a trade to its potential loss. Calculating the risk-reward ratio involves dividing the expected profit by the potential loss. For example, if you stand to gain $200 on a call option trade but risk $100, the risk-reward ratio is 2:1. Maintaining a favorable risk-reward ratio is essential for long-term success, as it ensures that the potential rewards justify the risks taken.

Lessons From a Loss

In the trading world, not every move leads to profit. Consider the case of a long call option on a biotech stock that seemed promising. The background of this trade is rooted in the biotech sector's inherent volatility and the allure of high returns from breakthrough drug approvals. Our trader, let's call him Mark, was captivated by the buzz surrounding a biotech firm on the verge of releasing a revolutionary drug. The initial setup involved buying a call option with a strike price of $75, anticipating that positive news would drive the stock price significantly higher. The expiration date was set three months out, providing ample time for the anticipated price movement.

The execution of this trade seemed straightforward. Mark selected the strike price of $75, slightly above the current market price of $72, to balance cost and potential gain. The expiration date was chosen to align with the expected regulatory announcement. However, market conditions took an unexpected turn. Despite initial optimism, the biotech sector faced broader market volatility, and regulatory delays compounded the uncertainty. The stock price remained stagnant, hovering around $70, well below the strike price. This unexpected stagnation was the first sign of trouble.

As the trade progressed, it became clear that several missteps contributed to the loss. The first mistake was overestimating the market movement. Mark was overly optimistic about the stock's potential, failing to account for the broader market conditions and the specific regulatory risks inherent in the biotech sector. The second issue was inadequate risk management. Mark didn't set a clear exit strategy or stop-loss order, which could have mitigated the losses as the stock price failed to rise. Lastly, there was a failure to adjust the position in response to changing conditions. As the stock price stagnated, Mark held on to the call option, hoping for a last-minute surge that never materialized.

The key takeaways from this experience highlight the importance of thorough research and analysis. Relying on hype without conducting comprehensive due diligence can lead to misguided decisions. Implementing better risk management strategies is crucial. Setting clear exit strategies and stop-loss orders can help limit potential losses. Being prepared to adjust trades as needed is another vital lesson. Flexibility in response to changing market conditions can make a significant difference in outcomes. For instance, rolling the option to a later expiration date or a different strike price could have provided a better chance to salvage the trade.

Mark's experience underscores the complexities of options trading and the importance of learning from losses. While setbacks are inevitable, they provide valuable lessons that can refine your trading approach. By incorporating these insights into your strategy, you can navigate the market with greater confidence and resilience.

Case Study: Calculating Risk in Options Trading

Consider a call option trade on a tech stock. The stock is trading at $150, and you buy a call option with a strike price of $155 for a premium of $3. The delta is 0.6, indicating the option will move $0.60 for every $1.00 move in the stock. If the stock rises to $160, the option's price will increase by $3 ($5 move x 0.6 delta), resulting in a $6 price for the option. Your profit would be $3 per share ($6 - $3 premium), and the risk-reward ratio is calculated as follows:

- **Potential profit**: $3 per share

- **Potential loss (premium paid):** $3 per share

- **Risk-reward ratio:** 1:1

Now, consider a put option trade on a retail stock. The stock is trading at $80, and you buy a put option with a strike price of $75 for a premium of $2. The delta is -0.5. If the stock falls to $70, the option's price will increase by $2.50 ($5 move x -0.5 delta), resulting in a $4.50 price for the option. Your profit would be $2.50 per share ($4.50 - $2 premium), and the risk-reward ratio is calculated as follows:

- **Potential profit**: $2.50 per share

- **Potential loss (premium paid):** $2 per share

- **Risk-reward ratio:** 1.25:1

Understanding and calculating risk in options trading is essential. Whether using the Greeks, VaR, or the risk-reward ratio, these tools help you make informed decisions, manage your portfolio effectively, and confidently tackle the complexities of the options market.

4.2 Setting Up Stop-Loss Orders

Imagine you're driving on a winding mountain road. You wouldn't think twice about using guardrails to prevent your car from veering off the edge. In options trading, stop-loss orders serve a similar purpose. They act as automated guardrails, preventing significant losses by selling your position once it hits a predetermined price level. This automation is crucial because it removes the emotion from trading decisions, ensuring you stick to your risk management plan even when market conditions become volatile. For instance, during sudden market downturns, a stop-loss order can automatically sell your position, preventing larger losses.

Different types of stop-loss orders are available, each with its specific applications. A traditional stop-loss order triggers a market order to sell once the stock reaches a specified price. This is straightforward but can sometimes result in selling at a lower price if the market moves rapidly. A trailing stop-loss order, on the other hand, adjusts itself based on the stock's price movements. It sets the stop price at a fixed percentage or dollar amount below the market price, moving up as the stock price increases but staying put if the stock price declines. This allows you to lock in gains while protecting against significant drops. Another type is the stop-limit order, which combines elements of stop-loss and limit orders. It triggers a sell order at a specified price but only executes if it can be filled at or above a predetermined limit price. This helps avoid selling at an unfavorable price but carries the risk of not executing if the limit price isn't met.

Setting effective stop-loss levels is an art that involves a blend of technical analysis, percentage-based criteria, and a deep understanding of market volatility. One approach is using technical analysis to determine key support and resistance levels. For example, if a stock has consistently bounced off a specific price level, setting a stop-loss just below this level can be effective. Another method is the percentage-based stop-loss, where you set the stop at a fixed percentage below the purchase price. This approach is simple and ensures you cap your losses at a manageable level. Volatility-based stop-losses consider the stock's historical price fluctuations. Stocks with higher volatility may require wider stop-loss levels to avoid premature triggers, while less volatile stocks can have tighter stops.

Examples of Stop-Loss Implementation

Consider a scenario where you hold a call option on a tech stock trading at $150. You decide to set a traditional stop-loss order at $140 to prevent significant losses. If the stock price drops to $140, the stop-loss order triggers a sale, minimizing your losses. In another scenario, you might have a put option on a retail stock trading at $80. You use a trailing stop-loss order set at 5% below the current price. As the stock price rises to $85, the stop price adjusts to $80.75, locking in gains while protecting against a sudden decline.

Adjusting stop-loss levels in response to market conditions is also crucial. If you notice increasing volatility, you might widen your stop-loss levels to avoid getting stopped out prematurely. Conversely, in a stable market, tighter stop-loss levels can help protect your profits more effectively. Imagine holding a call option on a stock during earnings season, a period known for heightened volatility. You might initially set a stop-loss at 10% below the purchase price but adjust it to 15% as the earnings announcement approaches to account for potential price swings.

By understanding and effectively implementing stop-loss orders, you can protect your investments, automate risk management, and master the intricacies of options trading with greater confidence and precision.

4.3 Diversifying Your Options Portfolio

Diversification is a key strategy for managing risk. By spreading your investments across different assets, you reduce your exposure to any single asset, which helps smooth out portfolio volatility. Think of it like not putting all your eggs in one basket. If one asset performs poorly, the others can help offset the loss, providing a more stable overall performance. For instance, if you have all your options tied to tech stocks, and the tech sector takes a hit, your entire portfolio suffers. But if you also hold options in healthcare, finance, and other sectors, a downturn in tech won't devastate your portfolio.

Several strategies are at your disposal to diversify an options portfolio. One effective method is to diversify across different asset classes, such as stocks, ETFs, and indices. Stocks offer specific exposure to individual companies, while ETFs and indices provide broader market exposure. For example, holding options on both individual tech stocks and an ETF like the S&P 500 can balance specific risks with general market trends. Another approach is to diversify across different sectors. By spreading your options across tech, healthcare, finance, and other industries, you mitigate the impact of sector-specific risks. If the healthcare sector underperforms due to regulatory changes, your tech and finance options can help cushion the blow. Additionally, using different types of options strategies, such as covered calls, vertical spreads, and straddles, can further diversify your risk. Each strategy has its risk-reward profile, and combining them can create a balanced portfolio.

Creating a diversified portfolio involves selecting a mix of underlying assets and balancing high-risk and low-risk strategies. Start by identifying assets that align with your market outlook and risk tolerance. Choose a combination of individual stocks, ETFs, and indices from various sectors. Next, balance your strategies. Use high-risk strategies, like buying calls and puts, for assets you believe will experience significant price movements. Pair these with lower-risk strategies, like covered calls and cash-secured puts, for more stable assets. This mix ensures you're not overly exposed to any single risk. For instance, if you have a bullish outlook on tech but want to mitigate risk, you might buy call options on individual tech stocks while selling covered calls on a tech ETF. This combination allows you to capture potential gains while generating steady income.

Examples of Diversification

Let's illustrate diversification with some real-world examples. Imagine you have a portfolio that includes options on tech and healthcare stocks. You hold call options on a prominent tech company known for its innovation and rapid growth. At the same time, you own put options on a healthcare stock that you believe is overvalued. This combination allows you to benefit from tech sector gains while protecting against potential declines in healthcare. Additionally, you might include an ETF, such as the SPDR S&P 500 ETF, to provide broad market exposure. By holding options on this ETF, you gain from overall market trends, adding another layer of diversification.

Another example involves using a mix of covered calls, straddles, and spreads. Suppose you own shares in a stable consumer goods company. You might write covered calls against these shares to generate income. Simultaneously, you could set up a straddle on a volatile biotech stock ahead of a major product announcement, capturing potential price swings in either direction. Lastly, you might implement a vertical spread on a financial stock, balancing risk and reward. This diversified approach ensures that your portfolio isn't overly reliant on a single strategy or market movement. If the biotech announcement is less impactful than expected, the income from your covered calls and the balanced risk of your vertical spread help maintain your portfolio's stability.

Diversifying your options portfolio is essential for managing risk and achieving consistent returns. By spreading your investments across different asset classes, sectors, and strategies, you create a balanced and resilient portfolio capable of weathering market fluctuations. This approach not only protects your investments but also positions you to capitalize on a wide range of market opportunities.

4.4 Hedging Techniques for Risk Management

Imagine you're sailing through a turbulent sea with waves crashing around you. Hedging in options trading is like having a lifeboat ready—it helps you reduce potential losses and balance your exposure to risk. Hedging involves taking an offsetting position in a related security to mitigate the impact of adverse price movements. It's a strategy that aims to protect your investments, ensuring that even when market conditions are rough, you have a safety net in place. This doesn't eliminate risk but manages it, reducing the impact of unforeseen events on your portfolio.

Common hedging strategies in options trading include protective puts, covered calls, and collars. A protective put involves buying a put option for a stock you already own. This strategy is akin to purchasing insurance; it allows you to sell the stock at the strike price, protecting against significant declines. Covered calls, on the other hand, involve selling call options against stocks you own. This generates income through premiums, providing a cushion against potential drops in stock price. Lastly, collars involve holding the underlying stock while simultaneously buying a protective put and selling a call option. This strategy limits potential losses and gains, offering a balanced approach to risk management.

Implementing these hedging strategies requires a step-by-step approach. For a protective put, start by selecting the stock you own and want to protect. Choose a put option with a strike price close to the current market price and an expiration date that aligns with your risk horizon. For example, if you own shares of a tech company trading at $150 and expect potential volatility, buy a put option with a strike price of $145 expiring in three months. Place the order on your trading platform, ensuring you accurately enter the details. For a collar strategy, you'll need to buy a put option and sell a call option on the same stock. Suppose you own shares of a healthcare company trading at $100. You buy a protective put with a strike price of $95 and sell a call option with a strike price of $110, both expiring in three months. This setup limits your downside risk while capping your potential upside, creating a balanced risk profile.

Hedging Examples

Consider a scenario where you hold a long stock position in a major tech company. The stock is trading at $200, and you're concerned about potential market volatility. To hedge this position, you decide to buy put options with a strike price of $190, expiring in two months. If the stock price drops to $180, your put options allow you to sell at $190, mitigating the loss. This protective put strategy provides a safety net, ensuring that your losses are limited.

Another example involves using covered calls to generate income while hedging. Suppose you own shares of a stable consumer goods company trading at $50. You decide to sell call options with a strike price of $55, expiring in one month. By selling these call options, you earn a premium, providing additional income. If the stock price remains below $55, you keep the premium and can sell another call option next month. If the stock price rises above $55, you sell your shares at the strike price, benefiting from the capital appreciation while still earning the premium. This strategy allows you to generate steady income while managing potential risks.

Hedging techniques are essential tools in your options trading toolkit. By understanding and implementing strategies like protective puts, covered calls, and collars, you can effectively manage risk and protect your investments. These approaches provide a balanced way to navigate market uncertainties, ensuring that you're prepared for whatever the market throws your way.

4.5 The Role of Volatility in Risk Assessment

Volatility is a key factor in options trading that you can't afford to overlook. It measures the degree of variation in the price of the underlying asset over time. Volatility can be categorized into two main types: historical and implied. Historical volatility looks at past price movements to gauge how much the asset's price has fluctuated. It's like reviewing the weather patterns over the past year to predict future storms. Implied volatility, on the other hand, reflects the market's expectations for future volatility, akin to weather forecasts predicting future conditions. Both types are crucial for understanding potential price swings and making informed trading decisions.

Volatility has a direct impact on options pricing. The relationship between volatility and option premiums is straightforward: Higher volatility leads to higher premiums. This is because increased volatility raises the likelihood of the option expiring in the money. Vega, one of the Greeks, measures an option's sensitivity to changes in volatility. A high vega means the option's price will significantly change with small fluctuations in implied volatility. For example, if you hold an option with a vega of 0.10, a 1% increase in implied volatility will raise the option's price by $0.10. Understanding vega helps you gauge how volatility will affect your options, allowing you to adjust your strategies accordingly.

Different volatility environments call for tailored strategies. In high-volatility markets, options strategies such as straddles and strangles become effective. A straddle involves buying both a call and a put option at the same strike price and expiration date. This setup allows you to profit from significant price movements in either direction. A strangle, on the other hand, involves buying a call and a put option with different strike prices but the same expiration date. It's a cheaper alternative to the straddle, offering potential gains from large price swings. For instance, during earnings season, when stock prices can be highly volatile, these strategies can help you capitalize on the price movements.

In low-volatility environments, strategies like iron condors and butterflies are more suitable. An iron condor involves selling an out-of-the-money call spread and an out-of-the-money put spread on the same underlying asset. This strategy profits from the lack of significant price movement as the options decay in value over time. Similarly, a butterfly spread combines both a bull spread and a bear spread with the same expiration date, profiting from minimal price movement in the underlying asset. These strategies are ideal when you expect the market to remain stable, allowing you to generate consistent income from premiums.

Examples of Volatility Analysis

Consider a high-volatility environment, such as the period leading up to a major earnings announcement for a tech company. You decide to set up a straddle by buying a call option and a put option at the same strike price of $100, expiring in one month. The high implied volatility increases the premiums for both options, but the potential for significant price swings makes the trade worthwhile. If the earnings announcement leads to a substantial price movement, either up or down, your straddle can yield significant profits.

208

Now, imagine a low-volatility environment where a major index ETF has shown minimal price fluctuations. You decide to set up an iron condor by selling a call spread with strike prices of $110 and $115 and a put spread with strike prices of $90 and $85. The low volatility means the premiums are lower, but the strategy profits from the ETF's price remaining within a specific range. As the options approach expiration without significant price movement, you collect the premiums, generating steady income.

Understanding the role of volatility in risk assessment is crucial for effective options trading. By tailoring your strategies to different volatility environments and leveraging tools like vega, you can navigate the complexities of the market with greater confidence. This approach helps you capitalize on market conditions, ensuring you're well-prepared for both high and low volatility periods.

Chapter Recap - True/False Quiz:

1. True or False: Stop-loss orders are used to limit potential losses in options trading.

2. True or False: Diversifying your options portfolio increases risk.

3. True or False: Volatility is irrelevant to risk assessment in options trading.

4. True or False: Hedging techniques are used to manage and reduce risk in options trading.

5. True or False: Calculating risk is unnecessary if you are using advanced trading strategies.

True and False Answers:

1.) True 2.) False 3.) False 4.) True 5.) False

Make a Difference With Your Review

First off, congratulations on diving into the world of options trading with **Options Trading for Beginners: Proven Strategies to Trade With Confidence, Master Risk Mitigation Techniques, and Maximize Profits for Financial Freedom**. You've taken an exciting step toward mastering a skill that could seriously transform your financial future. But before you move on to the next big thing in your trading journey, I want to ask you for a quick favor—one that could make a huge difference for other readers just like you.

People who give without expecting anything in return live longer, happier lives and often find success along the way. Are you willing to assist someone unfamiliar if it means receiving no recognition? Who is this person, you ask? They are like you—or, at least, like you used to be: curious, exploring new technologies, wanting to make a difference, and needing help but not sure where to look.

Our mission is to make **OPTIONS TRADING** accessible to beginners everywhere. All our efforts are grounded in this endeavor, intending to reach a broad audience, and this is where you play a vital part. Most people do, in fact, judge a book by its cover (and its reviews).

So, here's the ask: Could you take just a few minutes to leave an honest review? Feel free to share just a few sentences about what you found helpful, what you enjoyed, or even what you think could be improved. Every bit of feedback helps. To leave a review, simply scroll to the bottom of the product page on Amazon, look for the "Write a customer review" button, and let your thoughts flow. It's that easy!

Your review for this book would be greatly appreciated. This small act could significantly affect others, potentially aiding local businesses, supporting entrepreneurs, or helping individuals achieve their dreams. Your willingness to leave feedback makes a world of difference and can be accomplished easily by scanning the QR code below or using this link:

https://www.amazon.com/review/review-your-purchases/?asin=B0DK52N3M5.

CHAPTER 5

TRADING PSYCHOLOGY

Chapter 5:

Trading Psychology

Imagine you're on a roller coaster, strapped in and ascending that first colossal hill. Your heart is racing, your palms are sweating, and the anticipation is almost unbearable. This sense of thrill and anxiety is not unlike the emotions traders experience in the financial markets. Navigating the psychological landscape of trading is crucial for long-term success. Understanding and managing your emotions can be the difference between triumph and failure.

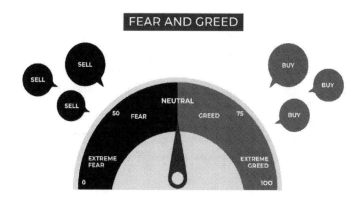

5.1 Overcoming Fear and Greed

The psychological roots of fear and greed in trading are deeply embedded. Fear often stems from the anxiety of losing money. This fear can paralyze you, leading to missed opportunities and hesitant decision-making. Picture this: You've invested in a promising tech stock, but recent market volatility makes you doubt your choice. The fear of seeing your hard-earned money evaporate can be overwhelming.

Greed, on the other hand, is driven by the desire for quick profits. This can lead to over-leveraged positions and reckless trading. Imagine hitting a hot streak with a series of winning trades—the temptation to go all-in on the next trade can be irresistible. Past experiences and market volatility further exacerbate these emotions. A previous significant loss can haunt you, while a volatile market can amplify both fear and greed, leading to impulsive decisions.

Having strategies in place to overcome fear is essential. Setting realistic expectations is a good starting point. Understand that losses are part and parcel of trading. No one wins all the time. Set goals that are achievable and grounded in reality. Using stop-loss orders is another effective technique. By setting a predetermined exit point, you limit potential losses, reducing the fear of the unknown. For instance, if you buy a stock at $50, set a stop-loss order at $45. If the stock dips to that price, the order will execute automatically, capping your loss. Practicing risk management techniques is also crucial. Diversify your portfolio and avoid putting all your eggs in one basket. By spreading your investments, you mitigate the risk of a single catastrophic loss, making the trading experience less nerve-wracking.

Managing greed requires a balanced approach. Setting profit targets and sticking to them is a fundamental strategy. Decide in advance the profit level at which you'll exit a trade. For example, if you aim for a 20% return, stick to that goal and resist the urge to hold out for more. Developing a disciplined trading plan is equally important. Outline specific criteria for entering and exiting trades, and adhere to them rigorously. Avoid over-leveraging positions by ensuring your investments are proportionate to your overall portfolio size. Over-leveraging can lead to significant losses, even if a single trade goes wrong. By maintaining a balanced approach, you safeguard against the highs and lows that can lead to rash decisions.

Real-life examples illustrate these points effectively. Take the case of Jane, a trader who faced a major loss in her early trading days. She invested heavily in a biotech stock that promised groundbreaking results. When the stock plummeted following a failed clinical trial, she lost a significant portion of her investment. Initially paralyzed by fear, Jane decided to rebuild her strategy. She set realistic expectations, used stop-loss orders, and diversified her portfolio. Over time, she regained her confidence and achieved consistent profits.

Conversely, consider Mark, who struggled with greed after a series of successful trades. Buoyed by his success, he began taking larger, riskier positions, hoping for even bigger gains. This overconfidence led to a significant loss when the market turned. Realizing his mistake, Mark implemented strict profit targets and developed a disciplined trading plan. By sticking to his targets and avoiding over-leveraging, he managed to achieve steady, sustainable profits.

Understanding and managing the psychological aspects of trading is crucial. By addressing the root causes of fear and greed and implementing consistent strategies, you can ride the emotional roller coaster of trading with greater confidence and success.

5.2 Building Emotional Resilience in Trading

Emotional resilience in trading is like having a mental armor that shields you from the market's turbulent swings. It's crucial for long-term success, enabling you to stay calm under pressure, recover from losses without emotional breakdown, and maintain focus and clarity. Imagine you're in the midst of a market downturn. The stock prices are plummeting, and panic is spreading among traders. Those with emotional resilience can handle this chaos without making impulsive decisions. They understand that market fluctuations are part of trading, allowing them to weather the storm with a clear mind.

Building emotional resilience requires practical methods. Regular self-assessment and reflection are fundamental. Take time to analyze your trades, not just the outcomes but the decisions and emotions that led to them. Reflecting on both wins and losses helps you understand your trading patterns and emotional triggers. Developing a support network is equally important. Surround yourself with mentors and join trading communities where you can share experiences and gain insights. These networks provide a sense of camaraderie and offer valuable advice during challenging times. Additionally, practicing stress-relief activities is essential. Engage in regular exercise, pursue hobbies, and take breaks to recharge. These activities help you manage stress and maintain a balanced lifestyle, which in turn enhances your trading performance.

Experience and continuous learning play a significant role in building emotional resilience. Each trade, whether successful or not, is a learning opportunity. Keeping a trading journal is a powerful tool for this purpose. Documenting your trades, including the rationale behind them and the emotions experienced, provides valuable insights over time. Continuous education through books, courses, and seminars also contributes to resilience. Staying informed about market trends and trading strategies boosts your confidence and equips you to handle different market conditions. Remember, resilience is built gradually through experience and learning, not overnight.

Case studies of resilient traders offer valuable lessons. Consider Tom, who faced a significant setback early in his trading career. He invested heavily in a startup, expecting high returns. However, the company went bankrupt, and Tom lost a substantial amount of money. Instead of giving up, he analyzed his mistakes and sought advice from experienced traders. By implementing their suggestions and continuously learning, he rebuilt his portfolio and eventually achieved consistent profits. Another example is Lisa, who maintained her composure during market crashes. She was trading during the 2008 financial crisis, a period marked by extreme volatility and uncertainty. While many traders panicked and sold off their assets, Lisa stayed calm. She relied on her well-researched strategy and support network, and she even took advantage of the market lows to make profitable trades.

Reflection Section: Journaling Prompt

Take a moment to reflect on your trading experiences. Write down a recent trade that didn't go as planned. What emotions did you feel? How did you respond? What did you learn from the experience? Use these reflections to identify patterns and areas for improvement.

Building emotional resilience is an ongoing process. By regularly assessing your trades, developing a strong support network, engaging in stress-relief activities, and continuously learning, you can enhance your ability to stay calm under pressure, recover from losses, and maintain focus. These strategies will not only improve your trading performance but also contribute to your overall well-being.

5.3 Developing a Trading Routine

Creating a consistent trading routine is like setting up a well-oiled machine. It brings structure and discipline to your trading activities, which is crucial for long-term success. Without a routine, you might find yourself making impulsive decisions that lead to inconsistent results. A structured routine helps reduce decision fatigue by standardizing your decision-making process. Imagine waking up each day knowing exactly what steps to take to analyze the market, place trades, and review your performance. This consistency enhances your focus and productivity, making your trading activities more efficient and less stressful.

An effective trading routine begins with premarket preparation. This involves researching and analyzing various factors that could influence the market. Start by reviewing economic indicators, news reports, and any relevant updates on the stocks or options you plan to trade. This initial research sets the stage for informed decision-making throughout the day. Next, set daily goals and objectives. These could be as simple as identifying key support and resistance levels or as detailed as planning specific trades based on your analysis. Regularly reviewing and adjusting your strategies ensures that you stay aligned with market conditions and your trading goals.

Incorporating daily and weekly rituals into your routine can make a significant difference. Begin your day with a morning market analysis and news review. This helps you stay updated on any overnight developments that could impact your trades. Mid-day check-ins are also essential. These allow you to adjust your positions based on market movements and ensure that your trades align with your initial analysis. At the end of the week, conduct a thorough performance review. Analyze your trades to identify what worked and what didn't. This weekly review helps you refine your strategies and make necessary tweaks for the following week.

Consider the routine of a successful day trader. Each morning, they start with a comprehensive review of market news, focusing on economic data releases and corporate earnings reports. By 9:00 a.m., they've identified potential trades and set specific entry and exit points. Throughout the trading day, they monitor their positions, making adjustments based on real-time data. By 4:00 p.m., they review their performance, noting what went well and what could be improved. This consistent approach ensures that they are always prepared and focused.

A swing trader's weekly schedule might look a bit different. On Sunday evenings, they spend an hour analyzing weekly charts and setting up potential trades for the week. Each morning, they review their positions and make any necessary adjustments based on overnight news and market movements. Mid-week, they take a closer look at their trades, ensuring everything aligns with their initial strategy. By Friday, they conduct a comprehensive review, analyzing their performance and planning for the next week. This routine helps them stay disciplined and focused, allowing for more calculated decisions and better results.

By establishing a consistent trading routine, you create a structured environment that fosters discipline and reduces the likelihood of impulsive decisions. From premarket preparation to daily and weekly rituals, each component of your routine plays a critical role in your overall success. As you develop and refine your routine, you'll find that it not only enhances your trading performance but also makes the entire process more manageable and less stressful.

5.4 Mindfulness Techniques

Mindfulness in trading can significantly impact your performance by reducing stress and anxiety, enhancing focus and concentration, and improving decision-making under pressure. Imagine navigating the fast-paced world of trading with a clear, calm mind, able to make rational decisions even in high-stakes situations. Mindfulness helps achieve this state by fostering a present-focused awareness, allowing you to respond to market changes with composure rather than react impulsively. When you reduce stress and anxiety, you free up mental space to concentrate on your trading strategies, making it easier to analyze market trends and execute trades with precision.

Mindfulness techniques tailored for traders can be straightforward yet highly effective. Deep breathing exercises are a quick and easy way to center yourself. Whenever you feel overwhelmed, take a moment to inhale deeply through your nose, hold for a few seconds, and exhale slowly through your mouth. This simple act can lower your heart rate and calm your mind, helping you regain focus. Meditation practices, even if just for a few minutes each day, can also be beneficial. Find a quiet space, close your eyes, and focus on your breath or a calming mantra. This practice trains your mind to stay present and reduces the mental clutter that can cloud your judgment. Visualization techniques are another powerful tool. Before the trading day begins, visualize yourself executing trades calmly and successfully. Picture the steps you'll take and the outcomes you aim to achieve. This mental rehearsal prepares you to act confidently and efficiently when the trading day starts.

Creating a mindful trading environment is equally important. Start by maintaining a clutter-free workspace. A tidy desk can help clear your mind and reduce distractions. Set up a dedicated meditation corner where you can retreat for a few minutes of calm before or during the trading day. This doesn't need to be elaborate—a comfortable chair and a quiet spot will suffice. Consider the colors and lighting in your workspace as well. Calming colors like blues and greens can create a serene atmosphere, while natural lighting can boost your mood and energy levels. These small adjustments can make a significant difference in your overall mindfulness and trading performance.

Examples of mindfulness practices integrated into trading routines can offer inspiration. Take the case of Alex, a trader who practices meditation every morning before the market opens. He spends 10 minutes in a quiet room, focusing on his breath and setting his intentions for the day. This routine helps him start the trading day with a clear and focused mind. During high-volatility periods, Alex uses deep breathing exercises to stay calm. Whenever he feels anxiety creeping in, he takes a few deep breaths, which helps him maintain his composure and make rational decisions. This consistent practice of mindfulness has improved his trading outcomes and overall well-being.

Another example is Emma, who incorporates visualization into her trading routine. Each morning, she visualizes herself analyzing market trends, placing trades, and achieving her trading goals. This mental rehearsal boosts her confidence and prepares her to handle the day's challenges. Emma also maintains a clutter-free workspace and uses calming colors in her office to create a serene environment. These mindfulness techniques have helped her stay focused and reduce stress, leading to more consistent trading success.

By integrating mindfulness into your trading routine, you can cultivate a state of calm and focus that enhances your decision-making and overall performance. Whether through deep breathing exercises, meditation practices, visualization techniques, or creating a mindful trading environment, these practices can significantly impact your trading success and well-being.

5.5 Maintaining Discipline

Discipline in trading is akin to the foundation of a skyscraper; it holds everything together and ensures stability. Without discipline, even the best trading strategies can crumble. Adhering to trading plans and strategies is the cornerstone of successful trading. When you develop a trading plan, it must be based on careful analysis and considered decisions. Sticking to this plan helps you avoid impulsive decisions that can derail your progress. For instance, if your plan dictates that you exit a trade when it hits a certain price, discipline ensures you follow through, regardless of market noise or emotional urges.

Avoiding impulsive decisions is critical. The market can be unpredictable, and emotions often run high. It's easy to get swept up in the excitement of a rising stock or the panic of a sudden drop. Discipline acts as a buffer, helping you stick to your plan and make rational decisions. This consistency is key to ensuring performance over the long term. A disciplined approach helps you build a track record of consistent results, which is more valuable than occasional big wins followed by significant losses.

To enhance discipline, set clear, achievable goals. These goals should be specific, measurable, and time-bound. For example, aim to achieve a 10% return on investment within six months. Such goals provide direction and a sense of purpose. Using checklists to follow your trading plans is another effective technique. A checklist ensures that you follow all necessary steps before entering or exiting a trade, minimizing the risk of forgetting critical tasks. Implementing strict rules for entering and exiting trades is also vital. Decide in advance the conditions under which you'll enter a trade, such as specific price levels or technical indicators, and stick to these rules rigorously.

Common challenges to maintaining discipline include dealing with emotional impulses, managing external distractions, and handling peer pressure in trading communities. Emotional impulses can be powerful, especially during volatile markets. To overcome this, practice mindfulness and stress-relief techniques, which help you stay calm and focused. External distractions, such as news headlines or social media buzz, can also derail your discipline. Create a distraction-free trading environment to maintain concentration. Peer pressure in trading communities is another challenge. It's easy to get influenced by others' trades or opinions. Stick to your trading plan and trust your analysis, regardless of what others are doing.

Examples of disciplined traders can provide valuable insights. Consider Sarah, a trader who follows a strict trading plan. She sets specific entry and exit points based on her analysis and never deviates from these points, even when the market behaves unpredictably. This disciplined approach has helped her achieve consistent profits while minimizing losses. Another example is John, who consistently meets his trading goals. He sets clear, achievable targets and uses a checklist to ensure he follows his trading plan meticulously. By staying disciplined, John has built a track record of steady performance, proving that discipline is not just about avoiding losses but also about achieving consistent gains.

Maintaining discipline is crucial for long-term success in trading. By adhering to your trading plans, avoiding impulsive decisions, and ensuring consistent performance, you build a strong foundation for profitable trading. Employing techniques to enhance discipline and overcoming common challenges further solidifies this foundation. Real-world examples of disciplined traders highlight the importance of this attribute and provide inspiration. Discipline is the bedrock upon which successful trading careers are built, and mastering it can set you on the path to achieving your trading goals

Chapter Recap - True/False Quiz:

1. True or False: Overcoming fear and greed is critical for long-term success in options trading.

2. True or False: Building emotional resilience has no impact on your trading outcomes.

3. True or False: A consistent trading routine can help improve your trading discipline.

4. True or False: Mindfulness techniques are irrelevant in the context of trading psychology.

True and False Answers:

1.) True 2.) False 3.) True 4.) False

RECURRING INCOME

Chapter 6:

Recurring Income

Trading options can sometimes feel like navigating through a maze. But what if I told you there was a way to turn this maze into a well-lit path that could lead you to consistent income? Meet weekly options— tools that offer frequent opportunities and flexibility, making it possible to generate regular income. Imagine having the ability to capitalize on market movements every week, turning short-term fluctuations into profit. That's the power of weekly options.

6.1 Strategies for Consistent Income

Weekly options, unlike their monthly counterparts, expire every Friday. This short lifespan presents unique advantages and risks. One of the biggest advantages is the frequent opportunities they offer. You can engage in new trades every week, allowing you to quickly adapt to changing market conditions. This flexibility is particularly beneficial for those of you who thrive on active trading and want to capitalize on market movements without waiting for monthly expirations. However, it's essential to be aware of the higher transaction costs associated with frequent trading and the rapid time decay that can quickly erode the value of weekly options.

When it comes to selecting suitable assets for weekly options trading, look for those with high liquidity and volatility. Stocks like Apple (AAPL) and Microsoft (MSFT) and index ETFs like the SPY are popular choices. These assets have active options markets, ensuring that you can easily enter and exit positions while benefiting from significant price movements.

Popular strategies tailored for weekly options include weekly covered calls, weekly cash-secured puts, and weekly vertical spreads. A weekly covered call involves buying 100 shares of a stock and selling a call option with a one-week expiration. This strategy allows you to collect premiums every week, generating consistent income. For example, if you own shares of a tech stock like Nvidia (NVDA) and believe the price will remain stable or experience a slight increase, selling a weekly call option can provide you with a premium while potentially allowing you to sell the stock at a higher price.

Another effective strategy is the weekly cash-secured put. This involves selling a put option with a one-week expiration while setting aside enough cash to buy the stock if the option is exercised. This strategy allows you to earn premiums while preparing to acquire stocks at a desirable price. For instance, if you're interested in buying shares of an index ETF like the SPY at a lower price, selling a weekly cash-secured put can generate income and potentially secure the shares at a discount.

Weekly vertical spreads, such as bull call spreads or bear put spreads, are also popular. A bull call spread involves buying a call option at a lower strike price and selling another call option at a higher strike price with the same one-week expiration. This strategy reduces risk while allowing you to profit from upward price movements. Conversely, a bear put spread involves buying a put option at a higher strike price and selling another put option at a lower strike price, benefiting from downward price movements.

Real-World Examples of Weekly Options Strategies

Consider a weekly covered call on a tech stock like Nvidia (NVDA). Suppose NVDA is trading at $200, and you own 100 shares. You sell a weekly call option with a strike price of $205 for a premium of $3 per share. If NVDA's price remains below $205 by the end of the week, you keep the premium and still own the shares. If NVDA's price exceeds $205, your shares are sold at $205, and you still keep the premium, resulting in a profit.

Another example involves a weekly cash-secured put on the SPY ETF. Suppose SPY is trading at $400, and you're willing to buy it at $390.

You sell a weekly put option with a strike price of $390 for a premium of $2 per share. If SPY's price remains above $390, you keep the premium without having to buy the shares. If SPY's price falls below $390, you buy the shares at $390, effectively acquiring them at a discount when considering the premium received.

By understanding and implementing these weekly options strategies, you can generate consistent income while managing risks effectively.

6.2 Generating Monthly Income With Covered Calls

Imagine having a strategy that allows you to earn a steady stream of income every month while holding onto stocks you believe in. This is the essence of the covered call strategy. A covered call involves owning a stock and selling call options against it. The primary purpose is to generate regular income from the premiums received by selling these options. This strategy is particularly effective in stable or slightly bullish markets where you expect the stock price to rise moderately or remain steady. One of the significant benefits of covered calls is the ability to earn consistent income, which can be especially appealing for those looking to supplement their regular earnings. Additionally, covered calls lower risk compared to other trading strategies, as the ownership of the underlying stock provides some degree of safety. However, it's important to note that this strategy also comes with a drawback: limited upside potential. If the stock price skyrockets, your gains will be capped at the strike price of the sold call option.

Selecting suitable stocks for monthly covered calls is crucial for maximizing the effectiveness of this strategy. You want to focus on stable, high-quality stocks that have a history of steady performance. These stocks are less likely to experience extreme volatility, which can make managing covered calls more predictable. Look for stocks with moderate volatility, as they provide a balance between potential premium income and manageable risk. Additionally, it's essential to choose stocks with liquid options markets. High liquidity ensures that you can easily enter and exit positions without significant price slippage, making the overall process smoother and more efficient.

Executing monthly covered calls involves a few straightforward steps. First, select the stock you want to use for this strategy and purchase the necessary shares, typically in increments of 100, as each options contract represents 100 shares. Once you own the shares, you can write (sell) call options with a one-month expiration. Choosing the right strike price is crucial; it should be slightly above the current market price to maximize premium income while still allowing for potential capital gains. After writing the call options, your primary task is to manage the position throughout the month. This involves monitoring the stock's performance and adjusting your strategy if necessary. For example, if the stock's price approaches the strike price, you may consider rolling the option to a higher strike price to capture additional premiums and extend the strategy.

Consider a real-world example of using covered calls to generate monthly income. Let's say you own 200 shares of a blue-chip stock like Procter & Gamble (PG), currently trading at $140. You decide to sell two call options with a strike price of $145 and a one-month expiration. The premium for each option is $2 per share, so you receive a total of $400 in premiums for the two contracts. If the stock price remains below $145 by the expiration date, you keep the $400 premium and continue to hold your shares. If the stock price exceeds $145, your shares will be sold at the strike price, but you still keep the premium, resulting in a total gain from both the premium and the capital appreciation of the stock up to the strike price.

By following these steps and selecting the right stocks, you can effectively use covered calls to generate a consistent monthly income while managing your risk. This strategy provides a steady income stream while also allowing you to benefit from the underlying stock's performance, making it a powerful tool in your trading arsenal.

6.3 Weekly Iron Condors for Steady Returns

Options trading can sometimes feel like trying to catch a fish with your bare hands—tricky and elusive. But what if there was a way to make your trading more predictable, generating steady returns with limited risk? This is where the weekly iron condor strategy comes into play. An iron condor involves selling an out-of-the-money call spread and an out-of-the-money put spread on the same underlying asset. Essentially, you're creating a range within which you expect the asset's price to stay. The beauty of this strategy lies in its ability to generate income through premiums while limiting risk. By design, the maximum loss is capped at the difference between the strike prices of the spreads minus the premiums received. However, the flip side is the potential for losses if the market moves significantly beyond the anticipated range.

Setting up a weekly iron condor involves a few critical steps. First, you need to select a suitable underlying asset, preferably one with high liquidity and relatively stable price movements. Index ETFs like SPY or QQQ are excellent choices due to their predictable price ranges and active options markets. Once you've selected your asset, the next step is to choose the strike prices for the call spread and put spread. For a balanced iron condor, you might select strike prices that are equidistant from the current market price. For example, if SPY is trading at $400, you might sell a call at $410 and buy a call at $415, while simultaneously selling a put at $390 and buying a put at $385. This setup creates a range within which you expect the price to remain, allowing you to collect premiums from both the call and put sides.

Executing the four option trades is straightforward. On your trading platform, you will enter the details for selling the call and put options at the chosen strike prices and then for buying the call and put options at the higher and lower strike prices, respectively. Ensure that all options have the same expiration date, typically one week out. This setup locks in your potential income from the premiums while defining your risk parameters.

Managing weekly iron condors requires vigilance and adaptability. Monitor market conditions closely, as significant news or events can cause unexpected price movements. If the asset's price starts approaching one of your strike prices, you may need to roll up or down the spreads. Rolling involves closing the current positions and opening new ones at different strike prices, allowing you to adjust your range and maintain potential profitability. For example, if SPY is moving towards your call spread, you might close the current call spread and open a new one at higher strike prices. Additionally, be prepared to exit positions early if the market moves significantly against you. This might involve closing the entire iron condor to limit potential losses.

Consider a real-world example involving an index ETF like QQQ. Suppose QQQ is trading at $350. You set up a weekly iron condor by selling a call at $360 and buying a call at $365, while selling a put at $340 and buying a put at $335. Your goal is for QQQ to stay between $340 and $360 by expiration. If it does, you keep the premiums from all four options. Let's say the premiums collected amount to $2 per share, and each spread has a width of $5. Your maximum potential profit is the total premium collected, while the maximum potential loss is the spread width minus the premiums, or $3 per share. By carefully monitoring and adjusting your positions, you can manage risk and aim for steady returns.

6.4 Leveraging Short-Term Volatility for Income

Short-term volatility can be a trader's best friend when it comes to generating income. This concept refers to the rapid and often significant price movements that occur over a short period. Volatility impacts options pricing by increasing premiums due to the higher risk of price swings. When volatility is high, options become more expensive, offering you the chance to earn higher premiums. However, this also comes with increased market unpredictability, making it essential to manage your risk carefully.

To leverage short-term volatility, you can employ specific strategies designed to capitalize on these rapid price movements. Straddles and strangles are popular choices. A straddle involves buying both a call and a put option at the same strike price and expiration date, allowing you to profit from significant price movements in either direction. A strangle is similar but involves buying a call and a put option with different strike prices, providing a cheaper alternative with a wider profit range. Short-term credit spreads, another strategy, involve selling an option with a higher premium and buying a similar option with a lower premium, aiming to profit from the difference. Weekly options strategies are also effective, as they enable you to quickly adapt to changing market conditions and capitalize on short-term volatility.

Implementing these strategies requires a step-by-step approach. First, identify high-volatility events such as earnings announcements or economic reports that are likely to cause significant price movements. Next, select appropriate strike prices and expiration dates based on your market outlook and risk tolerance. For a straddle, choose strike prices close to the current market price; for a strangle, select slightly out-of-the-money options. Execute the trades by entering the necessary details on your trading platform, ensuring you monitor and adjust your positions as needed. Managing your trades involves keeping an eye on market conditions and being prepared to exit positions early if the market moves against you.

Examples of Volatility-Based Income Strategies

Consider a straddle trade around an earnings announcement for a tech company. Suppose the stock is trading at $150, and you expect significant price movement following the earnings report. You buy a call option and a put option, both with a strike price of $150 and an expiration date shortly after the earnings release. If the stock price moves significantly in either direction, you can profit from the increased value of the call or put option, depending on the direction of the movement.

Another example involves a short-term credit spread during a volatile market period. Let's say you're trading an index ETF like the SPY, currently priced at $400. You expect the price to remain stable or experience only moderate movements. You decide to set up a credit spread by selling a call option with a strike price of $410 and buying a call option with a strike price of $415, both with a one-week expiration. The premium received from selling the call option is higher than the cost of buying the call option, allowing you to profit from the difference. If the SPY remains below $410 by expiration, you keep the premium and the trade is successful.

By understanding and implementing these strategies, you can effectively leverage short-term volatility to generate income. The key is to stay informed about upcoming events that could impact market volatility and to carefully manage your trades to minimize risk while maximizing potential returns.

6.5 The Role of Time Decay in Income Strategies

In options trading, time decay, or theta, is a crucial concept that directly impacts your trading strategies. Time decay refers to the reduction in the value of an options contract as it approaches its expiration date. Essentially, as each day passes, the time value of the option decreases, which is particularly significant for income-generating strategies. For options traders, understanding theta is vital because it affects the premiums of the options you hold or sell. As expiration nears, the rate of time decay accelerates, which can be both a benefit and a challenge depending on your position.

Time decay has a profound impact on options premiums. For sellers, time decay is an ally. The closer an option gets to its expiration date, the more its time value diminishes, allowing sellers to retain more premium if the option expires worthless. Conversely, for buyers, time decay is an enemy, as the option loses value each day, even if the underlying asset's price remains unchanged. This decay is particularly rapid in the final weeks leading up to expiration, making it a crucial factor to consider when designing your trading strategies.

Several strategies are specifically designed to capitalize on time decay. Selling covered calls, writing cash-secured puts, and implementing credit spreads are among the most effective. When you sell a covered call, you own the underlying stock and sell a call option against it. The premium received from selling the call is yours to keep, and as time decay erodes the option's value, you benefit if the option expires worthless. Writing cash-secured puts involves selling a put option while keeping enough cash on hand to purchase the stock if the option is exercised. Here, you earn a premium upfront, and as time decay sets in, the likelihood of the put being exercised decreases. Credit spreads, such as bull put spreads or bear call spreads, involve selling one option and buying another to limit risk. The goal is to profit from the net premium received, with time decay working in your favor as the options approach expiration.

Step-by-Step Guide to Time Decay Strategies

To execute these strategies effectively, start by selecting the underlying assets and appropriate expiration dates. For covered calls, choose stocks that you already own or are willing to own, and for cash-secured puts, select stocks you wouldn't mind buying at a lower price. Credit spreads work best with highly liquid assets with moderate volatility. Next, choose strike prices that align with your market outlook and risk tolerance. For covered calls, select a strike price slightly above the current market price. For cash-secured puts, choose a strike price below the current market price. For credit spreads, select strike prices that create a balanced risk-reward profile.

Execute the trades by entering the relevant details into your trading platform. For covered calls, sell the call option against your stock holdings. For cash-secured puts, sell the put option and ensure you have the cash to buy the stock if needed. For credit spreads, simultaneously sell one option and buy another at different strike prices. Monitor the trades closely, paying attention to how time decay affects the options' values. Be prepared to adjust your positions if the underlying asset's price moves significantly.

Real-World Examples of Time Decay Income Strategies

Consider a covered call benefiting from time decay. Suppose you own 100 shares of Johnson & Johnson (JNJ), currently trading at $150. You sell a call option with a strike price of $155 and an expiration date one month away, receiving a premium of $2 per share. As time passes, the option's value decreases due to time decay. If JNJ remains below $155 by expiration, the option expires worthless, and you keep the $200 premium without selling your shares.

Another example involves a credit spread profiting from rapid time decay. Let's say you set up a bull put spread on Microsoft (MSFT), currently trading at $300. You sell a put option with a strike price of $290 and buy a put option with a strike price of $285, both expiring in one month. You receive a net premium of $1 per share. As expiration approaches, time decay erodes the value of both options, but the sold put decays faster. If MSFT stays above $290, both options expire worthless, and you keep the $100 premium for a 100-share contract.

Understanding time decay and effectively using strategies that capitalize on it can significantly enhance your income-generating potential in options trading. Whether through covered calls, cash-secured puts, or credit spreads, time decay can work to your advantage, helping you generate consistent returns while managing risk.

Chapter Recap - True/False Quiz:

1. True or False: Weekly options typically offer less time decay compared to monthly options.

2. True or False: The strategy of selling covered calls is suitable for generating monthly income.

3. True or False: Weekly iron condors are designed to profit from significant price movements.

4. True or False: Time decay, also known as theta, plays a crucial role in income strategies using options.

5. True or False: Leveraging short-term volatility is irrelevant when using weekly options for income generation.

True and False Answers:

1.) False 2.) True 3.) False 4.) True 5.) False

CHAPTER 7

TECHNICAL
ANALYSIS

Chapter 7:

Technical Analysis

Imagine standing in front of a massive, intricate painting. At first glance, it appears chaotic, but with a closer look, you start to see patterns and shapes emerge, telling a compelling story. This is what technical analysis does for traders. It allows you to decipher the complex movements of the market, transforming apparent chaos into a structured narrative that guides your trading decisions.

7.1 Introduction to Technical Analysis

Technical analysis is a method used by traders to evaluate and predict the future price movements of a security based on historical price and volume data. Unlike fundamental analysis, which looks at a company's financial health and performance, technical analysis focuses on patterns and statistical trends derived from past trading activity. This approach operates on the belief that all relevant information is already reflected in the stock price, making price history a crucial indicator of future performance. By examining charts and using various technical indicators, you can identify potential entry and exit points, optimize your trades, and manage risk more effectively.

The core principles of technical analysis are built on three foundational ideas. First, the market discounts everything. This means that all known information about a security, including earnings reports, economic data, and other market factors, is already factored into its current price. Therefore, analyzing the price itself is the most efficient way to understand market sentiment. Second, prices move in trends. Whether it's an uptrend, downtrend, or sideways trend, recognizing these patterns helps traders align their strategies with the market's direction. Finally, history tends to repeat itself. Human behavior in the market often follows predictable patterns, which can be identified and leveraged through technical analysis.

To effectively apply technical analysis, you need to become familiar with several key tools and techniques. Charts are the primary tool, providing a visual representation of price movements over time. Line charts, bar charts, and candlestick charts each offer unique insights. For instance, candlestick charts, with their detailed depiction of open, high, low, and close prices, are particularly useful for identifying short-term price patterns. Technical indicators are another vital component. Moving averages, for example, smooth out price data to help identify trends and potential reversals. The Relative Strength Index (RSI) measures the speed and change of price movements, indicating overbought or oversold conditions. Trendlines and channels can also be drawn on charts to highlight support and resistance levels, guiding your trading decisions.

While technical analysis offers numerous advantages, it is not without limitations. One significant advantage is its ability to help identify precise entry and exit points, providing a visual representation of data that can simplify complex market trends. This can be particularly beneficial for traders who need to make quick decisions based on market movements. However, technical analysis is inherently subjective. Different traders might interpret the same chart patterns and indicators in varying ways, leading to different conclusions. Additionally, technical analysis does not account for fundamental factors such as a company's earnings, economic conditions, or industry trends, which can sometimes lead to incomplete assessments.

Reflection Section: Chart Analysis Exercise

Take a moment to practice analyzing a stock chart. Choose a stock you are familiar with and pull up its candlestick chart. Identify the trend (uptrend, downtrend, or sideways) and draw trendlines to mark support and resistance levels. Apply a moving average indicator and observe how it interacts with the price. Note any patterns, such as head and shoulders or double tops, and consider what these might indicate about future price movements. Reflect on how this exercise enhances your understanding of technical analysis and its application in real-world trading scenarios.

In summary, incorporating technical analysis into your trading strategy can transform how you view the market. By focusing on historical price and volume data, recognizing patterns and trends, and using key tools like charts and indicators, you can make more informed trading decisions. While it has its limitations, understanding and applying the principles of technical analysis can provide a significant edge in managing the complexities of the financial markets.

7.2 Understanding Chart Patterns and Indicators

Chart patterns are vital tools in technical analysis, offering visual representations of market psychology and investor behavior. These patterns are formed by the price movements of an asset over time, and recognizing them can provide insights into future price directions. Common chart patterns include head and shoulders, double tops and bottoms, and various types of triangles. Each pattern tells a story about the market's sentiment and potential future moves. For instance, a head and shoulders pattern often signals a reversal in an uptrend, indicating that the asset might soon decline. Similarly, double tops and bottoms suggest potential reversals, with double tops indicating a bearish reversal and double bottoms hinting at a bullish reversal. Triangles, on the other hand, can signal continuation or reversal, depending on their formation— ascending, descending, or symmetrical.

The psychology behind chart patterns is rooted in investor behavior. When you see a head and shoulders pattern, it's not just lines on a chart; it offers a visual representation of a market struggling to maintain an uptrend, with increasing resistance at the peak (the head) and two shoulders showing failed attempts to break higher. This pattern often leads to a bearish reversal as the market sentiment shifts. Double tops and bottoms work similarly. A double top forms when the price hits a high, retraces, and then hits the same high again before declining, which indicates strong resistance and potential bearish movement. Conversely, a double bottom suggests strong support and a potential bullish reversal. Triangles reflect periods of consolidation where the market is indecisive, with the breakout direction providing clues about future trends.

When you dive into the details of these patterns, you can uncover specific trading strategies. For example, in a head and shoulders pattern, you might look to enter a short position once the price breaks below the neckline, setting your stop loss above the right shoulder and your target based on the pattern's height. Double tops and bottoms offer similar entry points: A break below the support level of a double top or above the resistance level of a double bottom can be a signal to enter a trade. The height of the pattern can help determine your profit target. Triangles require a bit more patience as you wait for a breakout from the consolidation pattern. Ascending triangles often break upward, while descending triangles break downward. Symmetrical triangles can break in either direction, so it's crucial to wait for confirmation before entering a trade.

Technical indicators are another cornerstone of technical analysis, providing quantitative data to support your trading decisions. Indicators are categorized as either leading or lagging. Leading indicators, like the Relative Strength Index (RSI), predict future price movements by identifying overbought or oversold conditions. Lagging indicators, such as moving averages, confirm trends after they have begun. Moving averages smooth out price data to identify the direction of the trend, with crossovers between short-term and long-term moving averages often signaling potential entry or exit points. The moving average convergence divergence (MACD) is a momentum indicator that shows the relationship between two moving averages of an asset's price. When the MACD line crosses above the signal line, it indicates a bullish signal, and vice versa.

To use technical indicators effectively, you need to understand how to set them up and interpret their signals. Start with moving averages. A simple moving average (SMA) calculates the average price over a specific period, smoothing out fluctuations. When the price crosses above the SMA, it might indicate a buying opportunity. The RSI helps you identify overbought (above 70) or oversold (below 30) conditions. An RSI above 70 suggests the asset may be overbought and due for a pullback, while an RSI below 30 indicates it might be oversold and ready for a bounce. The MACD, with its histogram showing the difference between the MACD line and the signal line, provides insights into momentum shifts. A rising histogram suggests increasing bullish momentum, while a falling histogram indicates growing bearish momentum.

7.3 Analyzing Company Financials

Understanding the intrinsic value of a company is crucial for making informed investment decisions. This is where fundamental analysis comes into play. By evaluating a company's financial health, you gain insights into its long-term viability and growth potential. This analysis is essential not just for short-term trades but also for long-term investment decisions. It helps you distinguish between a company that is fundamentally strong and one that might be a poor investment despite short-term market hype.

The bedrock of fundamental analysis lies in three primary financial statements: the income statement, the balance sheet, and the cash flow statement. The income statement provides a snapshot of a company's profitability over a specific period. It details revenues, expenses, and net income, allowing you to assess how well the company manages its operations. The balance sheet offers a broader view, listing the company's assets, liabilities, and shareholders' equity at a particular point in time. This statement helps you understand the company's financial stability and how it finances its operations, whether through debt or equity. Lastly, the cash flow statement tracks the flow of cash in and out of the business, divided into operating, investing, and financing activities. This is crucial for understanding the liquidity and cash management practices of the company.

Financial ratios are indispensable tools in fundamental analysis. They distill complex financial data into more digestible metrics, offering quick insights into a company's performance. Earnings per share (EPS) is a key indicator of profitability, calculated by dividing net income by the number of outstanding shares. It shows how much money a company makes for each share of its stock, helping you gauge its profitability. The price-to-earnings (P/E) ratio is another critical metric, calculated by dividing the current stock price by the EPS. It gives you an idea of what the market is willing to pay for a company's earnings, helping you compare valuation across companies. Lastly, the debt-to-equity ratio measures a company's financial leverage by dividing total liabilities by shareholders' equity. A high ratio indicates that a company is heavily financed by debt, which could be risky, especially in volatile markets.

Let's consider a real-world example to illustrate how fundamental analysis works. Imagine you're analyzing a tech company that has just released its quarterly earnings report. You start with the income statement and notice that the company has reported a 20% increase in revenues year-over-year. This is a positive sign, indicating strong sales growth. Next, you scrutinize the balance sheet and find that the company has a healthy amount of cash and manageable levels of debt, suggesting financial stability. Moving on to the cash flow statement, you see that the company has positive cash flow from operations, which means it generates enough cash to sustain its business activities.

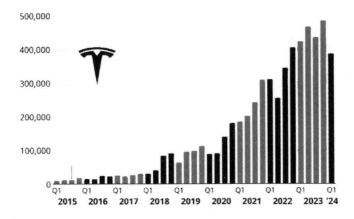

To dig deeper, you calculate the key financial ratios. The EPS comes out to $5, indicating solid profitability. The P/E ratio, based on the current stock price of $100, is 20. This is reasonable for a tech company with strong growth prospects. Finally, the debt-to-equity ratio is 0.5, showing that the company is not overly reliant on debt. These metrics collectively paint a picture of a financially healthy company with good growth potential.

Assessing the company's growth prospects involves looking beyond the numbers. Consider factors like market trends, competitive positioning, and management effectiveness. For instance, if the tech company is a leader in a burgeoning industry like artificial intelligence, it has a significant growth runway. Additionally, strong management with a track record of innovation and execution can further bolster the company's prospects. By combining these qualitative insights with quantitative analysis, you can make a more informed investment decision.

Incorporating fundamental analysis into your trading strategy provides a comprehensive view of a company's financial health. This approach not only helps you identify undervalued stocks but also enables you to make long-term investment decisions with greater confidence.

7.4 Using Economic Indicators in Options Trading

Economic indicators are vital statistics that reflect the overall health of an economy. Think of them as the pulse of the market, providing insights into various aspects of economic activity. They influence market sentiment and stock prices, guiding traders in making informed decisions. By understanding these indicators, you can anticipate market movements and adjust your trading strategies accordingly.

Among the most crucial economic indicators to watch are gross domestic product (GDP), the unemployment rate, the consumer price index (CPI), and Federal Reserve interest rate decisions. GDP measures the total value of goods and services produced within a country, serving as a broad indicator of economic health. A growing GDP suggests a robust economy, while a shrinking GDP signals economic troubles. The unemployment rate indicates the percentage of the labor force that is jobless and actively seeking employment. High unemployment can dampen consumer spending and economic growth, while low unemployment often boosts market confidence.

The CPI tracks changes in the prices of a basket of goods and services, reflecting inflation levels. Rising inflation can erode purchasing power and lead to higher interest rates, impacting borrowing costs and consumer spending. Conversely, low inflation can spur economic growth but might also indicate weak demand. Federal Reserve interest rate decisions are perhaps the most closely watched economic events. Changes in interest rates influence borrowing costs, consumer spending, and overall economic activity. Higher rates can cool off an overheating economy, while lower rates aim to stimulate growth.

Interpreting economic data requires a nuanced approach. For instance, GDP growth indicates economic expansion, which can boost investor confidence and drive stock prices higher. However, if GDP growth is too rapid, it might lead to inflationary pressures, prompting the Federal Reserve to raise interest rates. Unemployment data offers insights into the labor market's health and its impact on consumer spending. A rising unemployment rate can signal economic distress, leading to lower stock prices, while a falling rate typically boosts market sentiment.

Inflation data, as measured by the CPI, affects interest rates and stock prices. Higher inflation often leads to increased interest rates, raising borrowing costs and potentially slowing economic growth. For example, if the CPI shows a significant increase, the Federal Reserve might hike interest rates to curb inflation, impacting stock prices negatively. Conversely, low inflation might keep interest rates steady or prompt a rate cut, fostering a more favorable environment for equities.

Consider this example to illustrate how economic indicators can influence trading decisions. Suppose a quarterly GDP report shows robust economic growth, exceeding market expectations. This positive surprise can lead to a surge in stock prices as investors anticipate higher corporate earnings and increased consumer spending. In response, you might decide to buy call options on growth-oriented stocks, expecting their prices to rise.

Another example involves Federal Reserve rate changes. Imagine the Fed announces an unexpected interest rate cut to stimulate the economy. This decision can boost market sentiment, leading to a rally in stocks. In this scenario, you might adjust your strategies by closing short positions and initiating long positions, capitalizing on the market's upward momentum.

By closely monitoring economic indicators, you can gain valuable insights into market trends and make more informed trading decisions. Understanding how GDP, unemployment, CPI, and interest rate decisions affect the market allows you to anticipate shifts in investor sentiment and adjust your strategies accordingly. This knowledge empowers you to approach market complexities with greater confidence and precision.

7.5 Combining Technical and Fundamental Analysis

Integrating technical and fundamental analysis enhances your trading decisions, offering a comprehensive view of the market. By combining both approaches, you gain a balanced perspective that considers both short-term price movements and long-term financial health. Fundamental analysis helps you identify undervalued stocks with strong financials, while technical analysis provides precise entry and exit points. This dual approach allows you to make more informed decisions, minimizing risks and maximizing potential returns.

Let's explore how to develop a combined analysis strategy. Start with fundamental analysis to identify stocks with solid financials and growth prospects. Evaluate key financial ratios, scrutinize income statements, and assess cash flow. Once you've identified a promising stock, shift to technical analysis to determine the optimal times to enter and exit trades. Use charts, trendlines, and indicators like moving averages and RSI to spot favorable conditions. This combination ensures you invest in fundamentally strong companies while capitalizing on technical signals to enhance your timing.

Consider a real-world example involving a biotech stock. Imagine you identify a biotech company with strong financials, robust revenue growth, and promising drug pipelines. Fundamental analysis reveals an attractive P/E ratio, low debt-to-equity ratio, and positive cash flow. With this information, you recognize the stock as fundamentally sound. Next, apply technical analysis to refine your trading decisions. You notice a bullish head and shoulders pattern forming on the candlestick chart, combined with an RSI indicating the stock is not overbought. This alignment of favorable technical and fundamental factors suggests a strong buying opportunity.

To execute the trade, follow these steps. Start by buying shares of the biotech stock at the identified entry point, supported by the technical pattern and RSI levels. Monitor the stock's performance, keeping an eye on both financial updates and technical signals. If the stock's price rises and approaches the upper trendline, consider selling a portion of your holdings to lock in profits. Conversely, if the stock's fundamentals deteriorate or technical indicators signal a reversal, adjust your strategy accordingly. This flexibility ensures you can adapt to changing market conditions while adhering to your overall investment thesis.

Best practices for effectively combining technical and fundamental analysis include regularly updating your fundamental research. Keep an eye on quarterly earnings reports, changes in financial ratios, and industry trends. Continuously monitor technical signals to stay attuned to market movements. Employ tools like moving averages, trendlines, and volume analysis to confirm trends and reversals. Maintain flexibility in your strategy, adjusting your positions based on new information. For instance, if a stock's fundamentals improve unexpectedly, consider increasing your position. If technical indicators suggest an imminent downturn, don't hesitate to take profits or cut losses.

Combining both approaches offers a robust framework for making well-informed trading decisions. It provides a comprehensive understanding of the market, balancing short-term price movements with long-term financial health. By integrating fundamental and technical analysis, you are better positioned to excel in the options market.

In the next chapter, we'll dive into the essential tools and platforms that can help you implement these strategies effectively. From trading software to financial news sources, we'll explore the resources that can elevate your trading game.

Chapter Recap - True/False Quiz:

1. True or False: Technical analysis focuses primarily on analyzing company financials to make trading decisions.

2. True or False: Chart patterns are a key component of technical analysis in options trading.

3. True or False: Fundamental analysis is used to assess the overall economic indicators affecting the options market.

4. True or False: Combining technical and fundamental analysis provides a more comprehensive approach to options trading.

5. True or False: Economic indicators have no impact on options trading strategies.

True and False Answers:

1.) False 2.) True 3.) True 4.) True 5.) False

CHAPTER 8

TOOLS AND PLATFORMS

Chapter 8:

Tools and Platforms

Options trading is like driving a high-performance car; you need the right techniques to navigate the fast lanes and sharp turns of the financial markets. Choosing the right trading platform can significantly impact your trading success. Each platform comes with unique features, costs, and user experiences. Let's dive into comparing some of the most popular platforms available to traders today: E*TRADE, Fidelity, Interactive Brokers, and Robinhood.

8.1 Comparing Different Trading Platforms

DIFFERENT TRADING PLATFORMS

'eToro'   ↑ FIRSTRADE

E✱TRADE°   FⓄREX.com

E*TRADE is a well-known name in the trading world, offering a robust platform with a range of tools suitable for both beginners and advanced traders. known for its user-friendly interface and comprehensive educational resources, ETRADE provides real-time data, customizable dashboards, and advanced charting tools. The platform also offers a variety of investment options, including stocks, options, futures, and ETFs.

Fidelity is another heavyweight in the trading space, renowned for its excellent customer service and research capabilities. Fidelity's platform is intuitive, with real-time data and analytics that help you stay on top of market movements. Its customizable dashboards allow you to tailor your trading experience to your needs. Fidelity also offers a wide range of investment products and has a robust suite of tools for options traders.

Interactive Brokers is favored by professional traders and institutions due to its comprehensive offering and competitive pricing. The platform boasts advanced trading tools, real-time data, and extensive research resources. Interactive Brokers is known for its low commission fees, which makes it attractive for high-frequency traders. However, the platform's advanced features can be overwhelming for beginners.

Robinhood has gained popularity among younger traders for its commission-free trading and sleek, easy-to-use mobile app. While Robinhood offers real-time data and analytics, it lacks some of the advanced tools and research capabilities found on other platforms. However, its user-friendly interface makes it an excellent choice for novice traders looking to get their feet wet in the options market.

Key Features to Look For

When choosing a trading platform, several key features can enhance your trading experience. A user-friendly interface is crucial, especially if you're new to options trading. Look for platforms that offer real-time data and analytics, as these are essential for making informed trading decisions. Customizable dashboards allow you to tailor the platform to your specific needs, providing quick access to the tools and information you use most frequently.

Costs and Fees

Understanding the fee structure of each platform is essential, as costs can significantly impact your trading profits. E*TRADE charges commission fees for options trades, but it offers discounts for high-volume traders. It also has subscription fees for premium features and data feed costs for real-time market data.

Fidelity's fee structure is similar, with commission fees for options trades and additional costs for premium features and real-time data feeds. However, Fidelity is known for its competitive pricing and excellent value for money.

Interactive Brokers stands out for its low commission fees, making it an attractive option for active traders. It also offers tiered pricing, which can reduce costs further for high-volume traders. However, it charges subscription fees for some advanced features and data feed costs for real-time market data.

Robinhood's primary appeal is its commission-free trading, which makes it a cost-effective option for beginners and casual traders. However, they do charge for premium features through their Robinhood Gold subscription and for certain data feeds.

User Reviews and Ratings

User reviews and ratings can provide valuable insights into the strengths and weaknesses of each platform. Experienced traders often praise E*TRADE for its comprehensive tools and educational resources, but some note that the fees can add up for frequent traders. Fidelity receives high marks for its customer service and research capabilities, though some users find the platform's interface slightly cumbersome.

Interactive Brokers is lauded for its advanced features and low fees, but beginners may find the platform's complexity daunting. Reviews highlight the platform's suitability for professional traders and institutions. Robinhood is popular among younger traders for its simplicity and commission-free trading. However, some users express concerns about the platform's lack of advanced tools and research resources.

Reflection Section: Platform Comparison Exercise

To select the most suitable platform, reflect on your trading needs and preferences. Consider the importance of features like a user-friendly interface, real-time data, and customizable dashboards. Evaluate the impact of commission fees, subscription fees, and data feed costs on your trading strategy. Finally, read user reviews and ratings to gain insights into each platform's performance and suitability for your trading goals.

8.2 Utilizing Trading Software Effectively

When it comes to enhancing your trading efficiency, having the right software can make a significant difference. MetaTrader 4 and 5 (MT4 and MT5) are popular choices among traders for their robust features and flexibility. MT4 is renowned for its user-friendly interface and advanced charting tools, making it ideal for beginners. MT5, on the other hand, offers additional features such as more timeframes and order types, catering to more advanced traders. NinjaTrader is another powerful platform, known for its advanced charting capabilities and automated trading features. It provides extensive customization options, allowing you to tailor the platform to your specific needs. TradingView stands out with its cloud-based functionality, offering real-time data, social networking features, and a vast library of user-generated scripts and strategies.

Good trading software should offer advanced charting tools, which are crucial for analyzing market trends and making informed decisions. Look for software that provides a wide range of technical indicators, drawing tools, and customizable chart settings. Automated trading capabilities are another critical feature, allowing you to execute trades based on predefined criteria without manual intervention. This can help you take advantage of market opportunities even when you're not actively monitoring the markets. Backtesting functionality is essential for testing your trading strategies using historical data, helping you refine your approach and improve your performance.

Setting up and configuring your trading software for optimal performance involves several steps. Start with the initial installation and setup. Download the software from the official website and follow the installation instructions. Once installed, you can customize the charts and indicators to suit your trading style. This involves selecting the types of charts you prefer, such as candlestick or bar charts, and adding technical indicators like moving averages or RSI. Adjust the settings to match your analysis needs, such as changing the timeframes or colors. Setting up alerts and notifications is another crucial step. These can help you stay informed about significant market movements or alert you when certain conditions are met, allowing you to act quickly.

Integrating your trading software with other essential tools can enhance your trading experience. Syncing with your brokerage account is a must, as it allows you to execute trades directly from the software. This integration ensures that your trades are executed quickly and accurately, minimizing the risk of slippage. Importing and exporting data is another useful feature. You can import historical data for backtesting or export your trading data for further analysis in other software. Integrating with financial news feeds is also beneficial. Real-time news updates can provide valuable insights into market-moving events, helping you make more informed trading decisions.

Reflection Section: Software Setup Exercise

Take some time to explore the features of your chosen trading software. Customize the charts and indicators to match your trading style. Set up alerts for significant market movements or conditions. Sync your software with your brokerage account and configure the integration with financial news feeds. Reflect on how these features can enhance your trading efficiency and decision-making process.

8.3 Setting Up Your Trading Workspace

Creating an efficient trading workspace isn't just about aesthetics; functionality and productivity are paramount. A well-organized trading environment is crucial for reducing distractions and enhancing focus. Imagine trying to make a critical trading decision while your desk is cluttered with papers, coffee mugs, and random gadgets. Not ideal, right? A clean, organized workspace helps you concentrate on the market, making it easier to spot opportunities and make informed decisions.

First, let's talk hardware. Your setup should include multiple monitors. A multi-monitor setup allows you to keep an eye on various assets, news feeds, and trading platforms simultaneously. This setup can significantly enhance your efficiency and allow you to make quicker decisions. A high-performance computer is another must-have. Slow processing speeds and lagging software can cost you valuable time and, ultimately, money. Invest in a computer with ample RAM, a fast processor, and reliable storage. Lastly, a reliable internet connection is nonnegotiable. A slow or unstable internet connection can lead to delayed order executions, which can be costly in a fast-moving market.

Ergonomics play a significant role in maintaining productivity and comfort. Invest in an ergonomic chair that supports your posture, reducing the risk of back pain during long trading sessions. An adjustable desk allows you to alternate between sitting and standing, which can improve circulation and reduce fatigue. Monitor stands and keyboard trays are also essential. They help position your screens at eye level and your keyboard at a comfortable height, reducing strain on your neck and wrists. Proper lighting is crucial, too. Natural light is ideal, but if that's not an option, opt for adjustable LED lights that reduce eye strain and create a comfortable working environment.

Personalizing your workspace can make it more conducive to your trading style. Organize your trading tools and resources so they are easily accessible. Use whiteboards or sticky notes for quick references, jotting down important stock tickers, key market levels, or trading rules. This setup helps keep essential information at your fingertips, reducing the need to constantly switch screens. Consider setting up a dedicated trading space away from household distractions. This separation helps create a mental boundary between your trading activities and personal life, allowing you to focus better.

To make your workspace truly your own, think about what inspires and motivates you. Maybe it's a framed quote from a famous trader or a vision board outlining your financial goals. Personal touches can make your workspace a place you enjoy spending time in, which can positively impact your trading performance. Customizing your workspace also means having all the tools and resources you need readily available. Whether it's a specific type of notebook for tracking trades or a particular type of pen that you prefer, having these items within arm's reach can streamline your trading process.

Setting up your trading workspace involves more than buying the right equipment; the goal is to create an environment that supports your trading activities. From reducing distractions to enhancing focus and decision-making, every element of your workspace should serve a purpose. By investing in the right hardware, considering ergonomic factors, and personalizing your space, you can create a trading environment that enhances your performance and helps you achieve your trading goals.

8.4 Essential Tools for Technical Analysis

Technical analysis is a cornerstone of successful options trading, offering a way to interpret market data and make informed decisions. Among the most essential tools are candlestick charts, moving averages, and the Relative Strength Index (RSI). Candlestick charts provide a visual representation of price movements, showing the open, high, low, and close prices for a specific period. They help identify patterns and trends, making it easier to predict future price movements. Moving averages, on the other hand, smooth out price data to identify the direction of a trend. They come in various types, such as simple moving averages (SMA) and exponential moving averages (EMA). The Relative Strength Index (RSI) measures the speed and change of price movements, indicating whether an asset is overbought or oversold.

Good charting software is crucial for effective technical analysis. Real-time data updates are essential, as they provide the most current information, allowing you to react quickly to market changes.

Customizable chart settings let you tailor the visual representation to your preferences, enhancing your ability to spot trends and patterns. Technical indicators are also a must-have feature. They provide quantitative data that supports your trading decisions, including moving averages, RSI, Bollinger Bands, and more. Look for software that integrates these features seamlessly, offering a comprehensive suite of tools to analyze the market.

Using technical indicators effectively requires a solid understanding of their signals and how to interpret them. Setting up moving averages involves selecting the type of moving average and the time period. For example, a 50-day SMA smooths out price data over 50 days, helping to identify medium-term trends. A crossover between a short-term and a long-term moving average can signal a potential entry or exit point. The RSI, which ranges from 0 to 100, is used to identify overbought or oversold conditions. An RSI above 70 indicates an overbought condition, suggesting a potential sell opportunity, while an RSI below 30 indicates an oversold condition, suggesting a potential buy opportunity. Bollinger Bands consist of a middle band (usually a 20-day SMA) and two outer bands set two standard deviations away. They help identify volatility and potential reversal points. When the price touches the upper band, it may be overbought; when it touches the lower band, it may be oversold.

Integrating technical analysis into a comprehensive trading plan enhances your ability to develop effective entry and exit strategies. Start by using technical indicators to confirm trade signals. For instance, if you identify a bullish candlestick pattern, check the moving averages and RSI to confirm the trend. Backtesting strategies using historical data is another crucial step. This involves applying your trading strategy to past market data to see how it would have performed. Most charting software includes backtesting functionality, allowing you to refine your approach before implementing it in live trading. Combining these elements helps create a robust trading plan that leverages technical analysis for better decision-making.

Incorporating technical analysis into your trading routine can significantly improve your performance. Develop entry and exit strategies based on the signals provided by your technical indicators. Use moving averages to identify the direction of the trend and RSI to gauge the strength of the trend. Apply Bollinger Bands to assess volatility and potential reversal points. Regularly backtest your strategies to ensure they remain effective in changing market conditions. By integrating technical analysis with your overall trading plan, you can make more informed decisions, manage risk more effectively, and increase your chances of success in the options market.

Take some time to explore the technical indicators and charting tools available on your chosen platform. Practice setting up moving averages, using RSI, and applying Bollinger Bands. Experiment with different settings and timeframes to find what works best for your trading style. This hands-on approach will deepen your understanding and enhance your ability to leverage technical analysis for successful options trading.

8.5 Leveraging Financial News and Data Feeds

To succeed in the fast-paced world of options trading, staying informed is not just beneficial—it's necessary. Economic news can dramatically impact market movements, driving volatility and presenting opportunities or threats for your portfolio. For instance, a positive jobs report can boost market sentiment, leading to an increase in stock prices. Conversely, geopolitical tensions or unexpected economic downturns can create uncertainty, causing market sell-offs. Corporate earnings reports also play a crucial role. When a company reports earnings that exceed expectations, its stock price often rises, sometimes dramatically. On the flip side, disappointing earnings can lead to sharp declines. Staying updated on these developments helps you make informed decisions, aligning your strategies with current market conditions.

Reliable sources of financial news are indispensable for any trader. Bloomberg is a go-to for many professionals, offering comprehensive coverage of financial markets, economic data, and corporate news. CNBC provides real-time financial market updates, expert analysis, and interviews with industry leaders. Reuters is another trusted source, known for its speed and accuracy in reporting global news and financial data. The Financial Times offers in-depth analysis and commentary on economic news, market trends, and corporate developments. These sources provide a well-rounded view of the financial landscape, helping you stay ahead of market movements and informed about the broader economic environment.

Real-time data feeds are essential for staying updated on market conditions. Setting up these feeds on your trading platform ensures you receive the latest information as it happens. Most platforms allow you to customize alerts for significant market events, such as earnings announcements, economic indicators, or geopolitical developments. You can set these alerts to notify you via email, SMS, or within the trading platform itself. This real-time information enables you to react quickly to market changes and make timely decisions that can enhance your trading performance. Customizable alerts also help you stay focused on the most relevant news, filtering out the noise and zeroing in on the events that matter most to your trading strategy.

Incorporating financial news into your trading strategies can significantly enhance your decision-making process. Trading on earnings announcements is a common strategy. By following earnings reports, you can anticipate potential price movements and position yourself to capitalize on these changes. For example, buying call options before a company reports strong earnings can lead to substantial gains if the stock price jumps. Responding to economic indicators like GDP reports is another effective approach. Positive GDP growth can signal a strong economy, prompting you to adjust your portfolio towards growth-oriented assets. Conversely, a negative GDP report might lead you to adopt a more defensive strategy. Geopolitical events also require attention. Political instability, trade tensions, or natural disasters can cause market volatility. By staying informed and adjusting your strategies accordingly, you can mitigate risks and seize opportunities.

Reflection Section: News Integration Exercise

Take a moment to think about how you currently incorporate financial news into your trading decisions. Are there specific sources you rely on? How do you react to earnings reports or economic indicators? Consider setting up real-time data feeds and customizable alerts on your trading platform. Reflect on how these tools can enhance your ability to make informed decisions and improve your overall trading performance.

By leveraging financial news and data feeds, you gain a competitive edge in the market. Economic news, corporate earnings, and geopolitical events all influence market movements, and staying informed allows you to navigate these changes effectively. Reliable news sources, real-time data feeds, and strategic integration of news into your trading plan can significantly enhance your trading success. This proactive approach helps you stay ahead of market trends, make informed decisions, and ultimately achieve your trading goals.

Chapter Recap - True/False Quiz:

1. True or False: Trading software is essential for executing options trades efficiently.

2. True or False: Setting up a well-organized trading workspace can enhance your trading performance.

3. True or False: Essential tools for technical analysis include indicators such as moving averages and RSI.

4. True or False: Leveraging financial news and data feeds is unnecessary for successful options trading.

5. True or False: Choosing the right trading platform is irrelevant to your success in options trading.

True and False Answers:

1.) True 2.) True 3.) True 4.) False 5.) False

LEARNING
EXERCISES

Chapter 9:

Learning Exercises

Imagine being a pilot in a flight simulator. You can face turbulence, navigate storms, and practice emergency landings—all without ever leaving the ground. This kind of practice is invaluable, and the same principle applies to options trading. By using interactive learning tools and exercises, you can sharpen your skills, test your knowledge, and build confidence without risking real money. This chapter is designed to provide you with these vital tools, making your trading journey more effective and less daunting.

9.1 Test Your Knowledge

To ensure you grasp the key concepts we've covered, let's start with multiple-choice quizzes. These quizzes will help reinforce your understanding of basic terminology and test your ability to apply what you've learned. For example, you might encounter a question like, "What is a call option?" The answer would be straightforward: A call option gives the holder the right to buy an asset at a specified price before the option expires.

True/false quizzes are another effective way to reinforce fundamental principles. For instance, you might see a statement like, "Delta measures an option's sensitivity to the underlying asset price." This is true. Delta is a crucial Greek that helps traders understand how much an option's price will change with a $1 move in the underlying asset. Another statement could be, "An option's premium is only composed of intrinsic value." This is false. An option's premium consists of both intrinsic value and extrinsic value, the latter encompassing time value and volatility. True/false questions help clear up common misconceptions and solidify your foundational knowledge.

Another question could be scenario-based, such as, "Which strategy would you use in a bullish market?" The correct answer would involve strategies like buying call options or setting up a bull call spread. These quizzes are designed to challenge you and ensure you understand the material comprehensively. Scenario-based quizzes push your understanding further by requiring you to apply your knowledge to real-world situations. Imagine a question like, "Given a volatile market, which option strategy is most appropriate?" The correct answer might be a strategy that benefits from volatility, such as a straddle or strangle. Another scenario could be, "If a stock price rises, what happens to the value of a put option?" The answer would be that the put option's value decreases because puts gain value when the underlying asset's price falls. By tackling these scenarios, you can practice making informed decisions based on market conditions.

Feedback and explanations are crucial for learning from these quizzes. After completing each quiz section, please review the answers and note your personal feedback on your answer. For instance, if you give an incorrect answer, read the correct answer several times along with the question and then redo the quiz and the question until you ace the test! This approach will help reinforce the correct answer and help your learning. This immediate feedback loop style helps solidify your understanding and correct any errors in thinking.

9.2 Interactive Quiz Section

These quizzes are designed to be more than just a test—they are a learning experience. By engaging with these questions, you reinforce your understanding and gain confidence in your ability to make informed trading decisions. As you continue to work through these exercises, you'll find that your grasp of options trading concepts becomes more intuitive and second nature.

Multiple-Choice Quiz:

1. **What does the term "At-the-Money (ATM)" refer to?**

   a. An option where the strike price is higher than the current price of the underlying asset.

   b. An option where the current price of the underlying asset is equal to the option's strike price.

   c. An option where the current price of the underlying asset is lower than the option's strike price.

   d. An option that has already expired.

2. In a "Bear Put Spread," what is the main objective?

   a. To profit from an increase in the underlying asset's price.

   b. To minimize the bid-ask spread in a volatile market.

   c. To profit from a decline in the underlying asset's price.

   d. To protect an existing position from a sudden market drop.

3. Which of the following is a characteristic of a "Bull Market"?

   a. A decline of 20% or more in a broad market index.

   b. A market condition characterized by low volatility.

   c. A market condition where prices are stable.

   d. An increase of 20% or more in a broad market index.

4. What is the "Bid-Ask Spread"?

   a. The difference between the current market price and the strike price of an option.

   b. The difference between the highest price a buyer is willing to pay and the lowest price a seller is willing to accept.

   c. The spread between the bid and ask prices during after-hours trading.

   d. The fee charged by brokers for executing a trade.

5. What does "Implied Volatility (IV)" represent in options trading?

    a. The actual historical volatility of the underlying asset.

    b. The market's forecast of a likely movement in an asset's price.

    c. The amount of time remaining until an option's expiration date.

    d. The difference between the option's premium and its intrinsic value.

6. What is a "Covered Call" strategy?

    a. Buying a call option without holding the underlying asset.

    b. Selling a call option while holding a long position in the underlying asset.

    c. Buying a put option to protect against a decline in the underlying asset.

    d. Selling both a call and a put option on the same underlying asset.

7. What is the function of "Theta" in options trading?

    a. It measures how much the option's price is expected to move with the underlying asset.

    b. It measures the rate of change of delta with respect to changes in the price of the underlying asset.

    c. It measures the rate at which an option's value declines over time.

    d. It measures an option's sensitivity to changes in the volatility of the underlying asset.

8. What does "In-the-Money (ITM)" mean for a call option?

a. The current price of the underlying asset is equal to the strike price.

b. The current price of the underlying asset is above the strike price.

c. The current price of the underlying asset is below the strike price.

d. The option has expired with no value.

9. What is a "Straddle" in options trading?

a. An options strategy that involves buying a call and selling a put on the same underlying asset with different expiration dates.

b. An options strategy that involves buying both a call and a put option with the same strike price and expiration date.

c. An options strategy that involves selling both a call and a put option with the same strike price and expiration date.

d. An options strategy that involves buying a call option with a higher strike price and selling a put option with a lower strike price.

10.What does "Vega" measure in options trading?

a. The sensitivity of an option's price to changes in the price of the underlying asset.

b. The sensitivity of an option's price to changes in the volatility of the underlying asset.

c. The difference between an option's premium and its intrinsic value.

d. The amount of time until an option expires.

11. What is a "Put Option"?

a. A financial contract that gives the holder the right to buy an underlying asset at a specified price.

b. A financial contract that gives the holder the obligation to sell an underlying asset at a specified price.

c. A financial contract that gives the holder the right to sell an underlying asset at a specified price.

d. A financial contract that requires the holder to sell an underlying asset at the market price.

12. In options trading, what is the "Strike Price"?

a. The price at which the underlying asset is currently trading in the market.

b. The price at which the holder of an option can buy or sell the underlying asset.

c. The price at which the option was originally purchased.

d. The price difference between the bid and ask prices.

13. What is the primary purpose of using a "Protective Put" strategy?

a. To generate income from premium payments.

b. To protect against potential losses in an existing stock position.

c. To profit from an increase in the underlying asset's price.

d. To hedge against market volatility.

14. What is the "Expiration Date" in an options contract?

a. The date on which the option was purchased.

b. The date by which the option must be exercised or it becomes worthless.

c. The date on which the underlying asset reaches its strike price.

d. The date on which the market closes each week.

15. What does "Out-of-the-Money (OTM)" mean for a put option?

a. The current price of the underlying asset is below the strike price.

b. The current price of the underlying asset is equal to the strike price.

c. The current price of the underlying asset is above the strike price.

d. The option is profitable if exercised.

16. What is an "Iron Condor" strategy typically used for?

a. Profiting from large price movements in the underlying asset.

b. Profiting from low volatility in the underlying asset.

c. Hedging against significant losses in a stock portfolio.

d. Leveraging small price movements in a highly volatile market.

17. What does "Gamma" measure in options trading?

a. The sensitivity of an option's price to changes in volatility.

b. The rate of change of delta in response to changes in the price of the underlying asset.

c. The time decay of an option's premium.

d. The difference between the bid and ask prices.

18. Which of the following best describes a "Vertical Spread"?

a. Buying a call option and selling a put option on the same underlying asset.

b. Buying and selling two options of the same type with the same expiration date but different strike prices.

c. Buying a call option with a higher strike price and selling a put option with a lower strike price.

d. Selling both a call and a put option with different expiration dates.

19. What is a "Bull Call Spread" designed to do?

a. Profit from a decline in the underlying asset's price.

b. Minimize potential losses in a volatile market.

c. Profit from an increase in the underlying asset's price.

d. Hedge against currency risk in foreign markets.

20. **Which of the following best describes "Vega" in options trading?**

   a. A measure of the sensitivity of an option's price to changes in the price of the underlying asset.

   b. A measure of the sensitivity of an option's price to changes in the volatility of the underlying asset.

   c. A measure of how much an option's price is expected to move in response to changes in time.

   d. A measure of the difference between intrinsic and extrinsic value in an option.

21. **What is the primary use of "Weekly Options"?**

   a. To invest in long-term growth strategies.

   b. To execute short-term trading strategies.

   c. To hedge against annual earnings reports.

   d. To secure lower premiums in long-dated options.

22. **What does "Delta" represent in the context of options trading?**

   a. The time decay of an option's value.

   b. The sensitivity of an option's price to changes in the underlying asset's price.

   c. The difference between the bid and ask prices.

   d. The market's forecast of future volatility.

23. **What is a "Strangle" in options trading?**

    a. Buying both a call and a put option with the same strike price and expiration date.

    b. Selling both a call and a put option with different expiration dates.

    c. Buying a call and a put option with different strike prices but the same expiration date.

    d. Selling a call and buying a put option on the same underlying asset.

24. **What happens when a holder of a call option exercises the option?**

    a. The holder must sell the underlying asset at the strike price.

    b. The holder has the right to buy the underlying asset at the strike price.

    c. The holder is obligated to buy the underlying asset at the market price.

    d. The holder receives the premium paid for the option.

Multiple-Choice Quiz Answers:

1.) B 2.) C 3.) D 4.) B 5.) B 6.) B 7.) C 8.) B

9.) B 10.) B 11.) C 12.) B 13.) B 14.) B 15.) C 16.) B

17.) B 18.) B 19.) C 20.) B 21.) B 22.) B 23.) C 24.) B

All Chapters Recap - True/False Quiz:

Chapter 1: Laying the Foundation

1. True or False: The primary goal of options trading is to minimize risk and maximize profit.

2. True or False: A call option gives you the right to sell an underlying asset at a specified price within a certain timeframe.

3. True or False: The strike price is the predetermined price at which you can buy or sell the underlying asset.

4. True or False: In-the-money options have intrinsic value.

5. True or False: Market makers are responsible for providing liquidity in the options market.

Chapter 2: Basic Strategies

6. True or False: Buying a put option is beneficial in a bullish market.

7. True or False: A covered call strategy involves selling call options on stocks that you do not own.

8. True or False: Protective puts are used to safeguard investments against potential losses.

9. True or False: Cash-secured puts require you to have enough cash to buy the stock if the option is exercised.

10. True or False: The primary purpose of buying calls is to profit from a decrease in the underlying asset's price.

Chapter 3: Intermediate Strategies

11. True or False: A vertical spread involves buying and selling options with the same expiration date but different strike prices.

12. True or False: The butterfly spread strategy is most effective in volatile markets.

13. True or False: The iron condor strategy involves combining two vertical spreads to profit from low volatility.

14. True or False: In a bear put spread, you profit when the underlying asset's price rises.

15. True or False: Straddles are used to profit from significant price movements in either direction.

Chapter 4: Risk Management

16. True or False: Stop-loss orders are used to limit potential losses in options trading.

17. True or False: Diversifying your options portfolio increases risk.

18. True or False: Volatility is irrelevant to risk assessment in options trading.

19. True or False: Hedging techniques are used to manage and reduce risk in options trading.

20. True or False: Calculating risk is unnecessary if you are using advanced trading strategies.

Chapter 5: Trading Psychology

21. True or False: Overcoming fear and greed is critical for long-term success in options trading.

22. True or False: Building emotional resilience has no impact on your trading outcomes.

23. True or False: A consistent trading routine can help improve your trading discipline.

24. True or False: Mindfulness techniques are irrelevant in the context of trading psychology.

Chapter 6: Recurring Income

25. True or False: Weekly options typically offer less time decay compared to monthly options.

26. True or False: The strategy of selling covered calls is suitable for generating monthly income.

27. True or False: Weekly iron condors are designed to profit from significant price movements.

28. True or False: Time decay, also known as theta, plays a crucial role in income strategies using options.

29. True or False: Leveraging short-term volatility is irrelevant when using weekly options for income generation.

Chapter 7: Technical Analysis

30. True or False: Technical analysis focuses primarily on analyzing company financials to make trading decisions.

31. True or False: Chart patterns are a key component of technical analysis in options trading.

32. True or False: Fundamental analysis is used to assess the overall economic indicators affecting the options market.

33. True or False: Combining technical and fundamental analysis provides a more comprehensive approach to options trading.

34. True or False: Economic indicators have no impact on options trading strategies.

Chapter 8: Essential Platforms

35. True or False: Trading software is essential for executing options trades efficiently.

36. True or False: A multi-monitor setup can decrease your focus on individual tasks, making it less efficient for monitoring trading platforms and news feeds simultaneously.

37. True or False: Essential tools for technical analysis include indicators such as moving averages and RSI.

38. True or False: Leveraging financial news and data feeds is unnecessary for successful options trading.

39. True or False: Choosing the right trading platform is irrelevant to your success in options trading.

Chapter 9: Interactive Learning Exercises (THIS CHAPTER)

40. True or False: One of the most effective ways to test and reinforce your options trading knowledge is by applying a feedback loop approach.

41. True or False: Simulation tools allow you to practice options trading without any financial risk.

42. True or False: Checklists for successful trading are unnecessary if you have a good trading strategy.

43. True or False: While scenario-based quizzes enhance your understanding of theoretical concepts, the most effective way to build practical knowledge is through executing actual options trades.

44. True or False: Continuous learning is unnecessary once you have mastered basic options trading strategies.

Chapter 10: Learning and Improvement

45. True or False: Keeping up with market trends is essential for staying successful in options trading.

46. True or False: Trading simulations are only useful for beginners and offer no value to experienced traders.

47. True or False: Accessing ongoing education and being part of trading communities can enhance your trading knowledge.

48. True or False: Continuous improvement in trading strategies is key to long-term success in the options market.

49. True or False: A risk management checklist analyzes market conditions and confirms the strategy selection.

50. True or False: Mastering options trading involves not only understanding the basics but also consistently applying and refining your strategies.

True / False Quiz Answers:

Chapter 1: 1.) True 2.) False 3.) True 4.) True 5.) True

Chapter 2: 6.) False 7.) False 8.) True 9.) True 10.) False

Chapter 3: 11.) True 12.) False 13.) True 14.) False 15.) True

Chapter 4: 16.) True 17.) False 18.) False 19.) True 20.) False

Chapter 5: 21.) True 22.) False 23.) True 24.) False

Chapter 6: 25.) False 26.) True 27.) False 28.) True 29.) False

Chapter 7: 30.) False 31.) True 32.) True 33.) True 34.) False

Chapter 8: 35.) True 36.) False 37.) True 38.) False 39.) False

Chapter 9: 40.) True 41.) True 42.) False 43.) False 44.) False

Chapter 10: 45.) True 46.) False 47.) True 48.) True 49.) False 50.) True

9.3 Exercises for Real-World Trading

To truly understand options trading, it's not enough to just read about strategies; you need to practice them in real-world scenarios. Mock trading scenarios are invaluable in this regard. These exercises simulate real-world trading, allowing you to set up various options strategies like covered calls or straddles without the financial risk. For example, envision setting up a mock covered call strategy on a tech stock with a bullish outlook. You would select a stock you believe will rise modestly in price, buy 100 shares of it, and then sell a call option at a strike price slightly above the current market price. This way, you can collect the premium from selling the call while still holding the stock. Such simulations provide hands-on experience and help you understand the mechanics of different strategies.

Another crucial exercise involves evaluating the effectiveness of different trading strategies. This means analyzing their risk and reward profiles and comparing the outcomes. Imagine evaluating the risk and reward of a bull call spread versus a long call. With a bull call spread, you buy a call option at a lower strike price and sell another call option at a higher strike price. This limits your potential profit but also reduces your initial cost and risk. In contrast, a long call involves buying a single call option, which offers unlimited profit potential but comes with higher risk and cost. By comparing these strategies in a simulated environment, you gain insights into which approach aligns better with your risk tolerance and financial goals.

Managing an options trading portfolio requires a different set of skills. Portfolio management exercises help you focus on diversification and risk management techniques. For instance, you might create a diversified options portfolio with at least three different strategies. This could include a mix of covered calls for steady income, protective puts for downside protection, and iron condors for range-bound markets. Adjusting positions based on market changes is also crucial. If one sector faces unexpected volatility, having a diversified portfolio allows you to balance the overall risk. These exercises teach you to manage your investments more holistically, ensuring that you're not overly exposed to any single market movement.

Performance review exercises are perhaps the most reflective part of this learning process. By tracking and analyzing your mock trades, you can identify areas for improvement. For example, reviewing your mock trades over the past month can help you pinpoint the most profitable strategy. Perhaps your covered calls consistently generated income, while your straddles did not perform as expected. By documenting these outcomes, you can adjust your future trading plans accordingly. This practice not only builds your analytical skills but also instills discipline, helping you stick to strategies that work and avoid those that don't.

Interactive Exercise: Mock Trading Scenario

To put these concepts into practice, set up a mock trading account using a simulation platform like Thinkorswim's PaperMoney or the Investopedia Simulator. Execute a covered call strategy on a tech stock you believe will have a steady rise. Document each step: selecting the stock, buying 100 shares, selling the call option, and monitoring the position. At the end of the simulation period, review the performance. Note the premium collected, the stock's price movement, and any adjustments you made. Reflect on what worked well and what could be improved. This hands-on experience will deepen your understanding and prepare you for real-world trading.

9.4 Simulation Tools: Practice Without Risk

Using simulation tools for practice trading is like having a safety net while learning to walk a tightrope. You can experiment, make mistakes, and learn without the fear of losing real money. A risk-free environment for learning allows you to test various strategies and see how they play out in real time. Imagine using a trading simulator to practice options strategies. You can set up trades, monitor their performance, and adjust your approach based on the outcomes—all without the financial consequences of actual trading. This hands-on practice is invaluable for building confidence and honing your skills.

Popular simulation platforms offer different features to suit your needs. Thinkorswim by TD Ameritrade is a standout with its PaperMoney feature. It provides a comprehensive suite of tools, including advanced charting, technical analysis, and real-time data. The platform is user-friendly, making it ideal for both beginners and seasoned traders. Another excellent option is the Investopedia Simulator. This platform is great for those who want a straightforward, no-frills experience. It offers a wide range of assets to trade and provides educational resources to help you understand different strategies. Setting up a paper trading account on Thinkorswim is straightforward. You can quickly get started by creating an account, choosing your initial balance, and diving into the world of options trading without risking a dime.

To effectively use simulators, follow a detailed guide. Start by setting up a mock trading account on your chosen platform. This involves registering, selecting your initial balance, and familiarizing yourself with the interface. Next, place trades in the simulator. For example, you might execute a mock iron condor strategy. This involves selling an out-of-the-money call spread and an out-of-the-money put spread on the same underlying asset. You can monitor how the positions perform as market conditions change, making adjustments as needed. This hands-on practice helps you understand the mechanics of different strategies and how they respond to market fluctuations.

Tracking and analyzing simulation performance is crucial for improving your real-world strategies. Record each trade you make, noting the entry and exit points, the rationale behind the trade, and the outcome. Review performance metrics regularly to identify trends and areas for improvement. For example, analyze the performance of your simulated trades to understand which strategies worked best and why. You might find that your iron condor strategy consistently generated steady income while your straddle trades were more volatile. Use this analysis to refine your approach, focusing on strategies that align with your risk tolerance and financial goals. This iterative process of testing, reviewing, and adjusting is key to becoming a successful options trader.

Interactive Exercise: Simulation Performance Review

1. **Set up a mock trading account:** Choose a simulation platform like Thinkorswim by TD Ameritrade or the Investopedia Simulator. Create an account and set your initial balance.

2. **Execute a mock iron condor strategy:** Select an underlying asset, set up an out-of-the-money call spread and an out-of-the-money put spread, and place the trades.

3. **Monitor and adjust:** Track the performance of your trades as market conditions change. Make adjustments as needed to manage risk and optimize returns.

4. **Record and analyze:** Document each trade, including entry and exit points, rationale, and outcome. Review performance metrics to identify successful strategies and areas for improvement.

By engaging in these simulation exercises, you gain valuable experience and insights without the financial risk. This practice builds your confidence and prepares you for real-world trading, where every decision counts.

Chapter Recap - True/False Quiz:

1. True or False: One of the most effective ways to test and reinforce your options trading knowledge is by applying a feedback loop approach.

2. True or False: Simulation tools allow you to practice options trading without any financial risk.

3. True or False: Checklists for successful trading are unnecessary if you have a good trading strategy.

4. True or False: While scenario-based quizzes enhance your understanding of theoretical concepts, the most effective way to build practical knowledge is through executing actual options trades.

5. True or False: Continuous learning is unnecessary once you have mastered basic options trading strategies.

True and False Answers:

1.) True 2.) True 3.) False 4.) False 5.) False

LEARNING AND IMPROVEMENT

Chapter 10:

Learning and Improvement

Imagine yourself as a sailor steering through the vast, unpredictable ocean. Every wave, gust of wind, and change in weather must be anticipated and understood to ensure a successful voyage. Similarly, in the world of options trading, staying informed about market trends and developments is crucial for making sound trading decisions. In this chapter, we'll explore the importance of continuous learning and learn how to keep up with ever-changing market trends.

10.1 Keeping Up With Market Trends

Staying informed about market trends is not just beneficial—it's essential. The financial markets are dynamic, influenced by a myriad of factors ranging from economic data and corporate earnings to geopolitical events and changes in government policies. As a trader, your ability to anticipate and react to these changes can significantly impact your trading strategies and outcomes.

Understanding market trends allows you to make informed decisions, optimize your trading strategies, and seize opportunities as they arise. For instance, knowing that the Federal Reserve is likely to raise interest rates can help you position your trades accordingly, either by hedging against potential market downturns or capitalizing on sectors that benefit from higher rates. Moreover, staying informed helps you avoid pitfalls and minimize risks, ensuring that your trading decisions are well-grounded and strategic.

Reliable sources of market information are indispensable for staying updated. Financial news websites like Bloomberg and Reuters offer real-time updates, in-depth analysis, and expert opinions on market developments. These platforms cover a wide range of topics, including economic indicators, corporate earnings, and geopolitical events, providing you with a comprehensive view of the market landscape. Stock market analysis platforms such as Seeking Alpha offer detailed reports and analyses from seasoned traders and financial analysts, giving you insights into market trends and individual stock performances. Additionally, government and financial institution reports, such as those from the Federal Reserve or the Bureau of Economic Analysis, provide crucial economic data and forecasts that can influence market movements.

Integrating market updates into your daily and weekly routines is a great way to stay informed and prepared. Start your day with a morning news review and market analysis. Spend 15-20 minutes browsing financial news websites, checking for any significant overnight developments, and noting any economic data releases scheduled for the day. This routine helps you enter the trading day with a clear understanding of the current market sentiment and potential drivers of price movements. On a weekly basis, summarize market trends and adjust your strategies accordingly. Spend some time over the weekend reviewing the past week's market performance, analyzing any significant events, and planning your trades for the upcoming week. Using financial apps for real-time alerts is another effective way to stay informed. Apps like CNBC and Bloomberg offer customizable alerts for breaking news, earnings reports, and economic data releases, ensuring that you never miss critical updates.

Analyzing market trends requires a blend of technical and fundamental analysis. Technical analysis of market indices, such as the S&P 500 or the NASDAQ, helps you identify trends, support and resistance levels, and potential reversal points. Use charts and indicators like moving averages, RSI, and MACD to visualize price movements and make data-driven decisions. Fundamental analysis of economic indicators, such as GDP growth, unemployment rates, and inflation, provides insights into the broader economic environment and its impact on the markets. Combining multiple sources for a holistic view is key to making well-informed trading decisions. Consider integrating insights from technical analysis, fundamental analysis, and expert opinions to develop a comprehensive understanding of market trends and potential opportunities.

By keeping up with market trends, you arm yourself with the knowledge and insights needed to navigate the complex world of options trading. Staying informed helps you anticipate market movements, optimize your trading strategies, and ultimately achieve your financial goals. So, make it a habit to stay updated, analyze trends, and continuously refine your approach to trading. Your success in the markets depends on your ability to adapt and evolve with the ever-changing financial landscape.

10.2 Utilizing Trading Simulations for Practice

Picture yourself as a novice pilot in a flight simulator. You can maneuver through storms, practice emergency landings, and experience different weather conditions—all without the risk of crashing a real plane. This is the beauty of trading simulations. They provide a risk-free environment where you can practice and refine your trading strategies. Trading simulations allow you to test new approaches and understand market dynamics without the financial consequences of real-world trading. They offer a safe space to make mistakes, learn from them, and build confidence in your trading abilities.

One of the significant advantages of using trading simulations is the opportunity to test new strategies without financial risk. Whether you're trying out a new options strategy or tweaking an existing one, simulations allow you to see how these strategies perform under different market conditions. This experience is invaluable. It helps you understand the nuances of each approach and refine your tactics before applying them in a live trading environment. Additionally, simulations enable you to experiment with various asset classes and trading instruments, broadening your understanding of the markets and enhancing your versatility as a trader.

Several well-known platforms offer robust trading simulation tools. Investopedia's Stock Simulator is a popular choice among traders. It provides a user-friendly interface, real-time data, and a virtual trading environment where you can practice buying and selling stocks, options, and other securities. Thinkorswim's paperMoney, offered by TD

Ameritrade, is another excellent platform. It provides advanced charting tools, technical analysis features, and the ability to simulate complex options strategies. TradingView's simulator feature is also highly regarded. It allows you to backtest strategies, analyze historical data, and engage with a community of traders, all within a simulation environment.

Setting up and using trading simulations effectively involves a few key steps. First, create an account on your chosen platform and set your initial conditions. This might include selecting your starting balance, choosing the types of assets you want to trade, and setting any specific goals or parameters for your simulation. Next, start selecting assets and entering simulated trades. Treat this process as if you were trading with real money. Conduct thorough research, analyze market trends, and make informed decisions. As you enter simulated trades, monitor their performance closely. Pay attention to how market movements affect your positions and adjust your strategies as needed.

Analyzing the results of your simulated trades is crucial for improving your real-world trading performance. Start by reviewing performance metrics and results. Look at key indicators such as profit and loss, win rate, and average return per trade. Identify which strategies were most successful and which ones underperformed. Consider factors like market conditions, timing, and execution to understand why certain trades worked and others did not. Use this analysis to refine your strategies, making adjustments based on your findings. This iterative process helps build your confidence and experience, preparing you for live trading.

Trading simulations are a powerful tool for continuous learning and improvement. They provide a safe, risk-free environment to practice and refine your trading strategies, test new approaches, and build confidence in your abilities. By leveraging platforms like Investopedia's Stock Simulator, Thinkorswim's paperMoney, and TradingView's simulator feature, you can gain valuable experience and insights without the financial consequences of real-world trading. So, take advantage of these resources, analyze your results, and continuously refine your approach to become a more skilled and successful trader.

10.3 Checklists for Successful Trading

A solid checklist can be the difference between a successful trade and a costly mistake. It's like a pilot running through preflight checks—skipping even one step can have serious consequences. For traders, having structured checklists ensures that all necessary steps are completed, risks are managed, and trades are executed flawlessly. Let's start with a pre-trade checklist to ensure you're fully prepared before placing any trades.

First, always analyze market conditions. This involves checking the overall market trend, evaluating current economic indicators, and staying updated on relevant news. Confirming the suitability of your strategy based on this analysis is crucial. For instance, if you're planning to trade a bullish strategy like buying call options, make sure the market sentiment aligns with your expectations. If the market looks bearish, you might need to reconsider or adjust your strategy. This step helps you avoid entering trades that aren't supported by current market conditions.

Next, focus on risk management with a dedicated checklist. Setting stop-loss orders is a must. These orders automatically sell your position if the stock reaches a certain price, limiting your potential losses. Proper position sizing is equally important. This means not putting all your eggs in one basket. Ensure that each trade represents only a small percentage of your total portfolio. For example, you might set a rule that no single trade should exceed 5% of your investment capital. This approach helps protect your overall portfolio from significant losses due to a single poor trade.

When it comes to executing trades, having a checklist ensures everything goes smoothly. Start by reviewing all order details. Double-check the ticker symbol, option type, strike price, expiration date, and order type (market or limit). Confirming these details on your trading platform is crucial to avoid mistakes. For example, entering the wrong ticker symbol could result in buying an entirely different stock. Take an extra moment to verify everything before hitting the execute button.

This small step can save you from costly errors and ensure your trades are carried out as planned.

After executing a trade, a post-trade review checklist helps you evaluate your performance. Record all trade details, including entry and exit points, the rationale behind the trade, and the outcome. Assessing the performance and outcomes of your trades is essential for continuous improvement. For instance, if a trade didn't go as expected, analyze what went wrong. Was it a misjudgment of market conditions, an error in execution, or something else? Recording these insights helps you learn from each trade and refine your strategies.

Interactive Checklist: Pre-Trade Example

1. **Analyze market conditions:**

   o Check overall market trend (bullish, bearish, or neutral).

   o Evaluate current economic indicators (GDP, unemployment rate, etc.).

   o Review relevant news (earnings reports, geopolitical events).

2. **Confirm strategy selection:**

   o Ensure the chosen strategy aligns with market conditions.

   o Example: Verify the suitability of a bullish strategy based on current market analysis.

Interactive Checklist: Risk Management Example

1. **Set stop-loss orders:**

   o Determine the stop-loss level based on risk tolerance.

   o Example: Set stop-loss orders to limit potential losses on each trade.

2. **Ensure proper position sizing:**

   o Allocate a small percentage of the total portfolio to each trade.

   o Example: Limit each trade to no more than 5% of total investment capital.

Interactive Checklist: Trade Execution Example

1. **Review order details:**

   o Double-check ticker symbol, option type, strike price, expiration date, and order type.

   o Example: Double-check order details before executing a trade to avoid mistakes.

Interactive Checklist: Post-Trade Review Example

1. **Record trade details:**

   o Document entry and exit points, rationale, and outcomes.

   o Example: Record trade details and evaluate performance against expected outcomes.

Assess Trade Performance and Outcomes:

- ○ Analyze what went well and identify areas for improvement.

- ○ Example: Evaluate performance and pinpoint the most profitable strategies.

By following these checklists, you can ensure a disciplined and structured approach to trading. This method not only minimizes errors but also enhances your ability to make informed decisions, manage risks, and continually improve your trading performance. These checklists serve as a resourceful guide, allowing you to confidently tackle the complexities of options trading with greater precision.

10.4 Accessing Ongoing Education

To keep pace with the ever-evolving world of options trading, continuous education is not just beneficial—it's crucial. Market conditions change, new strategies emerge, and technology advances. Staying up-to-date with these changes helps you adapt and refine your approach. It ensures that you remain competitive and capable of effectively managing the market's complexities. By committing to lifelong learning, you not only enhance your trading skills but also stay ahead of the curve, ready to capitalize on new opportunities as they arise.

Educational resources abound for traders looking to deepen their knowledge. Online courses and webinars are an excellent starting point. Platforms like Coursera and Udemy offer a wide range of courses tailored to various skill levels, from beginner to advanced. These courses often include video lectures, reading materials, and interactive assignments, providing a comprehensive learning experience. Books are another valuable resource. Classics like *Options as a Strategic Investment* by Lawrence McMillan offer in-depth insights and strategies that have stood the test of time. Financial journals and articles provide ongoing education, keeping you informed about the latest research, trends, and developments in the field. Subscribing to reputable journals like *The Journal of Finance* or reading articles from respected financial analysts can significantly enhance your understanding and trading acumen.

Joining trading communities offers immense benefits for shared learning and support. Online forums and discussion groups, such as those on Reddit or Investopedia, provide platforms where traders can share experiences, ask questions, and learn from each other. These communities are invaluable for gaining different perspectives and insights into market trends and trading strategies. Social media platforms like Twitter and LinkedIn also host active trading groups. Following influential traders and participating in discussions can keep you updated on market movements and emerging strategies. Local trading clubs and meetups offer opportunities for face-to-face interaction, fostering a sense of camaraderie and support among traders. These gatherings can be particularly beneficial for networking and building relationships with other traders in your area.

Mentorship and networking opportunities are essential for personalized advice and growth. Seeking out experienced traders as mentors can provide you with guidance, feedback, and support tailored to your specific needs and goals. Mentors can help you avoid common pitfalls, refine your strategies, and accelerate your learning curve. Attending industry conferences and seminars is another effective way to expand your network and gain valuable insights. These events often feature presentations and workshops from leading experts, offering a wealth of knowledge and useful tips. Networking through professional associations and trading events can also open doors to new opportunities and collaborations. Building relationships with other traders, financial professionals, and industry experts can enhance your learning and growth, providing you with a support system and access to valuable resources.

In the dynamic world of options trading, continuous education and community engagement are key to staying informed, improving your skills, and achieving long-term success. By leveraging educational resources, participating in trading communities, and seeking mentorship and networking opportunities, you can keep pace with market changes and continually refine your trading approach. This commitment to lifelong learning not only enhances your trading performance but also empowers you with the confidence and agility needed to succeed in the market.

Chapter Recap - True/False Quiz:

1. True or False: Keeping up with market trends is essential for staying successful in options trading.

2. True or False: Trading simulations are only useful for beginners and offer no value to experienced traders.

3. True or False: Accessing ongoing education and being part of trading communities can enhance your trading knowledge.

4. True or False: Continuous improvement in trading strategies is key to long-term success in the options market.

5. True or False: Once you have learned the basics of options trading, further education is unnecessary.

True and False Answers:

1.) True 2.) False 3.) True 4.) True 5.) False

CONCLUSION

Conclusion

As we come to the end of *Options Trading for Beginners: Proven Strategies to Trade with Confidence, Master Risk Mitigation Techniques, and Maximize Profits for Financial Freedom*, it's time to reflect on the journey we've taken together. The primary goal of this book has been to demystify the often-complex world of options trading. We've aimed to equip you with actionable strategies and build your confidence, all in the pursuit of financial freedom.

Throughout this book, we've taken a comprehensive approach. We've covered everything from the basics to advanced strategies, all while keeping an eye on the psychological aspects of trading. Let's revisit the key points from each chapter to ensure you have a solid grasp of what we've learned.

In **Chapter 1**, we laid the foundation by introducing the fundamentals of options trading. We explored the basic terminology, the difference between call and put options, and the roles of strike prices, expiration dates, and premiums. We also discussed the critical distinction between in-the-money and out-of-the-money options. We examined the operation of options markets, the key factors influencing options prices, and the Greeks—delta, gamma, theta, and vega. We also covered the role of volatility and its impact on trading.

Moving to **Chapter 2**, we explored basic strategies for beginners. Here, we discussed buying calls and puts, covered calls, protective puts, and cash-secured puts. Each strategy was broken down step-by-step to ensure you could apply them confidently.

In **Chapter 3**, we introduced intermediate strategies. We covered vertical spreads, butterfly spreads, iron condors, and straddles and strangles. These strategies offer more sophisticated ways to manage risk and capture profits.

Chapter 4 focused on risk management and mitigation. We discussed setting up stop-loss orders, diversifying your portfolio, and employing hedging techniques. We also looked at the role of volatility in assessing risk.

Chapter 5 addressed trading psychology and mindset. We talked about overcoming fear and greed, building emotional resilience, and developing a consistent trading routine. Mindfulness techniques and the importance of discipline were also highlighted.

In **Chapter 6**, we explored weekly and monthly income strategies. We detailed using weekly options, generating income with covered calls, and leveraging short-term volatility. The role of time decay in income strategies was also discussed.

Chapter 7 took us into the realm of technical and fundamental analysis. We covered the basics of performing technical analysis, understanding chart patterns, and using technical indicators. We also delved into analyzing company financials and using economic indicators in options trading.

Chapter 8 was all about essential tools and platforms. We compared different trading platforms, discussed utilizing trading software effectively, and highlighted the importance of a well-organized trading workspace. Leveraging financial news and data feeds was also emphasized.

Chapter 9 focused on interactive learning tools and exercises. We provided quizzes, exercises, and simulation tools to help you practice without risk. Checklists for successful trading were also included to ensure you develop a disciplined approach.

Finally, **Chapter 10** encouraged continuous learning and improvement. We discussed staying informed about market trends, utilizing trading simulations, and accessing ongoing education and communities. The importance of mentorship and networking was also highlighted.

Now, it's time for action. Take the knowledge and strategies you've gained and apply them to your trading. Start with a practice account, refine your skills, and gradually transition to live trading as you gain confidence. Stay disciplined, manage your risks, and keep learning. The market is dynamic, and adaptability is key.

Finally, remember that every successful trader started where you are now. It's a journey, and persistence is crucial. You will encounter ups and downs, but each experience is an opportunity to learn and grow. Believe in yourself, stay committed, and keep pushing forward. Financial freedom is within your reach, and with the right mindset and strategies, you can achieve it.

Your review for this book would be greatly appreciated. This small act could significantly affect others, potentially aiding local businesses, supporting entrepreneurs, or helping individuals achieve their dreams. Your willingness to leave feedback makes a world of difference and can be accomplished easily by scanning the QR code below or using this link:

https://www.amazon.com/review/review-your-purchases/?asin=B0DK52N3M5.

Thank you for allowing me to be a part of your trading journey. Here's to your success and financial freedom!

References

AAPL Stock: Option Straddle Trade For Earnings
https://www.investors.com/research/options/aapl-stock-short-straddle-capture-volatility/

American vs. European Options: What's the Difference?
https://www.investopedia.com/articles/optioninvestor/08/american-european-options.asp

Backtesting with thinkorswim® OnDemand
https://www.schwab.com/learn/story/backtesting-with-thinkorswim-ondemand

Best Virtual Options Trading Simulators in July 2024
https://www.benzinga.com/money/best-virtual-options-trading-simulators

Best WEB Trader. (n.d.). Analyzing historical data for investment insights. Best WEB Trader. Retrieved from https://www.bestwebtrader.com/analyzing-historical-data-for-investment-insights/

Bizz Skills. Weighing the pros and cons of enlisting a forex broker. Bizz Skills. Retrieved from https://bizzskills.com/weighing-the-pros-and-cons-of-enlisting-a-forex-broker/

Blending Technical and Fundamental Analysis
https://www.investopedia.com/articles/trading/07/technical-fundamental.asp

Butterfly Spread: What It Is, With Types Explained & Example
https://www.investopedia.com/terms/b/butterflyspread.asp#:~:text=Example%20of%20a%20Long%20Call%20Butterfly%20Spread&text=The%20investor%20writes%20two%20call,priced%20at%20%2460%20at%20expiration.

Calendar Spread Strategy: A Step-by-Step Approach
https://www.motilaloswal.com/blog-details/calendar-spread-
strategy-a-step-by-step-approach/21887

Common Behavioral Biases in Trading & Finance
https://www.britannica.com/money/behavioral-biases-in-
finance

Covered Calls: A Step-by-Step Guide with Examples
https://www.lynalden.com/covered-calls/

Diagonal Spread: How Strategy Works in Trade - Acquire.Fi
https://www.acquire.fi/glossary/diagonal-spread-definition-
and-how-strategy-works-in-
trade#:~:text=The%20advantages%20of%20using%20diagona
l,risks%20associated%20with%20this%20strategy.

Financial Analysis: Definition, Importance, Types, and ...
https://www.investopedia.com/terms/f/financial-analysis.asp

Finra Financial Literacy Quiz | FINRA.org
https://www.finra.org/financial_literacy_quiz

*Forex Academy. (n.d.). What is moving average in forex trading? Forex Academy.
Retrieved September 2, 2024, from https://www.forex.academy/what-is-
moving-average-in-forex-trading/*

5 challenges women face across trade, treasury, and ...
https://www.tradefinanceglobal.com/posts/5-challenges-
women-face-across-trade-treasury-payments/

Getting Started - thinkorswim Learning Center
https://toslc.thinkorswim.com/center/howToTos/thinkManu
al/Getting-Started

How to Build a Multi-Monitor Trading Computer
https://www.tradingheroes.com/how-to-build-a-multi-
monitor-trading-system/

How to Hedge Your Positions with Long Protective Put
https://www.moomoo.com/sg/learn/detail-how-to-hedge-

your-positions-with-long-protective-put-a-case-study-of-tesla-108140-230569161

How to manage fear and greed in trading - IG
https://www.ig.com/en/master-your-trading-mind/managing-emotions/how-to-manage-fear-and-greed-in-trading

How to stay updated on market trends and developments ...
https://www.quora.com/How-do-you-stay-updated-on-market-trends-and-developments-and-what-sources-do-you-rely-on-for-financial-information

How to Trade Iron Condors on the SPY
https://www.cabotwealth.com/premium/magazine/how-to-trade-iron-condors-on-the-spy

How to Use Options as a Hedging Strategy
https://www.investopedia.com/articles/optioninvestor/07/affordable-hedging.asp

Iron Condor Options Strategy [Download Your Free Guide]
https://optionalpha.com/strategies/iron-condor

Iron Condor: How This Options Strategy Works, With Examples
https://www.investopedia.com/terms/i/ironcondor.asp#:~:text=An%20iron%20condor%20is%20an,middle%20strike%20prices%20at%20expiration.

Microsoft Stock: Covered Calls For Income (NASDAQ:MSFT)
https://seekingalpha.com/article/4487341-microsoft-stock-covered-calls-for-income

Option Greeks: The 4 Factors to Measure Risk
https://www.investopedia.com/trading/getting-to-know-the-greeks/

Options Trading for Beginners 2024 (The ULTIMATE In-Depth ...
https://www.youtube.com/watch?v=0GSB5YZx9ZE

Options Trading Terms and Definitions
https://www.nerdwallet.com/article/investing/options-trading-definitions

Options Trading: Basics of a Covered Call Strategy
https://www.schwab.com/learn/story/options-trading-basics-covered-call-strategy

Options Trading: How to Trade Stock Options in 5 Steps
https://www.investopedia.com/articles/active-trading/040915/guide-option-trading-strategies-beginners.asp

Options Trading: How to Trade Stock Options in 5 Steps
https://www.investopedia.com/articles/active-trading/040915/guide-option-trading-strategies-beginners.asp

Options Trading: How to Trade Stock Options in 5 Steps
https://www.investopedia.com/articles/active-trading/040915/guide-option-trading-strategies-beginners.asp

Protective Put: What It Is, How It Works, and Examples
https://www.investopedia.com/terms/p/protective-put.asp#:~:text=A%20protective%20put%20is%20a,a%20fee%2C%20called%20a%20premium.

Robinhood vs. thinkorswim - A Detailed Comparison
https://www.financialtechwiz.com/post/robinhood-vs-thinkorswim/

Short-term trading strategies for beginners - IG https://www.ig.com/en-ch/trading-strategies/short-term-trading-strategies-for-beginners-221109

Stop-Loss Orders: One Way to Limit Losses and Reduce Risk
https://www.investopedia.com/terms/s/stop-lossorder.asp

Technical Analysis - A Beginner's Guide
https://corporatefinanceinstitute.com/resources/career-map/sell-side/capital-markets/technical-analysis/

The 6 Best Books on Becoming an Options Trader
https://www.investopedia.com/articles/personal-finance/090716/top-5-books-become-option-trader.asp

The Best Online Trading Communities 2024
https://www.daytrading.com/communities

The Effect of Investor Bias and Gender on Portfolio Performance and Risk
https://www.researchgate.net/publication/256034847_The_Effect_of_Investor_Bias_and_Gender_on_Portfolio_Performance_and_Risk

The Importance of Diversification
https://www.investopedia.com/investing/importance-diversification/

The Psychology of Successful Traders
https://www.theinvestorco.com/post/the-psychology-of-successful-traders

The Top 10 Options Trading Simulators Today
https://wealthfit.com/articles/options-trading-simulator/

Top 10 Chart Patterns Every Trader Needs to Know - IG
https://www.ig.com/en/trading-strategies/10-chart-patterns-every-trader-needs-to-know-190514

Top-10 Female Traders Who Brought Value to the Financial ...
https://fxopen.com/blog/en/top-10-female-traders-who-brought-value-to-the-financial-industry/

Ultimate Guide to Options Trading Psychology - InsiderFinance
https://www.insiderfinance.io/resources/ultimate-guide-to-options-trading-psychology#:~:text=Mastering%20the%20psychology%20of%20options%20trading%20is%20essential%20for%20long,more%20rational%20and%20disciplined%20decisions.

VersaFi Professional Mentorship Program
https://versafi.ca/programs/professional-program

Weekly Options: How They Work, Advantages and ...
https://www.investopedia.com/articles/optioninvestor/11/intro-weekly-options.asp

What Is a Straddle Options Strategy and How Is It Created?
https://www.investopedia.com/terms/s/straddle.asp

Who are the players in the option markets? - Option Trading Tips
https://www.optiontradingtips.com/options101/who-trades-options.html

Whye.org. How do I stay updated on market trends and news relevant to my investments? *Whye.org*. Retrieved from https://whye.org/how-do-i-stay-updated-on-market-trends-and-news-relevant-to-my-investments

Made in the USA
Columbia, SC
12 January 2025

9547c69e-13fe-45f0-8d1f-e8babf551f7cR01